K-Speed

The Source of Korean Competitiveness

By

Jung Duk Lim

K-Speed: The Source of Korean Competitiveness

By Jung Duk Lim

This book first published 2023

Ethics International Press Ltd, UK

British Library Cataloguing in Publication Data

A catalogue record for this book is available from the British Library

Print Book ISBN: 978-1-80441-179-7

eBook ISBN: 978-1-80441-180-3

Table of Contents

About the author

Jung Duk Lim was born in Busan, Korea. He graduated from the Economics Department, Seoul National University, Korea. Ph. D in Economics, University of South Carolina, SC, USA.

He worked at Bank of Korea, Korea Southern Power Co. (Auditor), and currently works with DongHwa Entec Co. (Auditor). He taught at Wingate University, NC, USA, University of Maryland Asia Campus (Busan) and Pusan National University, Busan, Korea, where he is Professor Emeritus currently.

Served as President, Busan (Development) Institute, Busan, Korea. Visiting Fellow at East-West Center, Honolulu, HI, USA. Visiting Fellow at International Center for Southeast and East Asia, Kitakyushu, Japan. Member of International Advisory Committee, Asian Urban Information Center of Kobe, Japan. Dean for Planning and Research at Pusan National University. Member, Presidential Committee for Regional Development. Regular columnist of regional broadcasting companies and newspapers. Leader and member of many civil movement organizations.

Published about 15 books on mainly regional development, industry, and innovation. Published articles and academic papers, in and out of Korea.

Preface

Korea is a very unique country. Impoverished and underdeveloped, ravished from war, she is the only country in the world that has achieved both industrialization and democratization almost simultaneously within thirty years. This record is highly unlikely to be broken in the future. Unfortunately, some Koreans, particularly the generation that did not experience the war and the miraculous rebuilding process afterwards do not fully acknowledge and recognize this fact. Some even learn and teach that Korea's recent history is one of shame due to a period of military dictatorship.

The world is in a fierce competition economically, regardless of past or present. It is akin to running a marathon race. There is a leading group, middle group, and groups at the tail but all running together. Korea started from the tail group in this race, gradually accelerated, passing the groups ahead one by one, and has finally reached or nearly reached the leading group. It's an unprecedented and astonishing record in world economic history.

However, this race is an ongoing competition without a finish line and a merciless one where you must keep running without any award ceremony or medal presentation. If you cannot maintain your pace or fall behind relatively, the countries (competitors) next to or behind you would be pleased to overtake you. They won't deliberately slow down for you, or encourage you to push you forward.

In this competition, speed equates to competitiveness. Competitiveness encompasses all elements of outperforming your competitors (other countries). If you are competitive, you can move faster than others and lead in the competition. This competitiveness is a force that comes into play in all areas including politics, economy, management, culture, society, and education, etc... Therefore, this book is a product of an investigation into the source of Korean competitiveness and how it can be nurtured, maintained, and developed.

The author argues that Korean competitiveness lies in people's ability to act faster. Competitiveness comes from factors that make you perform better than others. The citizens, businesses, and organizations have been and still are clearly good at getting things done faster. Astounding accomplishments and miracles have resulted from demonstrating this speed in the economy, management, technology, learning, and lifestyle. Furthermore, the author also considers that what could be viewed as a negative flipside – the inability to wait – also being a driving force that has led to the simultaneous achievement of democratization and industrialization.

The Korean Peninsula is the only experimental ground that has tested the above argument, which is generally impossible in social science. Tragic and forced but experimentally a perfect example is the situation of South and North Korea. The past eighty years have proven that the Korean attribute of speed can only bloom to fruition in an encouraging environment and democratic system. The author explains through examples that when the boiling point is reached in sectors other than the economy, explosive results follow. The book also discusses the 'sequence' of industrialization and democratization, a feat every developing country hopes for. Simultaneous achievement of both is practically impossible.

Over time, Koreans have often misconstrued this speed as a drawback, focusing primarily on its side effects such as accidents. Typical expressions of this are 'quickly' or 'roughly'. While these are aspects that need to be corrected or improved, they should not be seen as a cause for shame. The ability to move relatively faster and perform better than competitors is a unique blessing.

Hence, this book is an attempt to reaffirm the source of Korean competitiveness – speed or quickness – from anthropological, historical, economic, statistical, and empirical as well as an academic perspective, and to provide a pathway to revive this source. Of course, there are apparent side effects and costs associated with speed, so these are introduced and discussed, along with suggestions for improvement. The book also explains the phenomenon of increasing tangible and intangible factors such as regulation and interference akin to slowing down the relative speed of a marathon runner by increasing body weight. It also discusses the phenomenon of self-reducing or blocking the speed, legally, institutionally, and habitually. Therefore, the author proposes that Korea should restore the previous speed it has used, but upgrade it to a safer, reliable, and more honest tool.

The author attempts to inform the younger generation by reflecting on the rapid changes in and outside the country that he experienced throughout his not-so-short life from a speed based perspective. Furthermore, he records his observations and feelings from his experience traveling in China and Russia at the early period of their opening and includes stories from his living experience in the United States, where he studied and worked, using a story-box format.

It is somewhat embarrassing that it took over two decades to complete this book, which was conceptualized when the author was the president of the Busan Development Institute, the municipal research organization, but hopefully time brings maturity and refinement. From this current standpoint, the author reconsiders the concept of 'completion' in all things as a fallacy, thus resolving to continue studying in the future.

The Korean edition of this book was published in 2022. This English version is basically a translation of the original book but with a substantial revision and editing. Readers who are busy are suggested to consider reading from Chapter 3 and coming back later.

For this English book, my daughter Kajin helped me a lot in refining my English. My son Yong provided with excerpt of his classroom examination for a story box. My granddaughter Natalie and her mom Hanna Chung were always the source of vitality. My wife Kwang-sun Ahn encouraged and helped this work with prayer and encouragement as usual. Gang-min Noh gave me various kinds of help in making figures and tables.

In the book, the Republic of Korea is called 'Korea' instead of South Korea. Many citations and references in the endnote come from Korean media and sources, mostly in Korean. Many foreign books and references also are translated in Korean which may be different from pages of original source.

Chapter 1

Speed – Another Name For Change and Progress

1-1 Thinking about the Meaning of Speed: In Lieu of an Introduction

Everything changes. Changes manifest in various forms. They occur physically, spatially, distantly, ideologically, institutionally, economically, functionally, culturally, and in all other realms. At the core of these changes lies speed. Climate change happens very slowly, making it difficult to feel the transformation, but nonetheless change is occurring.

What humanity is collectively experiencing now, is the increasing influence of acceleration. This influence manifests itself not only in technology, such as information and communication, but also in relatively slow natural phenomena such as climate change. The once long-lasting, gradual changes in the earth's environment and temperature are now accelerated due to rapid advancements in technology, industry, and income, affecting atmospheric conditions. Addressing or slowing down these consequences of industrialization is becoming difficult, demanding more effort at enormous cost.

All changes (speed and acceleration) are an inevitable process for humanity. We have typically defined these changes as progress or development. Simultaneously, almost all things related to human and human life have been structured to prefer and inevitably choose fast over slow. There have been reactions against the increasingly busy lifestyles and fast paced pressure, such as isolating oneself, deliberately pursuing and implementing a slow paced lifestyle.[1] Or cases like the recent COVID-19 pandemic experience, which forcibly slows down the pace of life. However, the vast majority of humanity does not resist or reject fast paced life or changes but even enjoys adapting. History has been moving in a direction of acceleration.

---

1 The Slow Food Movement or the lifestyle depicted in Henry David Thoreau's novel "Walden" (1854) are representative examples. There are also behaviors such as refusing to watch TV or deliberately avoiding the use of mobile phones.

If you narrow the discussion to an economic aspect, the logic becomes much clearer. We distinguish developed countries and developing countries by national income without thinking twice. High-income countries are recognized as developed countries without depending on complicated theories like the causality between economy, politics, society and culture. There have been considerable discussions and research on why most countries in the West became developed and why many countries in Asia, the Middle East, and Africa remained underdeveloped.[2] Various factors and conditions can be listed. However, when delving into the common cause of all factors, the essence lies in the speed of economic growth.

Economic development can be explained as an innovation process.[3] The three main factors of economic growth are capital, labor, and technology, but increasing labor and capital without technological change only leads to a simple increase in production, making it impossible to be competitive after a certain point due to diseconomies of scale. Of course, capital can play the role of 'embodied technology', so larger invested capital, like machines, can achieve competitiveness. However, most so-called developing countries have abundant labor but scarce capital. In this case, even if they produce goods at a low price, they cannot sell them freely in an open competitive market. Moreover, size and scale are a given constant that cannot be increased at will in a short period of time. In an open world where competition is essential, economic growth and development are relative concepts. Without the most up-to-date technology, it is not only difficult to develop in an open world economy but also to catch up with advanced competitors. We call this technology and the process of change, innovation.

South Korea (Korea hereafter)'s rapid ascent from one of the most underdeveloped countries in the world to an economic powerhouse in less than 50 years serves as a good example. In the early stages of the development

---

2 The works and papers of primarily Western scholars are often introduced. Recent discussions include Paul Kennedy's "The Rise and Fall of Great Powers" (1987), and Acemoglu and Robinson's "Why Nations Fail" (2014). It is also worth considering why the theories of economic development, which garnered significant attention from the 1960s, are hardly mentioned now.

3 While there are various theories and models related to economic development, the most persuasive explanatory model to date is that of the American economist Joseph Schumpeter. His main argument is that economic growth or development occurs through innovation caused by creative destruction.

plan that began in the 1960s, Korea entered the global economic competition system with its abundant low-wage labor force. Soon after, she adopted a strategy to catch up with advanced technology and production methods, and after reaching a certain level of development, entered with a fully competitive technology system (thus innovation). Now, as Korea enters a phase where it must lead rather than follow, she will inevitably face various challenges.

In this final stage, a different form of innovation is crucial for the growth and development of the Korean economy. To win in competition and/or survive or at the least not regress, innovation must be achieved in all areas, including manufacturing, service, administration, and the social system, etc. This is not an option but an inevitable requirement for staying in the ring (market) of the global economic arena. One of the most important reasons why the Korean economy has been in a relatively low-growth quagmire after passing through the high-speed growth phase is the decline of industrial competitiveness. In other words, the competitiveness of industries is declining because innovation might not be taking place properly on time.

Speed is the most important attribute that innovation or technological advancement pursues. Innovation can be defined as a method or approach that can accomplish things faster, easier, cheaper, better, more, and lighter than before. However, even the best innovations are mostly useless or ineffective if their results or ideas are not put forward faster than other competitors. The most dramatic example is the case of Alexander Graham Bell, who patented the world's first practical telephone, and Elisha Gray, who actually invented the telephone before Bell but was forgotten in the industrial and invention world because Gray's patent application was two hours late. For all companies, being the first in concept (idea) and the first to go to market as a result is absolutely necessary for survival. "No matter how good a mobile (computer) game is, if it drags on before its release and misses the timing, it will fail."[4] Therefore, the core factor determining the

[4] Interview with Netmarble's Chairman Bang Jun-hyuk, Chosun Economy, January 4, 2017, B2. Timing often plays a crucial role in the outcome. As mentioned above, apart from the invention of the telephone, there is another unsung pioneer in modern science who had a decisive influence on the theory of evolution. This is Alfred Russel Wallace (1823-1923), who penned his research results before Darwin. It is merely because Darwin's paper was published first that he is remembered as the founder of the theory of evolution. Alfred Russel Wallace (translated by No Seung-young), "The Malay Archipelago", Geo Book 2017.

success or failure of companies driving national economic growth is speed.

Keeping up or catching up is directly related to speed. Korea managed to quickly catch up with advanced technologies from its underdeveloped state, which led to its present-day success, but there are still many underdeveloped countries that cannot catch up with leading countries. Catching up with those who are ahead is about speed, as is the secret to not being caught up by those who follow. Therefore, the source of competitiveness is innovation, and the content of innovation is directly and indirectly connected to speed.

Speed is measured in time. Diverse concepts can be applied and compared to speed, but ultimately, they converge on the unit of time. Time is limited for everyone, so for humans, the war against time is an unavoidable fate.[5]

This book aims to ask what the secret to maintaining growth and development in the face of global competition is for Korea and to prove that the answer lies in speed. Over the past half-century, Korea has achieved miraculous growth and dazzling development recognized by the world thanks to its speed. But now the competitive advantage of speed we've had since the past is being exhausted, and its validity period has begun to expire. Therefore, we need to rediscover the source of our competitiveness with a cool-headed perspective and search for a better path. In other words, in the realms of industry and individual enterprise competitiveness, in politics and its institutional practices, and in social systems and their operation, most of the past advantages and competitiveness have been disappearing. Aspects that were once positive are now appearing as burdens, which is the reality of today.

To dismantle this reality, the answer lies in first identifying what Korea, Koreans, or Korean companies and public sectors can do best, individually or collectively, compared to other countries or societies. It's about rectifying the disadvantages or side effects that have emerged so far, fostering and developing the strengths, and utilizing them. This book seeks to recover Korea's past competitiveness by finding ways to revive and foster definitive competitiveness in Koreans.

More specifically, what can Korea or Koreans do better than other countries or ethnicities? Is it scientific thinking, philosophical background, or a

---

5 "Alexander Demandt, translated by Lee Deok-il, "The Birth of Time", Book Life 2018.

humanistic atmosphere? Exceptional artistic sense and emotional richness? Is it the relative superiority and strength of intelligence, technology, or physical strength? Is it historical, geographical, geopolitical advantages, and benefits? Cultural diversity or material and spiritual heritage inherited from ancestors? Diligence and character superior to other ethnicities?

The book begins with a discussion on the definition and characteristics of speed. In Chapter 1, we examine the changes in human life in the past and present, and analyze the role and importance of speed in all areas such as society and economy. Next, we examine the development process of economy, society, technology, knowledge, and lifestyle systems in relation to speed. In other words, it can also be expressed as a brief human history viewed through speed. As emphasized in various ways, the important role and outcome of speed appears in human life, sports, wars, living, and economic activities. Chapter 2 discusses more recent development and phenomenon and lifestyle changes in Korea. Chapter 3 presents evidence how quickly the so-called K-speed, which is the speed of Korea(n), has changed and transformed the Korean economy, society, and culture by eight categories. Speed is a relative concept, so the K-speed is proven to exist through comparison with other countries. In Chapter 4, we discuss how and to what extent speed plays an important role in corporate management, industrial competitiveness, and in Korean lives, specifically focusing on examples such as distribution and consumption life. Chapter 5 discusses the K-Culture and K-Wave (named Hallyu), which is a prominent cultural phenomenon in various fields in recent time, and examines it in relation to K-speed.

Human speed is a phenomenon or a characteristic inseparable from the genetic factors and/or society and culture of the subject. Chapter 6 examines the existence of K-speed as a genetic trait or ethnicity through examples and cultural phenomena, focusing on its form, content, and human and societal characteristics. In connection with this, Chapter 7 discusses the conditions for realizing K-speed and the possibility of its generalization for other countries as well. Korea is the only country in world history to have achieved both industrialization and democratization in a short period of time, and it discusses the possibility of generalizing this to other countries. At the same time, the order of industrialization and democratization is considered, questioning whether other countries can achieve both at the same time, following Korea's precedent.

The side effects and backlash of K-speed are also important topics to consider. Chapter 8 discusses the impact of this backlash on the Korean economy and society. In particular, it logically explains the impact and side effects of rapid population decline and aging of Korean society, describing them as a paradox and side effect of K-speed. An ancient expression 'too much is as bad as too little' is relevant here. Chapter 9 discusses the phenomena and causes that hinder and suppress K-speed, explaining the country's speed competitiveness by comparing it to a marathon race. It discusses the institutional factors, particularly various regulations, that suppress and reduce competitiveness, and gives examples from some industries. Chapter 10 is about the future speed Korea needs to regain, from now on. The book presents and discusses ways to upgrade it to a safe, reliable, and honest speed.

1-2 Preconditions and Conditions for Development

It is undeniable that Koreans possess many special traits. Although there may be room for counterarguments, it is widely known that Koreans rank first or second in the world in terms of Intelligence Quotient (IQ) in surveys of citizens from various countries. This higher average IQ may have enabled us to achieve rapid growth in the 20th century. However, there is no academic research or argument to date that claims a high average IQ of a nation is a necessary factor in economic growth or development. Although a high intelligence level has actually contributed to work efficiency, it might become a hindrance or suppression factor after a certain point.

Nevertheless, countries with high per capita income and so-called developed nations all belong to a group with relatively higher average IQ. There is no need to prove the causal relationship between these two variables, but it is clear that Korea has a favorable condition. The relatively higher average IQ of currently advanced countries can be observed empirically. For statistical data, one can refer to Table 6-1 in this book.

Another noteworthy factor is that in the 1980s and 1990s, significant research and discussions took place on the causes of the rapid economic growth of the Asian NIEs (Newly Industrialized Economies), consisting of Korea,

Taiwan, Hong Kong, and Singapore.[6] One common factor that emerged was the high educational fervor of these countries, which garnered considerable sympathy at the time.[7] During his tenure, U.S. President Obama often cited Korea's education system and high educational enthusiasm as an exemplary case. However, no one in Korea claims that its education system is successful or that the current system and approach should be maintained. Instead, there is a prevalent sense of frustration and dissatisfaction with the current state. It is difficult to consider high educational enthusiasm or the education system as a means of future competitiveness.

No one, domestically or internationally, would argue that Korea's politics, government, social system, culture, and custom are exceptionally exemplary and will be a great asset for the country's development not only in the past but also in the future. It is an undeniable historical fact that Korea's military regime in the 1960s and 1970s led to the rapid economic growth, however, there has been a strong movement to emphasize the negative aspect of military dictatorship and intentionally belittle its' achievement. It is likely that no one has the courage to say that individual diligence and sense of order served as a foundation for this.

Korea is indeed a unique country. The changes over the past half-century serve as clear evidence. Differences and speed are relative concepts. In terms of economic growth, social change, political change, change in international status, lifestyle change, and change in structure of consciousness, Korea(ns) is a country that has grown or changed faster than any other country. This book does not aim to discuss the pros and cons of these changes or the superiority of their outcomes but rather to properly recognize the facts and explore their sustainability. This is because a nation must continue to exist as long as the earth and humanity exist.

It is difficult to be convinced by the argument that we can utilize the rela-

---

6 In the 1960s and 70s, the rapidly growing economies of Korea, Taiwan, Singapore, and Hong Kong were collectively referred to as the 'Four Asian dragons'. Initially, they were called Asian NICs (Newly Industrialized Countries), but due to the national designation of Hong Kong, the term was changed to NIEs (Newly Industrialized Economies).

7 Academic research also has a significant degree of trendiness. After Korea's IMF economic crisis, such studies rapidly declined, presumably because there was not much to elaborate on regarding Korea's economic crisis.

tively higher intelligence level of Koreans or the overheated educational enthusiasm as a source of competitiveness for future development. The system and leadership that should lead and support an atmosphere conducive to innovation and development may instead be moving in the opposite direction. Ultimately if we cannot find what we can do best, we will have no choice but to walk the path of decline or stagnation among the global economies. Therefore, it is even more necessary to discover the source of competitiveness of Korea(n).

Development is measured by economic growth or increase in added value, and the principal agents for that are businesses. When the business sector grows and develops and thus produces, sells, employs, and exports more, it is concretely manifested as the growth of national income or GDP. Therefore, it is impossible to expect the economy to grow normally if the business sector lacks competitiveness. Korea, which has recently recorded an average annual economic growth rate of around 2- 3%, is predicted not to exceed this level in the future[8], which is an indicative of the future state of Korean industries and business competitiveness.

For Korea to develop, not only corporations but also the government, public sector, education sector, politics, society, and all other sectors must possess competitiveness. However, the realm in which competitiveness should most concretely manifest is the economy, more specifically in the industrial and business sectors. Of course, the advantage that can become the competitiveness of an entire country cannot and should not appear in just one sector. Nevertheless, strategically identifying and nurturing the leading sectors first is an inevitable strategic choice. Of course, companies are created and operated by people.

The main theme and conclusion that this book aims to argue is that the source of competitiveness for Koreans is speed (quickness). Koreans can comparatively get things done quicker and if this is a sole attribute unique to Korea it becomes an advantage in competition.

During the period of rapid economic growth, the merit of this speed

---

[8] The IMF projected the global economic growth rate for 2021, following the hit from the COVID-19 crisis in 2020. The global average was 6.0%, with Korea at 4.3%, which is relatively low among the advanced economies. (press materials from the Ministry of Strategy and Finance, July 27th 2021).

appeared in a slightly self-deprecating (negative) expression, such as 'PPali, PPali (quickly, quickly)' and 'Dae Choong, Dae Choong (roughly, roughly)' and was sometimes indicated as a defect of Koreans. Of course, there would be side effects that appear in the process of getting things done speedily. It is easier to make mistakes when doing things quickly to neglect details. Even if only one out of ten is neglected, the other nine may become useless together, and as in the case of architectural construction, the result could be fatal.

As briefly explained in the beginning, the central core of competitiveness through innovation is speed. Speed is also an essential prerequisite for innovation. If you are not faster than others, you cannot win. In order to grow and evolve, you must be ahead in every aspect. Until now, we have sometimes hesitated or failed to fully capitalize on what Koreans can do better by being overly conscious of the side effects. That being said, maintaining the same characteristic of speed as before may not be desirable in the future.

Therefore, in the future, the speed of Koreans should be fast but safe, a speed that everyone can trust, and an honest transparent speed for oneself and others. If these three criteria are met and at the same time our unique merit is utilized, it may become the foundation of competitiveness that will enable Korea to leap forward continuously. Of course, political, legal, and institutional improvement and support are necessary to realize that, and also the current education system must change, and certain cultural habits must change as well. In other words, we need to explore ways to preserve and utilize the intrinsic advantage while eliminating or reducing the side effects that we have experienced.

1-3 Speed and Acceleration: A Practical Clarification of Concept

Throughout history, humans have consciously or unconsciously yearned for speed, and this desire continues to this day. We want to move quickly, obtain things faster, earn money faster and grow quickly. We want to win, finish things as soon as possible, create things quickly and be the first to display it. We want to run fast and arrive fast. We even want to add the suffix 'er' to the word 'faster'. Thanks to this pursuit of speed, humanity has achieved an enormous outcome. As a result, speed has become synonymous with progress, victory, development, growth, or at least played a crucial factor in these achievements.

Thomas Friedman[9] explains that rapid computer technology development, globalization, market changes, and natural changes such as climate change have all contributed to an accelerated pace of change in the workplace, politics, geopolitics, ethics, and local communities. We live in an era of unstoppable acceleration. Acceleration has become a matter of survival, not a choice, for those who want to thrive in the world.

Peter Borscheid[10], in his book "The Tempo Virus," likened speed to viruses. The subtitle of the book is "The Cultural History of the Speed that Dominated Humans." One of the author's observations is that the richer a country is, the faster its citizens' move and the quicker their rhythm becomes. This implies that modern people seeking progress cannot escape the pressure of speed. "Time is life...the more people save time, the more they have it" (p540). Human history cannot be separated from speed. Being relatively faster means having more time.

However, Borscheid also points out that once the mechanism of acceleration is infected by an increasing amount of leisure time, it can hardly be stopped unless there is a tremendous disaster. The example of such a disaster could be the COVID-19 pandemic that the world experienced since the beginning of 2020. Moreover, the daily routine of speed and acceleration has already been achieved, and although the time spent on certain tasks has been reduced, and thus giving people more available time in absolute terms, there is a paradoxical phenomenon that people feel they have less time overall. Although this book's purpose is not to discuss humanistic considerations, it is clear that the acceleration of speed does not necessarily make people happier, however, it is also true that we cannot reject the acceleration of speed.

Speed can continuously accelerate(decelerate), stay in constant status, or leap forward(downward) in a revolutionary manner. Throughout human history, there have been instances of continuous growth, such as the development of agriculture, which increased crop yields over time, and instances

---

9 Thomas Friedman's Survival Guidebook (Thank You for Being Late by Thomas Friedman 2017), a worldwide bestseller, Chosun Ilbo, January 7th, 2017. A17

10 Peter Borscheid' "The Tempo Virus - A Cultural History that Ruled Humans" (translated by Du Hang Suk), Deul Nnyeok, 2008. In this book, the author maintains that the acceleration of speed is not necessarily always associated with happiness, but provides examples to demonstrate that speed dominates contemporary society.

of rapid leap such as the development of communication systems. Human communication has evolved from the actual speed of human walking to a state where information is transmitted and used in real-time, regardless of distance. We have reached a level where it can be said that distance and space have disappeared concerning communication[11]. In cases where human capabilities have clear limits, such as reading books or articles, machines and artificial intelligence have been developed to read and process information on our behalf. We now have no difficulty in obtaining, processing, and utilizing vast amounts of real-time data to acquire and process the necessary information based on big data. The development continues to the point where machines, rather than humans, independently judge and process information using artificial intelligence.[12]

(1) Perception and Consequences of the Speed of Change

Humanity has no choice or reason to refuse progress or growth. The source of physical and military power is speed, and the core of economic and industrial competitiveness is also speed. The common background encompassing the previous two sectors is technology, and the ultimate goal pursued by technological advancement is speed. In engineering, medicine, physics, and all other fields, the goals they seek to achieve are either speed itself or changes that can be acquired by speed.

There is a phrase we have always enjoyed quoting: 'time is money.' However, if time is replaced by speed, the expression 'speed is money' is becoming more natural and persuasive. For example, in financial transactions, which have already become a crucial function of modern economies, speed is vital. In cutting-edge financial transactions, competitiveness mostly stems from speed. As we will demonstrate later, the transmission speed of orders in stock or futures trading determines profitability, so the ordering function

---

[11] Of course, these phenomena vary by country and economy. In countries like Korea, where the communication infrastructure is well established, space and distance can often pose no actual barrier. However, in some regions or countries in Africa or the Amazon, there may be no means of communication or even roads to travel on, leading to the serious issue of the so-called digital divide.

[12] This is an issue related to the function and role of artificial intelligence (AI). It can serve as an example indicating that AI has the potential to progress beyond a supportive role for humans to a stage where it can make judgments and decisions.

needs to be close to the exchange computer to avoid disadvantages due to speed discrepancies. The difference in momentary split second connection determines the outcome of the transaction.

(2) Scientific Concept and Measurement Method

This concept can also be explained in terms of the natural science formula. Since speed is a physical phenomenon and attribute, if we use to explain it with the law of thermodynamics in physics, the formula for energy (vitality) would be:

$$E = \fallingdotseq \Sigma\, mv^2$$

In this formula:

Σ represents the sum

E represents energy or desired outcome (growth, income, output, etc.)

m represents mass or the size of the input (investment, revenue, scale, etc.)

v represents speed (rate of technological advancement, growing speed, etc.)

Thus, the size of energy (economic outcomes or vitality) is represented by the product of the mass (scale) of the object and the square of the rate of change (and its acceleration).

Applying this formula to the content we are discussing fits well. Energy can be replaced with any measurement or concern, such as national income, size of revenue, strength of military power, production, or competitiveness. In the formula, the mass represents the input subject being discussed, such as capital investment, input of production factors, military power expenditure, or economic scale, which are relatively stable values (constants) that do not change significantly in the short run. Speed represents the degree of change, such as the rate of technological advancement, the speed of innovation, the physical speed, or the growth rate, and the meaning of the square in the formula represents the accelerating effect of the speed itself, expressed as acceleration. For example, a company's output or sales increases as the speed of growth, technological advancements or innovation rate increases.

Of course, the size of production facilities, capital, economic scale, and other areas represented as the mass in the formula will bring greater results if they are relatively larger or abundant, but they play a role as constants in the short term, so the key lies in speed (and acceleration). In other words, the speed of change, rather than scale, determines competitiveness and the resulting consequence.

The formula can be applied not only to material aspects, but also to non-material aspects, such as culture[13]:

$$C = \Sigma\, E \times T,$$

C=Culture (level of culture)

E=Energy (energy extraction per person, per year. per capita GDP, for example)

T=Technology (efficiency of technical means for applying this energy to work)

The level of culture increases proportionally as the amount of energy humans (humanity) can extract (e.g., income) increases, and as the efficiency of technical means for applying this energy to work (e.g., IT technology) increases. This formula can be applied when explaining the Korean Wave(Hallyu) later.

The process of growth and development for entities and groups is the pursuit of 'more'. More faster, bigger, more stronger etc. In this expression, 'faster' represents speed, and 'even more' is represented as acceleration by squaring. If you have a relatively faster speed than your competitors, you have an advantage in competitiveness. In other words, if we borrow the physical formula shown above, while the size of the mass (bulk) itself needs to be large for the overall force (vitality) to increase, it is more important to note that any small scale can be compensated by the speed of acceleration. As an example, in the human history of combat, the key factor in determining victory or defeat was mostly speed (mobility) rather than the size of military power.

---

13 "Ian Morris, Foragers, Farmers, and Fossil Fuels (translated by Lee Jae-kyung), Banni, 2016". In the book Morris makes use of the equation suggested by Leslie White.

(3) Measurement by Economic Cost - Transaction Cost and Opportunity Cost

Another way to measure speed is cost in economic terms. The speed that this book aims to analyze and focus on is, of course, a speed related economic cost. Cost includes not only directly appearing and calculable price but also indirect or hidden cost. Representative costs are transaction cost and opportunity cost.

In economic theory, the transaction cost appears repeatedly. In all transactions, such as buying an item, the cost calculated for the consumer includes the time and transportation expenses spent going to and from shopping, and the time spent choosing the item, in addition to the price directly paid for the item. These are the hidden costs incurred for the transaction. Typically, since one does not directly pay this cost to oneself, it is referred to as an opportunity cost for the parties involved. Opportunity cost varies from person to person. The income or utility that one could earn or have by working or engaging in other activities instead of going shopping becomes that person's opportunity cost. Naturally, the higher the income, the higher the opportunity cost. Therefore, for such people, the time spent on transactions, that is, transaction cost becomes more important. Of course, shopping or dining out can be enjoyable and bring utility (pleasure) to the person engaging in that activity, despite the time and cost spent. Therefore, depending on the person, they may be willing to ignore the opportunity cost or transaction cost.

As income levels tend to rise, an individual's transaction cost and opportunity cost also increase at the same time. Therefore, time becomes more 'valuable' to everyone. Even if I am not doing anything but relaxing, the value of my time gradually increases. If someone provides a service that saves my time at a relatively low cost, I am willing to pay for that service. Thus, the rising transaction cost and opportunity cost that accompany one's income growth, along with the changing service cost, can create new markets. These markets may grow explosively if a 'non-face-to-face approach' like the COVID-19 situation is enforced or preferred.

The traditional saying 'time is money' has been used for a long time, but its meaning was more about the importance of not wasting time rather than its economic value. This was because there was little awareness of transaction cost and opportunity cost at that time, and the economic situation did not require people to be busy considering opportunity cost. Opportunity cost refers to the calculated loss of the value (money) that one could earn or create by doing other things during the time spent on a specific task. Thinking in terms of opportunity cost can significantly change an individual's life, and efforts for personal success can also be deemed to increase one's opportunity cost.

Therefore, the concept of opportunity cost has a more precise and cool meaning in business. In many cases, being faster than others (competitors) can secure more sales, profits, and customers. If you're not fast enough, you can often be left behind by competitors. This speed is represented by the time it takes to generate something, the time it takes to provide a service, the time it takes to use something, and the time it takes to connect. Therefore, time itself is competitiveness, encompassing all processes and procedures. Naturally, a faster high-speed train costs more than a slower train.

Transaction cost is also a subject of discussion in the same context. Time is spent on anything, such as shopping, commuting, eating, and so on, and this time or transportation expense should be calculated as the hidden cost to that individual. Going to a rural market in the past or voluntary shopping nowadays is not a problem if one enjoys the shopping itself and thus is willing to pay the hidden cost, but otherwise, the time spent shopping results in the opportunity cost. If you can save time and expense, you may calculate the corresponding expense(gain) anyway.

If time and effort can be saved, people are willing to pay money (expense). Examples related to daily life include electric rice cookers and robotic vacuum cleaners. And the core technology of the Fourth Industrial Revolution, Artificial Intelligence falls into the same category. The explosively growing delivery industry is another direct evidence of this. Numerous innovations, inventions, improvements, and efforts ultimately aim to suggest ways and directions to reduce time or cost compared to before. Since time is money, time itself is a competitive advantage.

1-4 Role and Importance of Speed in Economy, Society and Social Life

Throughout human history, the process of economic development has been an effort to increase productivity, and more specifically, progress has been rewarded by successfully reducing time. The industrial revolution, which can be considered one of the most important revolutions in human economic history, was a revolution that dramatically changed the speed of production and manufacturing. A paradigm-shift in production took place.

However, the perception of time and attitudes towards work in countries or regions that had not yet industrialized, whether before or during the Industrial Revolution, were completely different. In pre-industrial China and Korea, the expression "there is no need to hurry, as there is as much time as ox hair" was quite natural. However, now that industrialization dominates the world, no country can escape the rule of speed.

As is well known, the Korean economic growth rate is a world record.[14] The world evaluates the unprecedented growth from one of the poorest countries to an economic powerhouse with a per-capita GDP ranking around the top 10 worldwide as the 'Miracle on the Han River.' For a comparison, the United States, the world's number one economic power, increased its GDP scale by 35.7 times from 1960 to 2017, while Korea increased by 386.8 times during the same period. Every country strives to move from an underdeveloped or developing stage to an advanced level, but many of them fail to because growth rate is relative as well as absolute.

In other words, the key factor in economic growth and development is the relative growth rate. To win in competition, a country's economy must grow faster than other countries for a significant period, and this accumulation leads to actual development. In particular, if a country is not faster than its competitors in various areas, especially the economy, it cannot catch up.

---

[14] Jang Dae-hwan, What We Don't Know About Korea - Miracle Korea 70 Years, Maeil Business Newspaper Publishers, 2019. This book provides easy-to-understand statistical results and international comparisons on Korea's economic development.

1-5 Important Role of Speed in Transportation and Communication Development

When the author was young and his grandparents told stories about the past, they would always start with 'Once upon a time, a long, long time ago...' This was to describe a time that was definitely different from the present (at that time), and to emphasize that the world was somewhat different back then. Realistically the difference was minimal. However, now we live in an era where new expressions are created to describe recent events, such as last year, a few months ago, a few weeks ago, or even new technology that came out a few days ago. Moreover, the speed at which the world (society) changes has increased tremendously due to digitalization and the development of various social media. Transportation and communication are typical examples of this speed.

(1) Transportation

One of the most dramatic changes that have occurred over the past 200 years and that all humans have experienced in common is in the field of transportation. The primary means of transportation for humans on land was initially feet and then animal power, represented by horses[15]. However, for a long time, horses could not play the role of a universal means of transportation, except for military purposes. Although carriages were invented and played an important role in mass transportation in Europe and America, they did not reach the stage of significantly narrowing the space and distance as today's means of transportation do. Various types of ships played an important role in transportation across rivers and oceans since ancient times, but they relied on natural wind power or human power as an energy source until the invention of the steam engine. Therefore, they were significantly limited in size and speed, and faced many restrictions and risks of accidents due to natural conditions.

The invention of the steam engine, the emergence of railways and steam-

---

[15] Historically, depending on natural conditions or climate, animals like cows, camels, elephants, and dogs have served as main modes of transportation or subsidiary forces in living, especially in combat. However, universally speaking, horses were not only most widely used but also the most efficient means.

ships brought about a revolutionary change in the transportation sector, dramatically increasing human living space and travel distances. The geographical and spatial scope that nations, societies, and communities could influence expanded, resulting in major changes in all aspects of political system, social structure, community and individual lifestyle, consciousness structure and culture. The transition to modern society can be said to have been led by transportation and communication.

The invention of the automobile using an internal combustion engine was another revolution, and the subsequent emergence of airplanes opened up a new world of time and space concept. In particular, the invention of the train and automobile became a powerful means to expand the space and periphery within and between regions, creating modern cities, and promoting industrialization. At the same time, the emergence of steam ships and continuing development has facilitated the advent of today's globalized era. Without the invention of new means of transportation and the continuous increase in travel speed, today's urban formation and urban life would not be possible.

As mentioned earlier, since the industrial revolution, speed has begun to play a major role in the center of change. Of course, even before the industrial revolution, speed was valued and held a central position in competitiveness. For example, the constant innovation, improvement, and upgrade of faster feet, faster horses, and faster ships were absolutely necessary for economic and even more so for military competitiveness. Most of these improvements originated from military purposes. After firearms like guns and cannons were invented, speed competition, such as extending the range, reducing gunpowder reloading time, and enabling continuous firing, was absolutely crucial for military superiority, and performance competition continued fiercely. Nevertheless, the relative increase in speed before the Industrial Revolution was not comparable to that after.

The changes after the Industrial Revolution showed different dimensions in both quality and quantity. The acceleration has gone beyond what can be seen, reaching a level that surpasses imagination today. Automobiles limit their top speed for safety, but racing cars are approaching the speed of low-flying airplanes. Technology that goes beyond earth and into space is advancing to the point where space travel is being reserved as a tourism product. In the case of transportation, the use is limited not by the technology itself but by the legal, institutional, and infrastructure support needed to operate it.[16] Separate from the dimension of driving speed, the development of autonomous vehicles by artificial intelligence (AI) is making the distinction between the automotive industry, electronics industry, and communication and information industry unnecessary. Transportation methods like the Hyperloop, which can achieve faster speed than airplanes (1200 km/hour), are moving beyond the experimental stage and showcasing the possibility of commercialization.[17] Drones, which are gaining attention as one of the new industries in the era of the Fourth Industrial Revolution, are playing a leading role in the integration of land and air transportation, and can be interpreted as a preliminary stage for the miniaturization and autonomous flight of airplanes. Soon, there will be an inevitable need for an air traffic control system in the air, just like on the ground. Work to revolutionize the speed of airplanes is also becoming visible. As the scope of human life and travel space expands into outer space, space travel may become a common life.

(2) Communication

We have covered transportation first for convenience sake, but the development of communication has been far more dramatic and revolutionary than that of transportation. In the past, the speed of communication could not exceed that of transportation, as mail or messages were delivered by foot, horse, carriage, or ship.[18] The communication revolution began with the invention of the telegraph, telephone and through the establishment of optical communication networks.

---

16 At present, a flight from Seoul to New York takes over 12 hours, but technology that could make the flight possible in less than 2 hours is being developed. Considering that it took a month to travel this distance by ship before commercial airplanes were operational, we can gauge the impact of the acceleration of transportation speed.

17 'New York-Washington in 29 minutes. Bullet Train Hyperloop a Reality?' Maeil Business Newspaper (Maeil Business hereafter) July 22nd, 2017

18 Of course, a more diverse range of methods was used for military purposes. For example, carrier pigeons were used, and light and smoke from beacon towers were employed, as were communication methods using specific sounds or reflected light, but these were not universally used.

In the past in Korea, during the Joseon Dynasty (1392-1910), it took about a month to walk from Busan to Seoul(450Km), but now real-time communication is possible, not only through written correspondence but through conversation even while seeing the counterpart, which is a radical change that occurred in a very short time. Real-time communication is revolutionary as it is now possible with many points in the world. Another important point is that this real-time communication can be achieved at very low or relatively cheap communication charges. Of course, this was made possible because of the invention, discovery, and utilization of electricity, electronics, and radio waves.

By comparison, there has been no field in human history related to daily life that has shown faster change and progress than communication. In the case of Korea as an example, telephone calls were first introduced in 1882 and were used for communication between the palace and government ministries. Twenty years later, in 1902, the first telephone line was installed between Seoul and Incheon, and local telephone lines were established later. The number of subscribers was only a few hundred by 1905, mainly due to high prices. It was almost impossible to install a landline telephone in a private home until the 1960s due to the lack of infrastructure such as wired telephone network, and high cost. Before that period, it was an indirect connection method through a switchboard, not automatic exchange.

By the 1980s, landline telephones could be installed in any household. And also the first phase of mobile communication, the "beeper," emerged as a groundbreaking change. This method, which involved sending a signal (beep sound) to the mobile subscriber to request contact, was an amazing cutting-edge means at the time. Soon after, the early mobile phones(not like today's small, lightweight form but in a large, quite heavy form) began to spread in the United States, Korea and some other countries. The era of mobile communication began in the late 1980s, followed by the smartphone from the 2000s. In the last 100 years or longer, many people on earth, including Korea, have moved from a communication method that basically relied on their foot to equipping themselves with means that allow anyone to communicate in real time and anywhere.[19] This speed is frighteningly fast. In early 2019, when Korea became the world's first country to commer-

19 This tremendous technological advancement and device distribution inevitably lead to a digital divide among countries. Communication methods, regardless

cialize 5G, Hwang Chang-gyu, the chairman of Korea Telecom, predicted in his speech at the world's largest mobile exhibition MWC that "5G is not just about faster speed, but a technology that will change the manufacturing paradigm and become the driving force for the Korean economy."[20]

During the Napoleonic Wars spanning the 18th and early 19th centuries, the Rothschilds, a prestigious financial dynasty, acquired vast wealth in the stock and bond markets by securing information and news faster than the British government. They did this through the use of pigeons, express ships, postal carriages and competent informants. Their secret was speed. [21]

In the past, we have used the expression 'in the blink of an eye' to describe a very short time, which may be equivalent to about one second or less in our current time concept. Today's communication speed competes at a rate that is one-thousandth of a second (millisecond), which we can never perceive through our senses. Examples of this speed are found in stocks and futures trading as well as in sports.

---

of whether they are wired, wireless, or digital, require enormous infrastructure investment and service costs. If economic development is slow or lagging, the gap in communication methods poses a challenge. I published a paper discussing this issue in the 1990s. It is a question of which communication method to install as a national policy in developing countries where even the wired telephone system is not properly distributed yet. That is, whether to follow the development pattern of developed countries and install a wired network first, or to start with a mobile network. This question applies to many developing countries, and due to the characteristics and fast progress of technology, most countries are starting with digital methods. (Lim Jung-Duk, "Information and Communication Technology and Balanced Development", Urban and Regional Development Research Vol. 8, No. 1, 2000) This raises other possibilities for the theory of evolutionary adaptation methods. It is a question of whether there are any side effects or problems with the interaction with other sectors when using digital methods as communication means from the beginning. That is, if it is confirmed that there is no problem with starting with a digital method from the beginning, skipping the very important wired communication method in the process of the advancement (evolution) of communication means, it could be a very important reference for economic development theory. However, the interim evaluation is that a gradual path cannot be taken. There is no need to follow the countries that have gone ahead due to the speed of technological change. The acceleration effect of technological change results in astronomical cost reductions. It's like the principle that a country introducing cars for the first time has no choice but to choose electric cars.

20 Chosun Economy, February 26th 2019. B5

21 Hong Ik-hee, "The Story of New Yorkers", Chosun Ilbo, October 19th 2021. A34

The world's largest commodity futures exchange (CME) is located in Chicago, and the stock exchange (NYSE) is in New York, USA. Since stock and commodity futures prices influence each other, placing orders faster than others is a very important source of competitiveness. Nowadays, all transactions are carried out through electronic communication methods, so being even a few milliseconds ahead can result in winning a trade. As the speed of communication varies depending on the distance, the distance between the transmitting and receiving means is critically important.

The following illustration and description provide an interesting example of the communication speed war. It clearly demonstrates that the time spent for a single transmission, which is impossible for us to perceive in our daily lives, is the most important factor determining the success or failure of enormous financial transactions.

The 0.001-Second Tower War in a Small American City of 200,000 Residents

In Aurora, a city with a population of 200,000 located 60 km west of Chicago, a 'light-speed war' is in full swing. On street lamp poles in the northeastern suburbs of the city, where the interstate highway I-88 passes, dish antennas are mounted, and metal towers with multiple dish antennas continue to be installed on vacant lots. These are setups by companies that engage in high-frequency trading of various futures and derivatives at the Chicago Mercantile Exchange (CME), receiving and sending financial data to and from the NYSE and NASDAQ data centers in New Jersey via microwaves.

CME is the world's largest futures exchange, with around 20 million daily transactions involving commodities such as oil, grains, energy, and metals, as well as U.S. Treasury bonds, the S&P 500 index, the Nikkei 225 index, and a variety of futures, derivatives, and futures swaps. High-frequency trading firms use advanced algorithms to automatically trade securities, quickly placing orders for futures and derivatives on stocks with rising prices in the NYSE, as well as placing orders for futures with rising prices in the CME on NYSE or NASDAQ. Moreover, the CME data center is connected to nine stock exchanges worldwide, including Hong Kong, Tokyo, London, and Frankfurt, making it a necessary stop for global high-frequency financial transactions.

Speed is essential in this game. It's a competition to gain an edge by mere milliseconds, one-thousandths of a second. Microwaves only require a line of sight between antennas, so high-frequency trading firms connect U.S. mobile communication base station towers with microwaves and install their servers directly in the stock exchange data center. As a result, while fiber-optic transmission between Chicago and New Jersey data centers takes 6.55 milliseconds, microwave transmission takes only 4.25 milliseconds.

During the 2-3 milliseconds saved, the price fluctuation is a mere 0.08 cents on average. However, they trade tens of thousands of shares at a time and automatically conduct thousands to tens of thousands of electronic transactions around the clock to generate profits. This is why two high-frequency trading firms in Chicago leased a brick house site across the street from the CME data center for $14 million a year in May 2017 to attach dish antennas close together. In response, other competitors rented streetlights closer to the data center to install their dish antennas.

"A 0.001-second tower war in a small American city of 200,000 residents. What's going on?", Chosun Ilbo, April 26, 2019, Partially Reprinted

In Korea, the situation is similar. The headquarters of the Korea Exchange moved to Busan, 2nd largest city located at the southern tip of the Korean Peninsula in the 1990s. However, the computer trading function still remains at the same place in Seoul, because moving the server to Busan would result in longer communication times with major trading companies mostly located in Seoul.

In February 2021, the Bank of Korea announced its benchmark interest rate via Kakao-talk message which is the most popular communication device in Korea to reporters. They explained that Kakao-talk was chosen as the means of communication with the least margin of error to ensure fairness, since the benchmark interest rate is an extremely sensitive indicator that can shake the financial market and must be shared with all market participants simultaneously. In this case, the margin of error is 300 milliseconds. For email, the difference is said to be over 2 minutes.[22]

---

[22] Chosun Economy, March 7th 2021. B1

Nowadays, the pace of change in communication methods, technology, and equipment as well as the adoption cycle of related devices and technology is becoming shorter in less developed countries too. This trend of change, which can be referred to as a paradox or the 'latecomer advantage,' is primarily due to the fact that less developed countries can adopt state-of-the-art hardware and software from the start without having to bear the enormous sunk costs that advanced countries have invested in evolving facilities, equipment, and technology over a long period.[23]

The most astonishing aspect is not communication technology itself, but the ability and speed to collect, store, search, and process information, knowledge, and data, and in addition, the methods of transmitting, learning, and educating all of these things. The way knowledge is acquired, discovered, and transmitted has fundamentally changed from the traditional gradual, step-by-step evolutionary approach to one that is virtually different in dimension and means. The digital technology-related method (such as algorithm), which can also be described as 'customized,' not only makes life convenient for humans but also controls them.

The invention of the Internet is one of the most important achievements of the 20th century, and the PC has been widely acclaimed as its universal means of execution. However, PCs are now being replaced by smartphones.[24] By the end of the 20th century, five IT related devices - PDA, digital camera, Ultra mobile PC, landline phone, and MP3 player - were revolutionary inventions that were highly acclaimed and widely used, but they have either completely disappeared or are disappearing. The future of credit cards is also predictable. The disappearance of dictionaries, one of the most important pieces of human cultural heritage to be remembered and recorded, is an example of how information acquisition is changing beyond the traditional speed.

---

[23] The author's previous paper. This paper discusses whether there is a price to pay for leapfrogging in underdeveloped countries without going through the development process of advanced countries. For instance, when an underdeveloped country first introduces telecommunication facilities, they have no choice but to introduce mobile phones. The question is whether there could be any side effects to this.

[24] The question raised in footnote 17 also applies here. It's a question of judgment whether it is better to start with PC education for children in remote parts of Africa where personal computers have not yet been disseminated, or to start with smartphones.

Paradoxically, there is a saying that 21st-century humans are computer-bound (now more accurately smartphone-bound) peasants.[25] This refers to the reality that time is becoming more precious and expensive, so most tasks must be handled by individuals themselves using their phones. This can be seen as a shift from cost-effectiveness to time-saving ratio, and time is becoming more precious.

Technological advances and their actual and institutional application do not always coincide. Humanity has reached an era where the fundamental ways of acquiring and disseminating knowledge throughout human history are bound to change from a technological perspective. However, actually accepting and applying that change and its implementation is a different dimension.

1-6 Technological Change and Role of Speed

The length of one second has remained the same since humans started measuring time, and it will continue to be the same in the future. However, its relative length keeps increasing. The communication speed for financial transactions, as mentioned earlier, pursues and strives for a difference of 0.001 second, which is too fast for our bodies or senses to perceive. Technological advancement can be explained as a dimension that reduces the time required to complete a task.

The fundamental factor driving economic and social development is technological advancement. Transportation, communication, production, management, etc. have all changed and progressed as a result of technological advances. Therefore, it may be more reasonable to discuss technology from an integrated perspective rather than separating it. However, it is necessary to consider the basic science separately from the category of science and technology. Without the advancement of basic science, we could not enjoy the benefit of all technological progress we have today. Like technology, basic science is also characterized by its competitive nature in terms of speed. The reality is that if the result of research is not published and recognized before others, the outcome and result may differ as mentioned earlier in Bell telephone incidence.[26]

---

[25] Craig Lambert (Translated by Lee Hyun-ju), "Shadow Work: The Unpaid, Unseen Jobs That Fill Your Day," Min Um Sa, 2016

[26] For example, "Recently, a Korean neutrino experiment called RENO (Reactor

Of course, technology is not limited to manufacturing or production sectors. In all areas, including management, business administration, and organization, technology becomes the driving force for development and change. As its scope broadens, technology becomes a means and method for progress and improvement in every aspect of human life.[27] Regardless of the type or content, all technological advancements also represent concepts that are faster, cheaper, or more convenient than before.

Artificial intelligence is another aspect brought about by technological advancement. There is growing controversy over whether artificial intelligence will ultimately be dependent on humans or one that becomes equal to or even dominates humans. Since it is not unreasonable to imagine that AI (Chat-GPT, for example) is evolving and advancing on its own, if this imagination becomes a reality, our world will exist in a completely different dimension than before. The ability to control the speed of change arbitrarily is another dimension of the discussion. Control of speed will pose a significant challenge for humanity. We are experiencing the profound impact of big data on all aspects of human life, thought process, science, economy, and industry, more intensely every day. Speed matters.

Sociologist Zygmunt Bauman defined the current generation as living in a "liquid modernity" era, where for the first time in history, humans have to accept change itself as a permanent condition of life. "We are all becoming something new, and there has never been a better time in human history to start than now..."[28] This statement implies the need to embrace and actively create change as it is inevitable and unlike anything experienced in the past.

Experiment for Neutrino Oscillation) has been conducted at the Yeong Gwang nuclear power plant in Junnam Province. Meanwhile, research results from a facility with the same purpose at the Daya Bay nuclear power plant in China were announced first. Basic science may also be a fierce competition, and it might be a race against time." Chosun Ilbo, March 3rd 2012.

27 The term 'technology'" is also widely used in society, in contexts such as lifestyle or relationships. For example, it emphasizes 'technology' in terms such as presentation technology, political technology, conversation technology, dating technology, and marketing technology. Of course, when expressed in English, the 'technology' in this context is not 'technology' but 'technique,' so a distinction needs to be made. However, if we consider it as a concept of improvement or development, there's no issue with the Korean expression, and it doesn't hinder the logical progression of the argument.

28 Kevin Kelly, "The Inevitable," translated by Lee Han-eum, Chunglim Publishing, 2017.

So, how should we cope? David Allen, who published "Getting Things Done" in 2001 and released a revised edition 15 years later, explained the reason for the update as follows: "... The world has become faster due to digitalization and the development of social media. In the past, once you got a job and became familiar with your tasks, you could spend 1-2 years comfortably without change. Now, that period is only a day or two... There is a need to build and utilize an external brain, which is backed by cognitive science research."[29] Technology widens the spectrum of multiple generations experiencing current events simultaneously which explains the discrepancy and polarization of generations especially since Korea has recently undergone rapid changes.

In his 2016 book "Thank You for Being Late," Thomas Friedman attributes the dizzying pace of change to the rapid development of computer technology, the globalized market, and natural changes like climate change, all accelerating together, causing rapid changes in the workplace, politics, geopolitics, ethics, and communities.[30] Acceleration is the key word here.

Discussions on artificial intelligence and the future of humanity can be summarized into two main categories: the optimistic claim that there is no doubt that AI technology will enhance human life; and the pessimistic stance that humans will inevitably be dominated and subjugated by the AI they have developed. This book will not discuss this further as it goes beyond the established scope, but AI requires more attention and discussion.

In a book that predicts technological change and their impact on society, politics, economy, and culture, the author of "The Inevitable," Kevin Kelly, presents the following 12 points as deep trends:[31]

1) interacting, 2) cognifying, 3) flowing, 4) screening, 5) accessing, 6) sharing, 7) filtering, 8) remixing, 9) interacting, 10) tracking, 11) questioning, and 12) beginning.

These predictions are quite acute, and the world is changing rapidly in the direction predicted by the author.

---

[29] David Allen, "Getting Things Done: The Art of Stress-Free Productivity," translated by Kim Kyung-sub and Kim Sun-jun, Kim Young Publishing, 2016.
[30] Book Section, Chosun Ilbo, January 7th 2017. A17.
[31] The aforementioned book by Kevin Kelly.

1-7 Speed in Sports

Modern people are increasingly obsessed with speed in sports. Popular Western events like car racing and soccer games are prime examples of people wanting to see speed itself and achievements (scoring) through fast speeds. The core of all sports is 'faster.' In track and field, the person who reaches the goal line faster wins, and in most ball games, the person or team who scores more within the given time wins. Even in games like baseball, tennis, or volleyball, where various techniques are used to score more points, the key is to throw or hit faster, and those who run faster have a decisive advantage. In any sport, the slower player can never win.

In the 2015-16 season, the English Premier League saw the rise of the underdog team, Leicester City, whose success was attributed to the fact that five of their players ranked within the top 20 fastest players in the league.[32] This team, which never had any star players and had been perennially at the bottom of the league since its inception, combined the movement of explosive speed to win the championship that season. However, when their speed could not be sustained, the team quickly returned to its previous standing.

In baseball, major league teams are searching for pitchers with the fastest ball speed from all over the world. Both average and marginal pitching speed are continually increasing, thanks to advancements in science and technology. This trend will likely continue as faster speed makes it difficult for batters to hit the ball and because the public is fascinated by this. In order to speed up the game itself, the US professional baseball game has reduced practice time during pitcher change, professional basketball league has implemented a 14-second rule for offensive rebound, and professional volleyball league has introduced an 8-second rule for serving time of players. Added to this is increased audience enjoyment.

To boost speed, athletes optimize their physical fitness and conditioning, and enormous investments are made in equipment and clothing. This not only leads to individual glory and a significant increase in income for the athletes, but also brings massive wealth to the related industries. It is no

[32] "The whirlwind of the Fox Legion, the driving force is speed," Chosun Ilbo, November 27th 2015

exaggeration to say that the expansion of market size by the media industry's growth, the development of speed measurement technology, and the public's enjoyment of sports are all immersed in acceleration.

While speed improvements in sports cannot be infinite, rapid advancement in measurement technology will continue to push the boundaries, and humans will put more effort and investment into achieving those marginal speeds. In events like the Olympic, 100m race or short track competitions, rankings are determined by the time difference as small as one-hundredth of a second. However, most people do not experience such a small change in speed in their everyday lives. Sports games push athletes into an endless competition, using a time unit that is imperceptible to the average person. At the 2018 Pyeongchang(Korea) Winter Olympics, Korea's Cha Min-kyu lost the gold medal in the 500m speed skating event by a mere 0.01 second. When asked about the significance of the 0.01-second difference after the race, he responded, "My short legs."[33] In the 2022 Beijing Winter Olympics, there was a report of victory decided by a difference of 0.001 second.[34]

As previously cited, in the book "Tempo Virus," the author states that "speed has evolved independently from its original economic basis, becoming a leisure culture or a new kind of sport" (p. 156). Various technologies and resources are being mobilized to increase speed in sports. The world has changed drastically from the days when success could be achieved simply through physical strength, talent, perseverance, and personal effort.

The concept of speed is now being applied to the exercise methods of the elderly. The American College of Sports Medicine revised its guidelines, raising the importance of increasing muscle power in elderly exercise and influencing elderly exercise guidelines worldwide.[35] Even for the elderly, it seems that speed is now essential.

1-8 Speed in Wars

Regardless of whether it is a personal fight or a battle in wars, if you are asked to point out the most important factor that determines victory or

---

33 Chosun Ilbo February 21rst ,2018.
34 "Chosun Ilbo, February 22nd, 2022. A22"
35 "Chosun Economy, Issue No. 30273"

defeat, it is speed. If you can't cut, hit, shoot, or dodge faster than your opponent, you will die or suffer defeat. Of course, there are cases where even the most exceptional individuals or armies cannot win if they are weaker in terms of firepower, manpower, supplies, and equipment in the longer run, but even if they are disadvantaged in battle and have to retreat, speed determines the success of retreat. Therefore, speed is the most important factor in victory, survival, and domination in wars. The side occupying a strategically advantageous position first or capturing it faster wins, and this is true in ancient and modern battles and various disputes alike. One of the main elements of strategy, a surprise attack, also relies on speed. This principle applies not only to actual combat but also to mobile games enjoyed by modern people. Even in the game of Go, which is played by moving pieces with your hands while sitting still, the side that first secures a strategic position has a distinct advantage.

The key to the success of the 13th-century Mongol Empire, which achieved the largest territorial empire in history, was speed. At the time, the total population of Mongolia was around 2 million, so the actual combat force would have been much smaller. Instead, the entire army was composed of mounted infantry, and all were light cavalry. That is, they did not wear heavy armor, and their weapons mainly consisted of personal bows and crescent-shaped swords that could easily cut enemies. Food was provided through an individual supply system, allowing soldiers to drink horse milk and mature jerky under their saddles, making it possible to eat while on the move. They could even sleep on their horses. The movement speed of such cavalry was much faster than that of heavily armed cavalry, who had to wear iron armor and carry heavy weapons while also moving with supply troops and infantry.[36]

The Mongol army was said to have moved faster than rumors spread by human feet, which was not an exaggeration. This fast movement meant that all battles were like surprise attacks. In the slow-information medieval era, if an army arrived and attacked before information or intelligence could be

---

36 "Until the formation of the Mongol Empire and the establishment of the Yuan dynasty, which led to a sedentary lifestyle, families and livestock moved collectively like an army. The army moved first and the rest followed, making it pointless to employ strategies such as striking at the enemy's rear or base. Also, due to the difference in movement speed, even if a surprise attack was launched from behind, the forward-moving army could easily be turned back." (Kim Jong-rae, Millennium Man Genghis Khan, Dream Ends 2006, Jack

received, the outcome of the battle was almost certain. The Mongol army must have been an object of horror.

In the Middle Ages, Western knights, clad in heavy iron armor and wielding long iron lances, could not achieve faster speed even when riding horses. When Western knights faced the Mongol cavalry, the lightly armored Mongol fighters would first dodge the knights' long lance, swiftly move past them, and immediately turn around to shoot arrows at the knights' unprotected back, taking advantage of the weight of the armor and weapon that made it impossible for the knights to turn around quickly. This was done with lightning-fast speed, overpowering their opponents. This image of heavily armored Western knights appeared frequently in foreign movies popular in Korea until the mid-20th century, making it an easily recognizable scene for older readers. If Genghis Khan's army, which conquered the largest territory in the shortest period of time in history, had not halted their advance in Hungary during their European conquest, today's world history would be completely different.

Horse-drawn chariots and cavalry had long been indispensable in various battles in both the East and West. However, a strategy relying solely on cavalry could not remain effective indefinitely. Developments in new weapons and transportation methods due to technological advancements changed the way wars were fought and the nature of battles.

There are countless examples of battles in which the outcome was reversed due to unpredictable movement strategies or speed. Napoleon army's victories are attributed more to 'rapid operational actions and lightning-fast marches' than to dependence on the newly developed artillery and firearms of the time.[37] General MacArthur's Inchon landing operation during the Korean War (1950-1953) can also be classified as a surprise attack, a speed war. In both Eastern and Western wars, being the first to capture a key point first is one of the critical factors for victory. Therefore, speed was the key to winning wars. In the late 16th Century Admiral Lee Sun-Sin's tactics at the Battle of Myeongnyang (war against Japanese invasion) used the speed of water currents, where he defeated more than ten times as many Japanese ships with only 13 ships.

Weatherford, Woken by Genghis Khan, Four Seasons 2005)

[37] Borscheid, Tempo Virus, p 400

Throughout history of war, special operations that reversed lack of troop numbers, firepower, and disadvantageous situations were often carried out with lightning-fast movement. Special operations are small units executing missions in a short time in a confined area but these operations often play a crucial role in turning the tide of war.[38]

The innovation of ancient Roman war and battle concepts also lies in speed. Traditionally, building fortresses or constructing trenches served the purpose of defending against enemies. Therefore, methods were used, such as selecting high locations to hinder enemy access, building high fortresses, and constructing moats. However, Romans didn't build fortresses from the beginning. Instead, they built Roman roads that extended from Rome to each region and colony. Parts of the roads were not only for pedestrians but also sturdy and wide enough for chariots, paved with stones. In today's terms, they constructed highways. This allowed enemies to approach easily, so the strategy was to go out in advance, occupy advantageous terrain, and fight the invading enemy rather than waiting and fighting defensively. Such a strategy involved the concept of going out to fight and conquer the outside regions first. When the concept of warfare and the strategy of the country changed to defense rather than offense, Rome began to decline.

Roman road networks played a crucial role in the spread and exchange of economy, culture, and religion. Roads are the basic condition for the rapid movement of goods and people. The roads built by Rome played a decisive role in spreading Roman systems or Roman culture in various areas such as law, institutions, military organization, and battles, and in managing a vast range of colonies. In modern day this can be evaluated as speed-oriented management.

Also, Roman roads made a significant contribution to the spread of Christianity as a world religion, changing world history. If Paul, the most outstanding Christian theologian and missionary in history, hadn't been able to use Roman roads in the 1st century, it would have been impossible to make three missionary journeys across Israel's neighboring regions, Europe, and the Middle East (Asia Minor) in such a short time.

---

38 Yuval Harari, Translated by Kim Seung-ok, Bold Operation, Forest of Psyche, 2017

General McChrystal, who commanded the US military fighting against Al-Qaeda from 2003 to 2008, reorganized the US special forces into smaller units to respond to Al-Qaeda, which restructured its organization in real-time. He delegated authority broadly so that teams on the ground could share information, become their own brains, and adapt. This was to adapt to the 4th generation warfare characterized by 'acceleration of speed,' 'rapid increase of variables,' and 'expansion of interdependence.'[39]

The key to winning battles, business, and decision making is information, and the core of gathering information is speed. The victories and defeats in wars, commercial transactions, and financial transactions in the East and the West depended on the quality and quantity of information, as well as the speed of transmission and acquisition. Zhuge Liang (Kongming), who would be called the god of war in the Chinese novel 'Story of the Three Kingdoms', set in the history of the 3rd century AD, excelled in information collection and utilization method. In the novel, Zhuge Liang is described as overcoming military disadvantages and winning most battles through outstanding use of information such as human intelligence, geographic information, weather information collection and use, and predictions based on astronomy (mainly changes in constellations). In modern terms, he could be described as an exceptional expert using GIS and GPS technology.

Silicon Valley, which is leading the world's technological innovation, can also be compared to a battlefield. There is an argument that likens the secret to success in Silicon Valley to Blitz-scaling.[40] The term is a combination of Blitzkrieg, which means a surprise attack, and scale-up, which means expanding the scale, and refers to a strategy of growing a company at an enormous speed to secure an overwhelming competitive advantage. Examples include Amazon, Google, and Meta.

---

[39] Kim Kyung-jun, 'Cellular Organization, Speed Race, Weekly Biz, Chosun Ilbo, April 15th 2017, B 13

[40] Reid Hoffman, Chris Yeh, translated by Lee Young-rae, 'Blitzscaling', Sam & Parkers, 2020

1-9 Relationship between Development and Speed- A Summary

Acceleration is an expression of progress. Not only physical speed, but when changes or growth occur quickly, we typically express it as progress or rapid pace of development. Human culture has continuously developed along with technological changes. Competition was the catalyst that promoted technological advancement for that development. The more intense the competition, the faster the speed.

It is self-evident that the economic development of Korea over the past 50 years, unprecedented in world economic history, has been driven by speed. Today's Korean economy exists because Korea's economic growth rate has been consistently higher than other competing countries in a short period of time.

The opposite case that stops or slows down the speed of development is the restriction or prohibition of competition(innovation) by customs, laws, or institutional devices. Various institutional mechanisms to oppose and limit competition have been operating continuously from the past to the present. The Luddite movement, which refused and sought to destroy mechanization due to the Industrial Revolution, is a representative example. In the same context, from a political or institutional perspective, the system is a very important factor in determining the speed of progress in diverse tasks. "At the end of the 14th century, ships sailing on the Rhine River were subjected to 64 inspections. In the lower Danube in Austria, there were as many as 77 inspections, and 74 inspections on the Loire River between Loire and Nantes in France."[41] This can also be explained by the conflict and contradictory relationship between micro and macro perspective, which will be discussed later.

Regulations imposed on corporate activities in Korea and other countries and societies around the world can be seen in the same dimension. Every regulation in this world has its own reason. In fact, a country or society cannot be an organization that only pursues competition. The problem is the decline in competitiveness that arises when one country stubbornly insists on regulations that other countries do not impose in a globalized

41 Borscheid, Tempo Virus, p.65

modern society. In such cases, the change in the system can reduce or stop the speed of economic activities, hence becoming an example of slowing down the speed of development. The inspection of ships sailing in old Europe or the regulation on Korean corporate activities nowadays can be examples of change that actually decrease speed, so it can be said that development and speed do not always go hand in hand.

Until the cold war era, Russia was called the Soviet Union and belonged to the advanced powers as one of the G2, alongside the United States. At that time, China was a backward country called the People's Republic of China. After China's open-door policy and the subsequent collapse of the Soviet Union, the status of the two countries rapidly reversed, and now China is overwhelmingly surpassing Russia in almost all areas except for asymmetric military power. Let's take a look at an example based on contrasting experiences in terms of system and administrative service speed.

An Experience of Speed – Institutional and Administrative Service: Crossing the Russian Border

Far East Russia shares a border with the northeastern region of China. In 2009, during an official business trip, I crossed the border from Vladivostok in Far East Russia to Hunchun City in China by land. To cross the Russian border, we had to gather at a designated place in a designated area at the border region by 9 am, and from there, we could only cross the border zone by taking a bus provided by the Russian side. Because of this, we left our hotel in Vladivostok around 5 am, arrived at the gathering point early, and waited for a long time for the appointed hour. When the time came, we took the designated bus and passed the Russian border checkpoint. During the very short journey, there were several Russian military units stationed at various locations, and at each base, there was a checking process where soldiers would come up and look around the bus and check passports. We were passing through the same Russian zone and most of the passengers on the bus, which was directly operated by the Russian side, were Chinese. Although Sino-Russia relations were not hostile, numerous checkpoints caused significant delays.

Finally, we had our passports checked again at the last Russian border office and then entered the Chinese immigration office in the adjacent building. Surprisingly, there were no immigration officers at the entrance, passports

> *were automatically scanned by machines, and luggage was found and carried out in the same way as domestic flights through a baggage claim conveyor belt.*

Accidents or disasters brought about by speed can also result in resistance or refusal to accelerate. The sinking of the Titanic in 1912 may have temporarily dampened the fervor for speed competition. There was a backlash against compromising safety for top speed, but in the long run, the speed of all means of transport, including ships, has continuously and rapidly increased despite countless accidents and risks, both large and small. The rapid spread of the Corona pandemic in 2020 unleashed an unexpected force that effectively halted or slowed down numerous movements worldwide, but it does not mean that the importance or necessity of speed in other areas has diminished. It can be said that it has provided an opportunity for reflection on modern life, which is like a train racing forward with only the track ahead in sight.

For people who stay ahead by adapting to technological changes, a prediction states that "the human evolution that has been taking place over hundreds of thousands of years will be shortened to a matter of days." In particular, there is the argument that "although the pace of progress may seem slow when looking at a single technology, it is not when considering the simultaneous changes occurring in numerous sectors."[42]

[42] Interview with Peter Diamandis, CEO of Space Tourism Company, Weekly Biz, Chosun Ilbo, March 4th, 2017. Two quotations.

Chapter 2

Speed in Modern Times

2-1 Speed in Everyday Life

There may be nothing more important than speed among the factors that have transformed human life. Speed has completely changed human life in all aspects such as the movement of people and objects, household chores, communication, and learning. The absolute 24-hour a day remains unchanged, but relative time has changed entirely. There is a tremendous time difference in task completion from earlier days to current, and in cases like overseas travel, comparison is impossible. Moreover, the time it takes to understand and utilize space and distance, the concept of energy and its use, the awareness and utilization of microscopic subjects such as bacteria and viruses, acquisition and application of knowledge and information, and the time required to handle tasks or relevant issues has all been gradually decreasing. This means that the amount of available time overall for an individual has relatively increased compared to before.

However, this does not mean that humans have become more leisurely or gained more free time. On the contrary, life is more hectic. By today's standard, not knowing countless information or news in real-time means falling behind and not being able to compete. Society is gradually changing to one where survival is impossible unless you are always on the run and involved with the current issues.[43] All the contents and information provided by radios, televisions, SNS and now smartphones may be completely optional and free to watch, listen to, or read, but in reality, most modern people are voluntarily enslaved to these media and communication tools. Ironically,

---

[43] Ignoring an obituary or wedding invitation in Korea is very difficult. Especially since the obituary is always sudden, it was difficult to disseminate widely, meaning that funerals were usually limited to family or close relatives. In contrast to the era when people relied on telegrams, letters, and landline telephones, now mass, instant notification through smartphones or emails has become possible. This has significantly expanded the scope of notifications. People adhering to old lifestyles and values have become busier due to these changes too.

human beings are becoming the busiest in history communicating, holding dialogues and transactions even while walking.

It is essential to note that speed is relative in all aspects. Although the time given is the same, as one becomes older, time seems to pass rather quickly. This is because of the difference in nerve cell transmission speed.[44] When young, neuronal transmission is much faster, making it seem like watching slow motion on a video. Flies and mosquitoes have much faster nerve cell transmission speed than human, so when a fly sees a person's hand coming to catch it, it appears in slow motion, allowing the fly to evade easily.

The most symbolic change in everyday life is smart devices, especially smartphones.[45] Smartphones are the epitome of revolutionary changes that have fundamentally altered the concept of time and speed. Smartphones are magic boxes that compress time and space, making most aspects of life real-time and localized (on-screen). Acquiring real-time necessary information and knowledge, including news, is essential, and they solve numerous transactions within the palm of one's hand. One of the most representative examples is online shopping and financial transactions. As previously explained, all transactions incur transaction cost, with the most significant part being the opportunity cost of time. If individuals had to visit financial institutions regularly and go to the counter to carry out necessary transactions instead of using electronic financial transactions, one could guess how fundamental the change has been. Department stores and markets still function, but the proportion of online shopping and transactions is continuously increasing, especially in Korea. The increase in non-face-to-face transaction method can also be seen as decisively accelerated by the 'social distancing' campaign resulting from COVID-19.

The changes in speed in general life, especially in the linguistic area, are

---

[44] Kim Dae-sik, 'Brain, Reality, and Artificial Intelligence', Weekly Biz, Chosun Ilbo, March 28th-29th, 2015, C4

[45] Depending on the perspective, one might argue that the computer, particularly the PC, and the World Wide Web (WWW) could be seen as more significant precursors. However, no one can deny the advantages of the functions, roles, and uses of smartphones. While it's true that smartphones evolved from previous devices, systems, and technologies, they have developed much faster and beyond our imagination. Applying this process (model) to the case of artificial intelligence could lead us to conclude that we cannot be solely optimistic about the impact artificial intelligence will have on humanity.

particularly noticeable in Korea. "Language comes in massive amounts. We are in an era where language is measured in bytes... Not only in quantity, but also in tremendous speed through channels like SNS. Due to this amount and speed, it has become extremely difficult to refine, ruminate on, and think about language. For the first time in human history, we are facing a 'language crisis' stage."[46] Another example that makes the speed of language change palpable is the countless abbreviations produced every day in Korea. These abbreviations could be indistinguishable from a foreign language or extraterrestrial language especially for the elderly and 'mom and pop' generation.

Speed brings on and enables this trend. The increase in data processing speed and storage capacity is a typical example. More and more sectors are becoming intelligent and automated, especially the artificial intelligence at the center of continuing debates with growing expectations and concerns over its capabilities and limitations. However, legal mechanisms or social consensus that can hinder its development and usage may not be easily made, even disregarding ethical and technical issues, which could lead to significant contradiction and confusion. In other words, accelerating technology and its application could reach a state of uncontrollable chaos beyond our imagination.

We can imagine that humans might live in an era where they can only move and live according to the command of robots created by artificial intelligence. It is uncertain whether George Orwell's novel "1984" imagined a world dominated by artificial intelligence under the 'Big Brother' regime. Further discussion will be in a later chapter.

2-2 Speed of Change in Knowledge and Education

Since the dawn of time, humans have been continually accumulating and building up knowledge. Some of the knowledge from the past has been incorrect or flawed, but has been significantly advanced by new experiences and research, either by improving upon the existing accumulation, or by correcting and modifying it. There have been occasional major transitions, such as the fundamental shift in thought from the geocentric theory

---

[46] From an interview with Noma Hideki by Choi Bo-sik, Chosun Ilbo, March 6th, 2017, A31.

to the heliocentric theory of the middle ages. However, the cycles and durations of these changes were relatively long, both in absolute and relative terms, and the time it took to adapt to the new knowledge system was also quite extensive. In other words, the process of increasing knowledge or correcting and passing down accumulated erroneous knowledge took place over several generations.

With this context, the recent speed of change in knowledge, particularly its acceleration, is shocking. The rate at which new knowledge and acquisition methods are increasing and the rate at which existing knowledge is being discarded or becoming obsolete is much faster than we are conscious of. Samuel Arbesman of Cornell University, in his book "The Half-Life of Facts: Why Everything We Know Has an Expiration Date", argues that the time it takes for our previously recognized knowledge to increase or become obsolete is becoming incredibly shorter. Table 2-1 quoted from his book, shows the time it takes for knowledge to double in various fields, as well as the number of practitioners, discoveries, and the time it takes for knowledge to double.

Sector	Doubling time
• Number of people listed in the U.S. Biographical Dictionary	100 years
• Number of universities	50 years
• The number of important findings, the number of known chemical elements, the accuracy of the instrument	20 years
• The number of scientific journals, the number of known compounds, the number of members of scientific research institutes	15 years
• The number of known asteroids, the number of American engineers	10 years

「The half-life of facts」, Samuel Arbesman, p29, Table 1. KPI Publishing.

Table 2-1 *Doubling Time in Major Fields (Some Interested Sector)*

From ancient times, inventions and discoveries required a long period of time and effort. Likewise, the discovery and identification of chemical elements, the basic components of matter, would take a relatively long time. As an example, however, the above book argues that it takes only 20 years for those inventions and discoveries to double in content and quantity. This means that new knowledge, discoveries, and inventions are not as rare as they used to be, but could be commonplace, and their speed of change has increased substantially. Although there are no separate statistics or reports on Korea, making direct comparison impossible, the terms of scientific data are identical. Additionally, those who are lagging behind in pace may face the phenomenon of new knowledge invalidating existing knowledge without fully acquiring the current knowledge. Many other surprising statistics are presented, and it's difficult to deny them since the author has published them under his own name. The turnover speed is quite shocking.

Sector	Doubling time
• Wireless Communication (Bits/Sec)	10 months
• Digital Camera (Pixel/USD)	12 months
• Pixel (Array)	19 months
• Hard Drive Capacity (Gigabytes/USD)	20 months
• DNA Sequencing	22 months
• Frequency Band (Kilobytes/Sec/USD)	30 months

「The half-life of facts」, Samuel Arbesman, p83, Table 4. KPI Publishing.

Table 2-2 *Doubling Time in Technology (Communication, etc.)*

Furthermore, as shown in Table 2-2, the doubling time of communication and related technologies is much shorter than that of knowledge, discoveries, and inventions, being reduced to months instead of years, and that tends to accelerate. We have now reached a point where we are no longer surprised by this speed and accept it as a matter of course. We are already accustomed to the acceleration of technology, expecting competition and even enjoying the atmosphere it creates.

In another dimension, the obsolescence speed of different disciplines representing traditional knowledge also surpasses our imagination. The half-life of leading knowledge disciplines introduced in the above mentioned book, such as physics, mathematics, and history, is even more shockingly short. Many achievements of various disciplines built upon the foundation of knowledge accumulated by humanity over thousands of years have recently lost their authority and faced the destiny of having to exit the stage. This content would undoubtedly apply to the academia in Korea as well. Although there may be counterarguments regarding the author's research and measurement method, validity, and actual estimates, it is difficult for anyone to deny that the speed at which knowledge increases or its effectiveness becomes obsolete has become incredibly shorter.

In this era of knowledge transformation, we can clearly see that the systems we have cherished and nurtured so far - for example, the education system, teaching method, and human resource development system - need to change as soon as possible. Even if we understand the necessity theoretically or conceptually, implementing social change such as an education system with its history and tradition is quite difficult. Changing an established system is not easy, and experiments or trial tests face resistance, slowing down the progress. That is especially true in democratic societies that require institutional social-consensus. However, the unexpected pandemic forced such an experiment recently, resulting in varied outcomes and enabling prediction on the future. One of these is the possibility and inevitability of non-face-to-face education through virtual space or video.

It is difficult for a system that is perfect in every aspect beyond that point of time, to actually exist. Even if it does, it would be impossible or very difficult to properly test it under realistic conditions, and there would be many well-founded opposing reasons and practical constraints. In this respect, an unexpected situation like the COVID-19 pandemic could present the result of forced experiment, promoting change or accelerating its pace. In the case of the education system in Korea, since the first half of 2020, an unexpected experiment such as remote online lectures and classes have been conducted in all levels of schools from university to kindergarten. Despite the numerous problems, pros and cons, the experiments have been carried out, and now some form of change is inevitable. It is up to politics and policy whether Korean speed can fulfill its function.

2-3 Speed of Change in Lifestyle, Trend and Culture in Korea

The process of growth that the Korean economy achieved in just 30 years of the 20th century is referred to as 'compressed growth.' This expression means that Korea has leapfrogged stages of growth and development that took other countries over 100 years, 200 years, or even longer, and which many countries still have not achieved yet. No faster pace has been recorded in the history of the world economy so far. As the economy shifted, all other sectors have also undergone rapid changes and continue to evolve at a fast pace. Let's examine this from the perspective of living, lifestyle and trends in Korea.

(1) Food and Eating

If we look at the changes in human life from the standpoint of living through trends, we can discover both astonishing changes and significant contradictions. Let's start with eating. The traditional Korean expression 'eating and thus living' implies several meanings. Considering the previous case of Korea, we have pursued a life where we need to eat to survive for a very long time. The old expression 'If I could at least put a paste of grass in my mouth...' signified a desperate wish in the face of difficult realities, even if it meant barely eating.

The problem of eating and living in Korea was most likely resolved around the late 1970s or early 1980s. Until the late 1970s, there were two days of 'limited menu in restaurants' per week in Korea. On Wednesday and Saturday, restaurants could only serve meals made with no-rice during lunchtime.[47] The reason was implementation of a policy to replace rice, which was in short supply, with imported flour from US aid. After rapid industrialization, the problem of sustenance was completely solved. This was because the country was now able to import rice or other alternative foods. However, as a side effect, obesity and adult diseases related to excessive nutrition began to emerge.

Throughout human history, the global food supply has generally been insufficient to meet demand. Therefore, the primary concern of humanity was the issue of eating. Of course, there were significant differences depending on the country or region, and even within the same country, there was a clear distinction depending on the socioeconomic class. However, on a national or global scale, even if distribution was fair, the supply was still insufficient. In the late 20th century, advances in agricultural technology led to a dramatic increase in food production, enabling a balance or excess supply capacity for humanity as a whole. In other words, for the first time in human history, the shortage problem of food could be solved in terms of total quantity on a global scale.

[47] The 5-day work week and 40-hour work system, which we take for granted, was fully implemented in Korea from July 1, 2011. Up to the 1980s, working until Saturday morning and overtime were common, so dining out was also a routine for office workers, even for Saturday lunches.

However, this does not mean that the problem of food for humanity has been solved. The proportion of starving people in the world is still incredibly high. According to a survey by the United Nations Food and Agriculture Organization, in 2021, between 702 and 828 million people were suffering from food shortages or malnutrition, with children being the primary victim. In other words, although the conditions for solving the food problem have been met in terms of total quantity, issues of distribution remain unsolved. The problem of food remains a significant unresolved issue due to obstacles such as the conditions divided by individual countries, delivery and transportation method, transaction cost, and political and social system.

For the first time since the beginning of history, the global increase in food production has caught up with the rate of population growth. However, the problem of sustenance still remains as a serious issue for humanity due to the cost of distributing and trading food, as well as issues related to borders and distances. If many underdeveloped countries in the world cannot achieve a certain degree of economic growth or development, this problem will inevitably remain as an ongoing challenge. Korea surprisingly had an early breakthrough to overcome this challenge.

(2) Clothing

In some respects, clothing may be considered more important than food. The oriental expression 'clothing, food and shelter' might suggest that clothing comes before food for a reason beyond mere coincidence. Historically, clothing has provided more than just a simple function of regulating temperature, protecting the skin, or covering and emphasizing important body parts. From the beginning of human life, clothing has also been used as a means of distinction or discrimination between individuals. Clothing has played a significant role as a means to distinguish specific tribes, ranks, or individuals, or as aesthetic means for women. Those engaged in battle, hunting, or fishing would have worn functionally appropriate clothing or uniforms. Furthermore, clothing and adornments have been used from the outset as a way to demonstrate power, superiority, social status, or wealth. While nowadays anyone with money can wear whatever clothing they like, in the past, societies with strict social hierarchies had regulations regarding the materials, colors, and designs of clothing one could wear, making it possible to distinguish social status by clothing alone.

Looking back at the Joseon Dynasty (1392-1910), clothing and hat size, shape and materials were regulated according to social class or individual status, which might explain why the traditional expression of clothing comes before eating. The issue of clothing, which would have been considered more urgent than sustenance, was also a matter of governance and social order. The historical fact that government's occasional bans and debates on the size, materials, and length of women's clothing and accessories continued throughout the Dynasty indicates that as one's social status and rank changed, clothing became a more important issue and concern than food.

When examining the development of clothing in relation to its speed, we see that fashion has changed with the advancement in material, dyeing, processing, and manufacturing technology. In particular, the development of woven textile and the subsequent invention of synthetic fiber had a revolutionary impact on clothing. As a result, fashion spread across all economic and social classes, and the pace of expressing and promoting individuality accelerated.

The main content of the changes related to fashion is speed. Since the transition from custom-made and bespoke clothing to the era of mass production and mass consumption, a prominent recent phenomenon is the rapid spread of small-scale production and private consumption patterns. The paradigm of clothes manufacturing, distribution, and consumption has changed. The East-Gate Apparel Market in Seoul in the 1990s is an example of a place that quickly responded to and led those changes by speed. By altering the production and distribution paradigm, the fashion industry itself has continued to show changes that seemed impossible before. It is no exaggeration to say that new leaders in the clothing industry, such as Zara and H&M, which instantly reflect consumer trends in design, production, and distribution, have completely changed the long-standing management practices of this industry.

The pace of change will continue to accelerate. Development in 3D printing technology and AI will not bypass clothing and fashion. We can easily imagine cases where people design or obtain designs online to create or order their own custom-made clothes. The process of selecting custom clothes using virtual reality has already begun. The day when we subscribe to AI-coordinated outfits is not far off. In the case of clothing, the revolutionary change in production technology has enabled diverse small-scale production, making it possible to drastically shorten the cycle of trend.

(3) Housing

Housing has also undergone tremendous changes. However, the speed of these changes is relatively slower compared to food and clothing. Perhaps this is because housing, in terms of scale and cost (economic capability), is incomparably larger than the other two categories. In Korea, the changes were slow and gradual from ancient times until the end of the Joseon Dynasty, but with the introduction of Western-style housing and the increase in income that enabled individual construction easier, the pace of change has accelerated relatively quickly.

One aspect related to housing is urbanization speed. Statistically, the urbanization rate in Korea, which was less than 30% before the economic development plan began in 1962, already exceeded 80% in 1995. In just about 30 years, the character of the country changed from an absolute rural-centric society to an urban-centric society due to rapid industrialization. This speed is unprecedented in any country worldwide and is unlikely to appear in the future.

Even when comparing the changes in the three East Asian countries of Korea, China, and Japan, the differences are clear. Among these three countries, Korea achieved urbanization in the shortest time, with the speed being outstanding regardless of desirability, results, and side effects. Although there are differences in national policies, economic development speed, and cultural conditions, Korean speed has played a significant role in the process.

The most distinctive and symbolic aspect is the change in urban living and housing style centered around apartments. In fact, until the early 1960s, before the five-year economic development plan policy began, there was virtually no concept of apartment-style housing in Korea. However, in less than a generation (30 years), apartments have become the most preferred housing lifestyle in Korea and in particular, the most reliable means of wealth formation. This record is also unprecedented in the world. Housing is not easy to build or change, and it is the largest asset in personal or family life, but the apartment preference happened rapidly in Korea. Now, it is difficult to find a house with a traditional Korean-style (Han-ok) appearance, regardless of interior structure, anywhere in Korea. Regardless of whether it is desirable or not, this is also a manifestation of Korea's speed(K-speed).

The figure below shows the growth rate of apartment construction in Korea since the early 1970s. From the early 1970s to the early 2000s, the construction and supply of apartments have shown a steep growth rate that is unprecedented anywhere in the world over the course of 30 years. The fact that housing, the most substantial and valuable of all durable goods, and not merely consumer goods or fad items, has changed at such a pace is unique to Korea.

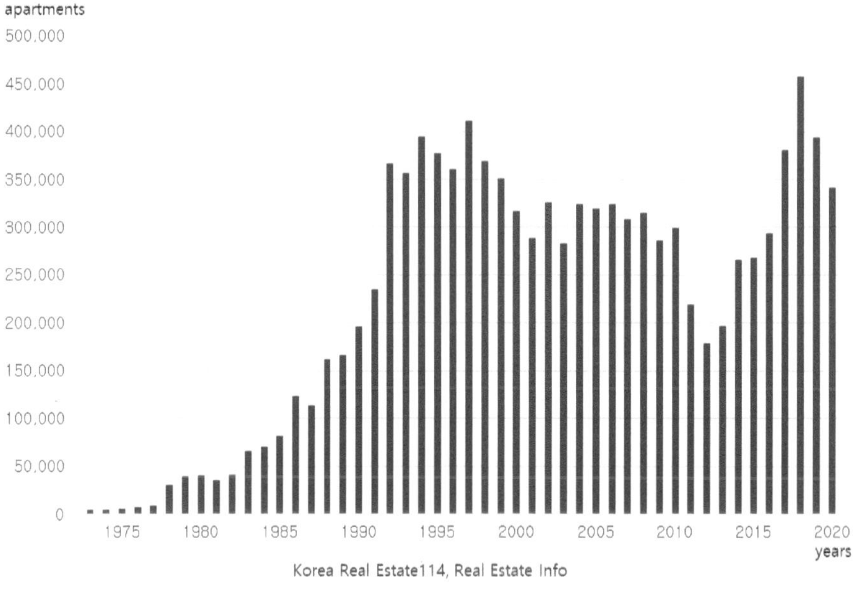

Figure 2-1 *Apartment Supply in Korea*

By 2020, the proportion of apartments in Korean housing exceeded 50%. Contrary to expectations, this change in housing preference may be the fastest and most characteristic K-speed in living and lifestyle.

Unfortunately, we miss out on many things when things move quickly. The phenomenon of traditional Korean houses being difficult to find not only in cities but also in rural areas is an example. In contrast, traditional Japanese-style houses can be easily seen even in major cities in Japan. There will likely be a need to prevent, or at least slow down, the rapid disappearance of the unique advantages of Korean-style living such as Ondol (traditional room heating system), for example.

(4) Tea Room and Coffee Shop

Korea is clearly distinguished from other countries and ethnicities in other ways as well. Once a certain cultural trend or method is introduced and reaches a tipping point, the absolute or relative speed of its distribution and dissemination is so fast in many areas that it is difficult to compare with any other countries. One of the most representative examples is the dissemination of coffee beverages and the proliferation of coffee shops. In the past, there were tearooms everywhere in urban areas, serving as a social hub. But more coffee shops have moved in recently and replaced tearooms completely. At the same time, the main customer base has experienced a complete generational turnover in the shortest possible time. During the heyday of tea rooms, the main customers were middle-aged males, and coffee was used as one of the beverages consumed in return for using the tea room, rather than the actual enjoyment of taste.

And until then, the representative beverage that Koreans enjoyed at tearoom was not coffee but rather black tea or traditional Korean tea. It can even be said that there was no such thing as going to a tea room just to taste coffee. Until then, served coffee was a powder mix of instant ground coffee, and the method of adding more sugar or milk (cream) was preferred. Around the year 2000 or a little bit later was when the number of tearooms peaked and withered abruptly.

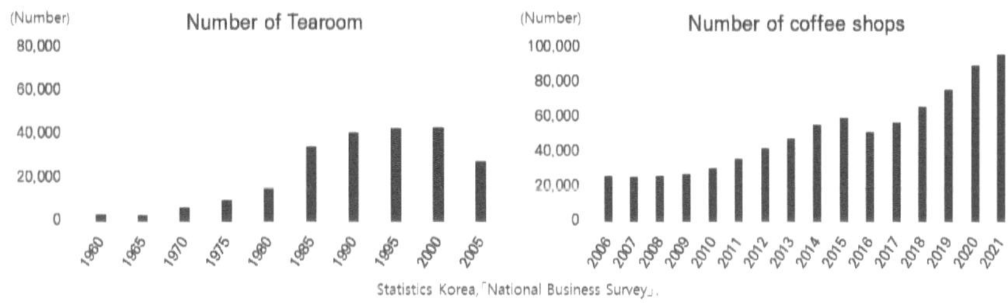

Figure 2-2 *Tea rooms and Coffee Shops in Korea*

For a very long time, in Korean conversations, expressions such as 'let's have a cup of tea...' or 'having a cup of tea while...' were naturally used to indicate an appointment or familiarity. However, as coffee emerged as the main beverage, this phrase has gradually changed to 'coffee' instead of 'tea'. The users themselves may not even be aware of this change. It is another example of the power and influence of K-speed.

As seen in the Figure 2-2 above, the number of coffee shops increased faster and more significantly than the number of tea rooms decreased, and the decreasing speed of tea rooms and increasing speed of coffee shops are, of course, the fastest in the world. In fact, coffee shops replaced tea rooms completely. China has recently shown a pace that is comparable to Korea in many areas, and the increase in coffee consumption and specialty coffee shops in China, which has a developed tea culture, is another example. However, when compared to the population size, the pace is incomparable to that of Korea.

Yeongdo District in Busan, which used to be an industrial area centered on shipbuilding, is now transforming into a coffee island. In the past decade, the number of specialty coffee shops has increased 30 times, from 7-8 to about 220. The Yeongdo district office plans to make the coffee industry the representative industry of the district and establish a coffee R&D center and a coffee mall.[48] This is another example of K-speed.

48 Chosun Ilbo, February 28th, 2022, A16

Memories of Tearoom

From 1970 to 1976, I worked at the main office of the Bank of Korea, the nation's central bank, in Seoul. At that time, there were very few private cars and no subways either, so the public transportation, like the bus, was quite inconvenient. As a result, everyone commuted to work by taking the bank-provided commuting buses. When the buses arrived at the office in the morning, passengers almost invariably headed straight to the nearby tearooms, crowding the area. A regularly visited tea room naturally became packed during early morning before office hours. The primary beverage at that time was black tea, which was consumed in a smoky atmosphere. The taste was nothing special by today's standard, since people didn't visit for the taste but rather for a social gathering spot.

Waitresses (called 'lady' in Korean pronunciation) would remember the regular's preferred drink, and bring coffee or other customized drinks without even taking orders. Tearooms were common not only next to major buildings in cities but also in country town centers.

Until then, tearooms served as places where people could meet, communicate, and spend their free time, more likely today's cafe. The main clientele was middle-aged and older male. Since customers had to be able to afford the comparatively expensive tea price at the time, clientele was limited. Some customers would order a cup of coffee or tea and sit for hours, drawing the glare of the manager (called 'madam'). For a long time, tearooms offered delivery service as well. Unlike today's delivery services, the waitress would wrap the drinks in a bundle, visit the place and personally serve them, wait until they finish, and then collect the cups back.

Tearooms at that time served three main functions. First, they acted as meeting places where most encounters took place, functioning as personal offices as well, and also performing secretarial tasks for clients during a time when telephones were scarce. Telephones of the tearooms were the only communication means for many customers, especially for in-coming calls. Tearooms were also the primary location for blind dates and setups between young men and women, especially for the marriage process. In the 1960s, it was trendy for university students to arrange group meetings between different departments or clubs of different sex, and these meetings usually took place in tearooms.

Second, tearooms acted as a cultural space. They served sometimes as an art studio or music listening room often hosting artists and playing popular music of the time. Lastly, they functioned as a recreational space for people with little to do, particularly unemployed but educated young adults (called 'room-fans'), but only those who could afford the tea price could partake.

During my college years in the early and mid-1960s, few friends or acquaintances could afford to visit the tearoom that often. However, music listening rooms that primarily played classical music were popular amongst college students for meeting, dating, and socializing. There were also different music listening rooms that played mostly foreign pop songs, trending at the time. I remember that music listening rooms charged an entrance fee, and customers had to pay separately for beverages. In general, tearooms offered various beverages, including coffee, not for the taste but primarily as a price to use a seat.

(5) Changes in the Mindset, Lifestyle, Social Life, and Language of the Millennials

While real-time conversation and communication through SNS is not unique to Korea, the trend of shortening and simplifying words or characters is incomparable to any other country. The new terms created by taking the first letters of Korean or foreign words make it difficult for older generations to communicate with younger ones unless they make a special effort to learn the lingo. This is another serious factor contributing to the generation gap in communication in contemporary Korea. Shortened expressions exist in any language and any era, but in Korea, it has become pervasive among younger generations, and the advent and widespread use of SNS has pushed this trend to the extreme. Even daily newspapers, broadcasts, and other media outlets use abbreviations, reflecting the typical Korean speed culture in language use. Of course, the unique nature of the Korean language, Hangul, makes this possible.

The generational differences in thought process and cultural trend are usually symbolized by language. As mentioned earlier, people today live in the same world and era but actually have different cultures and ways of thinking. The generation born between 1977 and 1997 is sometimes called the N Generation (Net Generation or Digital Native). Don Tapscott, the founder of Wikinomics, interviewed over 6,000 people, including Facebook founder Mark Zuckerberg, and summarized the characteristics of this generation as follows[49]

"1) They value freedom of choice (Freedom). 2) They want to customize everything, including products and services, to suit their tastes (Customization). 3) They are comfortable with collaboration (Collaboration). 4) They seek to verify any issue (Scrutiny). 5) They value integrity (Integrity). 6) They always pursue fun, even at work or school (Entertainment). 7) They prioritize speed (Speed). 8) They don't want to settle for the status quo(Innovation)"

The N Generation mentioned here largely overlaps with the Millennial generation (mid-1980s to mid-1990s in terms of birth year). A typical classification divides people into Baby Boomers, Millennials, and Generation Z(born between 1995-2004), identifying and connecting their characteristics. Since these classifications are not theoretical, they can be used as needed. Now, instead of the N Generation, they are often called the M Generation or the MZ Generation in Korea.

The eight characteristics mentioned above are also applicable in Korea. Therefore, it is essential to acknowledge that these characteristics are a new trend as well as cultural change, and that the wisdom to predict changes in acceleration is required. Additionally, the advent of a hyper-connected society due to rapid technological advancement could also be a keyword that intersects with the eight characteristics.

Moreover, these eight characteristics correspond to or contrast with the features introduced earlier in the context of technological changes and speed, and the direction and overall flow of change. Generations have always been distinguished by differences, and people refer to the 'generation gap' between older and younger generations. However, in today's age concept, the distinction between generations is characterized by a much narrower interval, leading to further distinction within existing classified generations. It is another face of speed. In particular, Korea exhibits more dramatic occurrences. Prioritizing personal life by rejecting promotions or

---

[49] Don Tapscott, 'Grown up Digital: How the Net Generation is Changing Your World', Foreign Book Review, Weekly Biz, Chosun Ilbo, February 21rst-22nd, C2

choosing voluntary job changes in work life is one example of rapid change. It could be a sign that predicts changes in the way people work in the future.

Consequently, the employment trend is seeing a rapid increase in gig workers who work only as much as they need and when they want. The explosive growth of the delivery industry is a major means of providing such opportunities. In contrast, manufacturing industries are facing labor shortages.[50] The phenomenon of changing jobs according to working conditions is also on the rise. A noticeable difference is that for these generations, moving from a large corporation to a startup is not a difficult decision in Korea. According to the analysis of monthly average household microdata by the National Statistical Office, the expense of purchasing lottery tickets for people in their 20s increased by 313% in 2021 compared to before the COVID-19 pandemic.[51] The surge in participation in the art, stock, and cryptocurrency markets is also in the same vein. To resolve disputes and legal grievances, the number of cases using online content certification through post offices has increased about threefold in three years.[52] This method is mainly used by the MZ generation.

In the 2022 presidential election, the most coveted demographic was the MZ generation, particularly voters in their 20s - an entirely new phenomenon. This signifies that these generations are becoming the agents of change, at the center of societal changes, undergoing the fastest transformations and instigating change as well.

As another example, Korea has unexpectedly become a leading center for the trends in clothing and luxury goods including China and Southeast Asia, as young people with purchasing power are sensitive to trends and are changing their consumption patterns. The speed of change in Korea is so rapid that she is becoming the number one travel destination for the global millennial generation.[53] The prediction that Korea will lead the way in the travel industry ,TV sets, smartphones and K-pop is somewhat convincing.[54]

---

50 Maeil Business, December 13th ,2021, A1
51 Maeil Business, December 14th 2021, A1
52 Chosun Ilbo, December 20th, 2021, A10
53 Interview with CEO of luggage company, Rimowa, Chosun Ilbo, October 6th, 2021, A16
54 Interview with Airbnb Vice President Lee Hane, Maeil Business, December 4th, 2021, A35

Chapter 3

K-Speed: The Fastest-Changing Aspects and Contents of the Korean Economy, Society, and Culture

Recently, there has been a trend to use the term 'K-00' to collectively refer to the Korean way of thinking, Korean culture, service method, genres such as K-pop and K-drama. Furthermore, the use of the prefix 'K' in relation to Korea-related events, incidents, and policies has become more frequent. In this context, it is not awkward to call the rapid change in the Korean economy and society, as well as the character possessed and demonstrated by Koreans, 'K-speed.'

Can we confidently assert that K-speed exists? If so, is it innate or cultivated? Does this speed manifest differently across generations and time? Whether it is innate or cultivated, the aim is to demonstrate its existence and present its specific content. Naturally, the discussion will focus on speed itself more than other factors.

3-1 Korean Economic and Social Development and Speed

The genetic traits, constitution, culture, and ethnic characteristics of the Korean people, also discussed in Chapter 6, are ultimately manifested at the macro level as a nation. The features of the country called Korea and her constituent, Koreans, are expressed as a result of processes involving internal and external factors such as geographical, historical, and genetic elements; living environments and its development processes; responses to global and regional changes; changes in international relation and positioning; national governance structures, and political system, as well as the interaction between individuals and groups within the country, and more.

History may be seen as a documentation of process and outcome. Analyzing history in relation to speed can yield many interesting discoveries. A country (macro-level observation target), in general, does not document change earlier than the individuals or individual groups (micro-level observation target) belonging to it. Even if there are significant and rapid changes in personal, hierarchical, and economic aspects within a country, there is no particular alteration when viewed at the national level. A country may experience significant economic and social changes internally, but when viewed globally, her relative status and position compared to other countries may not change much. For example, even though present underdeveloped or developing countries have tried to make efforts for development and change in their own way, most internal and domestic changes did not turn out to be prominent, particularly on the international level, despite the effort of individuals and firms.

Korea boasts a long history, but in the late 110 years of the modern era, she was a colony of Japan for 36 years. After liberation in 1945, she experienced a series of difficulties, such as the division of its territory into South and North by superpowers and the war between them for more than 3 years (1950-1953). North Korea, still under communist regime, belongs to the group of underdeveloped countries. To objectively measure and compare K-speed, it is appropriate to start with South Korea from the 1960s, after the Korean War. The 1960s also coincides with the period when the world began to experience an acceleration of change, as the so-called Second Industrial Revolution matured, and the world entered the early stage of the information age.

The following descriptions and examples summarize how (South) Korea has changed over the past 60 years. Despite her relatively small size and poor conditions, she underwent rapid changes in a short period of time in the late 20th century, transforming from an underdeveloped to an advanced country. The key word to understanding this change is unquestionably speed and acceleration.

All items introduced here are not organized using any particular academic model or method but are a collection of representative examples and statistics from various sources including official statistics, newspapers, magazines and others. There may be countless other pieces of evidence or examples, but the facts and statistics listed here are sufficient in proving the point. It is a shame, some Koreans do not properly acknowledge or recognize these achievements, fail to assess the accomplishment accurately, or foolishly disparage the efforts, achievements, and results of their predecessors.

3-2 Korea: A Very Fast and Unique Country in World Development History

By examining the characteristics of various fields listed below, it is clear that Korea is unique, and her speed of change so far is incomparable.

(1) History

- A country that is geographically peripheral to China and although subjected to intervention, attack and influence historically, maintained an independent country-name and individual system since its inception.

- An undivided state for over a millennium since the Unified Silla Kingdom, and a country with an independent culture and original language even before that.

- The only country in history that has risen to the ranks of world powers in just half a century after suffering colonial rule from early to mid-20th century, liberation, and a three-year period of war (1950-1953) between North and South Korea.

- The only country in the world that achieved industrialization and democratization simultaneously within one generation (30 years).

- Currently the only divided country in the world that has been in existence for over 78 years and is still technically at war (cease-fire).

After World War II, four divided countries emerged: North and South Korea, East and West Germany, North and South Vietnam, and North and South Yemen. Currently, Korea is the only divided country. She has an unprecedented history of achieving the 'Miracle on the Han River' and rising to the ranks of major powers in a short period of time, from a state where its industrial base was thoroughly destroyed after fighting a three-year war due to a reckless invasion from North Korea(and China).

(2) General Indicators

- Hangul: The language of more than 10,000 possible characters with the most phonetic letters (reference: about 400 for Chinese), and the most suitable script for digital technology.

- Hangul is adopted as a second foreign language in schools in 43 countries and 1,699 schools worldwide (as of 2020).

- Average IQ over 100 and an illiteracy rate below 1%, ranking 1st or 2nd in the world.

- Approximately 7.32 million overseas residents in 193 countries (as of 2021) (reference: about 60 million overseas Chinese).

- Ranked 17th out of 163 countries in the 2020 Social Progress Index (SPI) for the best countries to live in (2020).

- One of the two Asian countries, along with Japan that have joined the OECD and G-20.

- The only country where the first Catholic Church was started by natives instead of foreign missionaries in the 18th century.

- The only country in the world where approximately 25% of the population became Christian church members within 100 years of Christian missionary activity.

- Yoido Full Gospel Church, recorded as the world's largest Protestant church with 700,000 members in 1992, after starting as a tent church in 1958 (Guinness Book of Records).

- Emerged as the world's second-largest dispatch missionary nation within 100 years of foreign in-coming missionaries (currently dispatches over 20,000 missionaries overseas, 2nd in absolute numbers, 1st in population proportion).

- The only country in the world where early morning prayer meetings are held daily in all Protestant churches.

- One of the six countries that have achieved the Sports Grand Slam (hosting Summer and Winter Olympics, World Athletics Championships, and the World Cup).

- 211 World Taekwondo(traditional martial arts) Federation member countries, over 3000 instructors; training and competition terms use the Korean language.

- Ranked 1st for 8 consecutive years at the World Skill Olympics.

- Korea's e-government technology ranked 1st in the world.

- The country with the highest internet speed, technology, and distribution (penetration) rate in the world

- Patent registration reached one million in just 62 years (compared to 121 years in the United States and 97 years in Japan), with 700,000 in the last 10 years, 52% of which are IT related.

- Record for most international conferences held worldwide in 2017.

- Visa-free travel available to 190 countries (world's 2nd highest) transforming international status in the shortest time.

The above examples clearly demonstrate the speed of Korea. Factors and conditions for the achievements are varied so that other countries or groups cannot challenge or compare on level ground but there is a common thread that no ethnicity can replicate which is shown here in a few examples.

(3) Economy and Others

- Record of fastest economic growth: No. 1 in compressed growth

Per capita GDP	increase 573 times	during 1962-2021
Vehicle registration	increase 49 times	during 1966-2021
Average life-span	increase 21.2 years	during 1970-2020
Export	increase 3,790 times	during 1965-2021

- The world's first country to transform from a recipient to a donor of aid in modern world history

- The first country from receiving food aid from the World Food Program and US agricultural surplus products (PL480) to becoming a donor country

- The only country that has leaped to the top 10 in GDP within half a century from being one of the world's poorest countries (per capita income of $82 in 1961)
- The first country in the history of United Nations Development Program to be classified as a developed country from a developing country (2021)
- The only country to change its status in the UNICEF classification, currently ranking 4th in fundraising scale
- One of the seven countries in the world's 30-50 club (income of $30,000 or more - population of 50 million or more)
- A country that has economically surpassed seven of the 16 countries that participated in the Korean War, now providing assistance to them
- A country that has successfully overcome two recent economic crises (IMF financial crisis in 1998 and 2008 global financial crisis)
- A country who quickly succeeded in restructuring after using the IMF financial crisis as an opportunity for a turnaround
- A nation where citizens voluntarily participated in the gold collection movement to overcome the IMF financial crisis in a short period of time
- Ranked 1st in Bloomberg's Global Innovation Index (2021)
- Ranked 2nd among 157 countries in the World Bank Human Capital Index (2018)

Today's elderly generation over 75 and above have experienced an unparalleled historical path such as living through the analog era, famine, the Korean War, foreign aid, and poverty, but now enjoying the benefits of industrialization, affluence, welfare system, and state-of-the-art digital technology. The case of utilizing the IMF financial crisis as an opportunity for industrial restructuring and a major transformation, especially the voluntary submission of gold by citizens to repay foreign debt, is rare in world history and likely to remain so.[55]

(4) Human Power, Talent, Education

- The country with the highest passion for education in the world: from past to present
- Continuously producing global stars in the fields of culture, arts, and sports
- Dominating world charts in a short time through movies, dramas, games, webtoons, pop-songs and more
- Rapid spread of the Korean Wave(Hallyu) with BTS, Black Pink, etc., topping the US Billboard charts, American Music Awards, Grammy Awards, etc.
- Continuous recognition in prestigious international film festivals, winning Academy Awards for Best Picture, Best Director, Best Supporting Actor, etc.
- Continuous entry, advancement and rapid rise to the prominence of talent in international organizations (e.g., UN Secretary-General)
- Transition from sending students to long-term overseas programs to a sharp increase in the number of international students coming to study in Korea
- Building and maintaining a dominant position in the LPGA and continuously maintaining a high level of competitiveness
- Doubling the number of overseas workers in 5 years, doubling the number of adult volunteers in 5 years, doubling the number of patent registration in 10 years

---

55 The author was serving as a dean at the university headquarter at the time, and relinquished the gold button and gold ring he received as gifts at his wedding from his in-laws.

- Continuously recording impressive results in the World Skill Olympics, Mathematical Olympiad, and other events

These examples demonstrate the abilities of Koreans as a group and as an individual to possess 'talent', 'fun' and 'wits' and to display 'swiftness' and 'speed'. The difference between swiftness and speed lies in persistence. As explained elsewhere in this book, these capabilities slowly simmer and then explode when the economic conditions provide support.

(5) Living, Lifestyle

- All newborns are born in hospitals, most grow up in nurseries or kindergartens, and enjoy the status of 'royalty' while receiving early training cultivating talent and education

- Adolescents are virtually forced to receive various extracurricular lessons and sports activities outside of regular school hours

- In a short period, establishing and continuously improving the social security system, including national health insurance and national pension

- World's highest record of apartment supply rate, with more than half of the houses being apartments with convenient living environment and cultural facilities

- The world's fastest car penetration speed. All family members own smartphones, and overseas travel becoming a part of everyday life

- World's highest number of coffee shops per capita with coffee becoming a national beverage and essential drink. Early development of the coffee powder mixes became popular worldwide.

In terms of lifestyle, the standard of living for Koreans is the highest or top tier in most aspects. The per capita income level, as measured by purchasing power, has already reached the world's upper level. In particular, the change in Korea compared to other advanced countries during the past 50 years is unparalleled. Those who have not experienced this first hand may find it difficult to fully comprehend. Foreign veterans of the Korean

War who re-visit Korea are more often than not amazed by the extreme transformation from ruins. They cannot help but feel admiration, a sense of accomplishment, and a high pride.

(6) Politics, Society, Welfare

- In a short period of time, well-established social infrastructure such as road and transportation networks prioritized the quality of life, and the establishment of health insurance and social security system provided the basic framework of a welfare state
- Supply-related problems caused by chronic material shortages from the past are hardly encountered in the present
- Freedom of the press and civilian demonstration rights are guaranteed, and anonymity is further protected in cyberspace
- The only developing country to experience peaceful regime changes of the right and left wing parties back and forth through election several times after World War II
- Legal and institutional guarantee for consideration of the disabled and other vulnerable minority groups
- The mandatory military service period for young men is continuously shortened, and the living conditions of the military camps improves continually
- Administrative digitalization ranks first in the world, making the speed of e-government the fastest in global standards
- The widespread use of credit cards and electronic payment methods has made it possible to automatically prevent tax evasion by businesses and individuals
- In a short period of time, the country has transitioned from a state of absolute food shortage (especially staple food like rice) to a surplus country
- More than half of the population has attained a college education or higher (20-30 years old generation ranks first in the world)

- All citizens naturally accept and recognize the status given as a Korean citizen from a global standpoint

The improvement in economic level inevitably leads to changes in the social system. The sequence or causality of these two factors is that industrialization and economic development precede or accompany social change. As shown by Korea, industrialization leads to democratization in developing countries, not vice versa. So far, there has never been a case in the world where the opposite was true. The problem of making a decent living must be properly solved first in order to realize and sustain democracy.

(7) Industry-Hardware and Software

- Rising as a shipbuilding powerhouse, with Korean shipyards ranking from first to sixth in the world.

- Emerged as one of the top five car-producing countries in the world in just one generation.

- In the manufacturing of DRAM semiconductor, which is considered the main composition of the industry, it holds a solid first place in the world and is a semiconductor powerhouse with competitiveness in non-memory areas too.

- Shipbuilding, automobiles, aerospace and semiconductors were industries that did not exist in Korea until the 1970s, but now Korea is the world's leading manufacturer of those mentioned.

- One of the few countries that exports nuclear power technology and plant[56]

- Transformed from a chronic international balance of payments deficit country to a surplus country through industrial development in a short period of time.

---

56 The entire nation has been experiencing a predicament of Korea's nuclear industry due to the declaration of a nuclear power phase-out by President Moon Jae-in upon his inauguration in 2017.

- One of the leading countries in the development, production, and use of smartphones, an essential item for human life; one in four people in the world uses a mobile phone made in(by) Korea.
- 43% of large ships floating in the world's oceans were built in Korean shipyards.
- Koreans developed Kakao Talk, a SNS program and supplied it to more than 100 countries worldwide.
- Emerged as a cultural powerhouse leading and showing prominence in the shortest time in the fields of culture, art, entertainment, and more, from a manufacturing-oriented international competitiveness.
- Samsung Electronics' brand value rose to 6th in the world (2022).
- One of the countries in the leading group of production technology of batteries, the driving force of next-generation electric vehicles.
- The 7th country in the world to launch satellites
- Delivery culture, including rocket (same day) delivery and dawn(early morning) delivery, has become commonplace.

The short time period in which Korea emerged as a strong player in the world economy through industrialization is clear evidence of K-speed. Until the early stages of industrialization, most domestic products (Korean made or produced) were not the preferred choices, but rather objects of avoidance including industrial products, daily necessities, food, and consumables. Now at present, national industrial products are the public's favorite. Korea has been a very rare case in world economic history where this opposite phenomenon occurred in such a short time span.

(8) Culture and so on

- Hangul (Korean Language) becomes 7th foreign language studied in the world
- In North America, 30 universities opened Korean culture related departments or degrees

- There are 53 Korean language departments in Vietnam (2021)
- Hangul became the number one foreign language taught in Vietnam
- Increase in issues of Hangul teaching license 4.5 times, 2011-2021
- Increase in Hallyu (Korean culture) fan 17 times, 2012-2022
- The photo of Korean-built nuclear power plant printed in UAE's largest-denomination bill
- World Intellectual Property Organization(WIPO) recognized many Korean items such as Hanbok (costume), Soju (liquor), Gimbap (food), Doenjang soybean paste(source)… as official name of goods
- The fast and widespread diffusion of K-foods worldwide

The examples given above are not systematically or statistically arranged but are randomly selected based on various types of data source, media reports, and more. The focus is on its speed. Most Koreans, however, may not properly recognize or feel this outcome, because those who are in the vortex of change may not recognize the relative speed of change.

An Experience of Speed - Korea (1): Memories throughout 70 years of Personal Experiences

I was born in 1945. I was a newborn baby in the midst of liberation from Japan's colonial rule and was in Busan (southern-end city) during the Korean War that broke out in 1950. I don't have any specific memories of those chaotic times during the liberation or the experiences that all South Koreans had to go through during the refugee period. I vaguely remember that several refugee families came to our house and each shared one room per family. One memory I have of the 1940s is that there were trams on the streets of Busan, but there were also horse-drawn carriages. Until proper industrialization took place, a significant number of urban households had young female helpers from the countryside including ours, who were mostly unpaid but properly fed. It must have been an effort to reduce the number of mouths to feed in rural households.

I attended elementary school (called 'national school' at the time) and middle school in the 1950s. Of course, I walked to school. The middle school was about 3-4 Kms away from where I lived. There were many students who walked even further to attend school. The high school I attended was on the same campus as the middle school. Students who came far away from Busan, where connecting roads and transportation systems were not properly established, commuted by train. It must have taken a tremendous amount of time to commute.

Electricity and water supply were barely available for in-house use, and even if they were, the supply was limited and only available for a short period of time during the day. Electricity was low voltage, so the lighting was dim, and there were frequent blackouts or flickering. At the time, in order to save electricity bills, many households would punch a hole in the upper part of the wall between adjoining rooms and hang a not-so-bright light bulb in the middle. Household electric fans that became popular in the late 1970s were a luxury item that was difficult to use due to their high price and electricity bill. Telephones were introduced early on, but I had never seen an in-home telephone until high school. The church I attended was far from home, near my high school, and for messages or emergency meeting calls, the church administrative staff would deliver messages to each elder's house on foot. Urgent messages were sent by telegram, which of course required a trip to the far-away post office and taking a considerable amount of time for the sending process and for the recipient to receive the delivery by the postman.

In rural areas, people had to walk a long distance to the post office in the township to apply for a telegram, and it took even more time for the telegram to be delivered. Telegram fees were determined by the number of characters, so schools taught students how to write short telegrams (the basic fee was for 10 characters or less).

In the 1960s, I attended high school and college. The clothes and shoes I wore in high school were of poor-quality school uniform and pants, relief supplies sent from the United States, dyed military work clothes, and worn-out military boots.

Photographs were rare and expensive, and you had to go to a photo studio to get them. Up until high school, there was a photographer at the school campus who occasionally took photos of students, and after work, he developed and printed black-and-white photographs in his home-darkroom. He often accompanied students on picnics and field trips and sold the photos.

In 1963, I went to a university in Seoul, and during my first semester, I stayed in a private boarding room near the school. At that time, tensions between the US and Korea government led to a disruption in the aid-supply of rice and flour, so we had to have an early summer vacation. There was a small cafeteria on campus, but if you didn't go back to the boarding house for lunch, you had to skip the meal. In the mid-1960s, telephones began to be available in ordinary households, but having a telephone at home was a rare and valuable symbol of wealth and status of that family.

High birth rates, low national income level, and a desire to venture out into the world contributed to the beginning of planned emigration. This was mainly family-based agricultural emigration to South America, especially Brazil and Argentina. This Korean diaspora took place under government policy and encouragement. Around the same time, highly educated but unemployed people went to Germany as miners and nurses, and the Korean government decided to participate in the Vietnam War in the 1960s. Individuals with family connections or specific skills, such as a medical doctor, had the opportunity to emigrate to the United States. From the 1960s onwards, studying in American universities became more common, mainly due to scholarship benefits from American universities and the government.

When I first went to the university in Seoul in 1963, I remember there were about 10 bus routes, and the number of routes quickly increased after a while. At that time, trams were also an important means of transportation. The main alcoholic beverage for students and workers was called makgeolli traditionally made from rice , but there were rumors that it was made from carbide rather than grain. Korea was a poor country.

In the late 1960s, I served as an army officer at the division headquarter stationed in the Demilitarized Zone, and at that time, the subordinate units apart from the division headquarter mainly relied on manual radio communication, which was used during the Korean War. The military communication used switchboards, and it gradually changed to direct lines. I remember living in a Bachelor Officer's Quarter at my first post in the regiment headquarter, with broken windows and no proper heating in the midst of the winter cold at the frontline.

In 1970, I joined the Bank of Korea, which was equipped with state-of-the-art facilities at the time. We used a shared internal phone number for our department, and documents were mainly written with fountain pens or ballpoint pens. Although a typewriting machine was available, they had no copy or edit functions. Of course, there was a mimeograph room in the bank with professional typists. There were separate delivery persons for document orders and deliveries within the bank. Communication with foreign countries or remote locations mainly used international telegrams and telexes, and there were separate communication experts for that purpose. To make an international call to foreign countries, you had to visit a telephone and telegraph office, regardless of public or private business. There you had to apply, and wait for your turn and connection afterwards. The waiting time was unpredictable. Of course, it was known that international calls were also made in a similar way even in other countries like the United States at that time.

As a surprising discovery in the 1970s when working at the bank was a refrigerator sized copy machine made in Japan. The copy paper and ink were expensive, but it was the first time seeing a state-of-the-art device that could duplicate documents. With the widespread use of ballpoint pens, office environments that relied on pens and ink were significantly improved. Abacuses were prevalent, but electronic calculators began to be distributed, making it possible for those who did not graduate from a commercial high school(trained specifically for exclusive abacus calculation method), to handle standard banking and calculating tasks. There were no computers at the time, so I remember pounding on a calculator to perform regression analysis for deposit prediction. All documents had to be sent mainly by post-mail or messenger delivery. There was one telephone at the dormitory for single-employees in the bank and it was a large building with dozens of rooms. If there was an urgent call, the manager would come to the room to find the person.

In 1976, I was promoted to a junior manager, and a privilege of the promotion was having a desk telephone. Around that time, the supply for home telephones began to increase. There were two types of home telephones at the time: white phones, which were freely available for buying and selling, and blue phones, which required permission of the state for installation and could not be transferred to others. The relatively cheap blue phones had fierce competition, while white phones were very expensive and rare.

In 1976, I went to study in the United States. At Gimpo Airport (Incheon International Airport was established later), there were at least 50 or more people sending me off, including family members and relatives from remote regions. There was no direct flight to the destination in the US, so I had to go through Tokyo for transfer. I received a scholarship for my graduate study up to Ph. D degree. There were no telephones in the student apartments at that time. Since the United States was a well-off country at the time, graduate students were allowed to copy books and materials for free, which was a huge benefit, especially for those from underdeveloped countries. However, the system was abolished soon afterward because of unaffordable costs.

In 1981, I was employed as a professor at a university in the United States, and that university still had a shared phone system for the professors' offices, so when a call came in, someone had to pick it up from their office and connect it to the intended recipient in various ways. Until then, the primary means of communication within the department and school in my university was through posting notices on public bulletin boards or delivering typed or copied documents. Professors had to provide their own typewriter, which was equivalent to a personal computer nowadays. Needless to say, correction tapes for fixing typing errors were highly valued at that time.

From the 1970s, computers were introduced to US universities. In the early stages, these computers had a very small capacity compared to today's standard but were very big in size. The State university and State Government jointly shared the computer system in my case. Users punched holes in input cards and fed them into the card reader to run basic programming languages like Fortran or COBOL. Teaching those computer languages and operating methods was the main subject in the computer science course. Data processing or calculations using a computer were required for my thesis work, but the capacity of the university's system was so small that if I worked during the day time it would take several hours to get a simple error message. Naturally, I had to go to the computer room after midnight for work, which caused my health to deteriorate.

The university I joined in the United States in 1981 had a small student size and did not have its own computer facilities, so it had to borrow and utilize functions from other venues. Before returning to Korea in early 1984, I hesitated whether to buy the newly released Apple PC but decided not to, due to its high price, which I later regretted. Since Korea was not an affluent country yet, I brought back all my belongings and household appliances from the United States in a container.

Upon arriving at Pusan National University, in Korea, I was surprised to see that direct–dial phone service with premised campus numbers was provided for each professor's office. This phenomenon is an example of the latecomer advantage in economics, where less developed countries like Korea, which had lagged in telecommunication service, could start installing cutting-edge facilities from the outset, thus modernizing tele-communication systems more quickly than other advanced countries. It is highly likely national universities were treated similarly to government agencies, which may have accelerated the early adoption. Commercial copy-service stores began to emerge, offering typing services as well as copying and binding. The implementation of intellectual property was not yet fully established by that time, so copying various materials was common those days. I remember there were even specialized shops for copying and selling a whole foreign textbook. Subsequently, an individual computer (desktop) was provided to each professor's office, enabling researchers to work independently.

In early 1984, when I joined Pusan National University, not many faculty members owned cars. In my case, I bought a used car from a colleague, but for most people, driving a personal car was not common. However, it didn't take long for personal cars to become widespread, and soon after, students also began driving personal vehicles.

From the 1980s, a form of mobile communication called "beeper" was introduced. This involved sending a beeping signal to a receiver carrying a tiny device, who would then use a payphone or another telephone to call the sender. Although primitive by today's standard, it was a groundbreaking means of mobile communication at the time.

The internet was introduced and began to spread in Korea almost the same time as advanced countries. Not many people at the time would have imagined the function and usage we enjoy today. Among them, imaginative and adventurous young innovators founded giant corporations like Microsoft, Apple, and Google, changing the landscape of global business and life. Similarly, in Korea, start-ups founded by creative and imaginative individuals have become leading conglomerates today.

I was a visiting fellow at the East-West Center in Honolulu, Hawaii, for a year from the summer of 1989. What amazed me at the time was seeing mobile phones. They were very large, almost the size of a small wooden pillow or military communicator, and quite heavy. According to written data, a similar mobile phone service started in Korea on July 1, 1988. It's quite surprising.

From the mid-to-late 1990s, mobile phones began to be used, and my first mobile phone was provided by the university in 1997 when I took the position of the university dean. The main function of the phone was mobile communication, and since the use was not yet widespread, one of the essential functions at the time was receiving calls or summons from the president in real time. From 1998 to 2001, I served as the president of the Busan Development Institute, the city's think tank, using a Motorola mobile phone with similar functions. Subsequently, smartphones were introduced, absorbing or replacing the function and role of computers. In between, there were several devices like MP3 players and tablet PCs, but rapid technological advancements virtually eliminated the intermediate stages.

Until then, mobile phones did not have camera function like smartphones, so separate cameras were used, and subsequent film and photo development processes were necessary. Even though cameras continued to become smaller and more powerful, their basic function did not change. Early on, Kodak introduced a groundbreaking innovation such as developing and printing photos simultaneously while shooting, and other innovations like high-pixel and multi-functional photography continued. Although innovations like mobile cameras, video shooting and recording continued, they used tape or film, which was a completely different approach from today's smartphone.

The era of smartphones began in the mid-2000s with the introduction of the iPhone. In addition to communication and photography functions, it performed the functions of a computer, and now, utilizing artificial intelligence, it continues to evolve into a device that directly interacts with humans, performing tasks and acting as a personal assistant or close friend. Because of smartphone's func-

tions related to learning, such as information search and storage utilization, all the printed dictionaries and encyclopedias that can be considered part of humanity's cultural heritage have disappeared. Now equipped with the ability to instantly share self-produced or received materials including photos and videos, and use of social media , lifestyles are changing every moment.

So far, the content I have described is based on my personal experiences and memories, and I have tried to organize the events and changes that come to mind. The timeline and content may not be accurate, and my memories could be incorrect. The purpose of writing this is not to create documents based on accurate records, but to roughly observe and record the truly astonishing changes experienced or witnessed by an individual throughout the latter part of the analog era and the beginning of the digital era.

The speed of change during this relatively short period is faster and more revolutionary than the cumulative changes humans have experienced over tens or hundreds of thousands of years, with technological advancements at the center.

To summarize the past 70 years, I was born in Korea, a very underdeveloped country that had just emerged from colonization during the middle and latter stages of the global industrialization era. I participated in and benefited from the rapid economic development process of Korea, which was unprecedented in world history during the latter part of the global industrialization era. I experienced the overlapping and continuity of the information age, and I now stand at the intersection of the digital age and the fourth industrial revolution. I was also fortunate to live through the end of the 20th century and the beginning of the 21st century, and belong to a rare, lucky generation that experienced the millennium transition.

The content and speed of these changes are certainly something that no one before could have experienced or even imagined. Our generation, which includes myself, can be called the 'lucky generation' since there probably won't be another opportunity for future generations to experience these changes all at once. The current technological changes, including artificial intelligence, may change the world faster than in the past, but not everyone will experience multiple revolutionary changes as was in my case, so my feelings that come with them are unique.

3-3 Speed and Distinctiveness of Korea (and Koreans) through International Comparison

All economic and social phenomena and outcomes are relative. If other countries had developed faster during the same period, we would still be relatively underdeveloped. To compare Korea's speed and distinctiveness from other countries, two recent statistics were used. First, we compare Korea's speed and her differences using international labor-related statistics created by the OECD. Second, comparing Koreans' characteristics by health related international statistics. The comparison is mainly with the United States, which leads the world in many cases, and Japan, which has been the undisputed number one in Asia. In some other cases, we compare it with a few OECD countries and some other countries. To share the conclusion in advance, Koreans have clearly different characteristics and distinctiveness from other developed countries (and their citizens) , and the speed generating such differences is most certainly faster.

(1) Comparison by Labor-related Statistics

1) Hourly wage index and purchasing power of wages

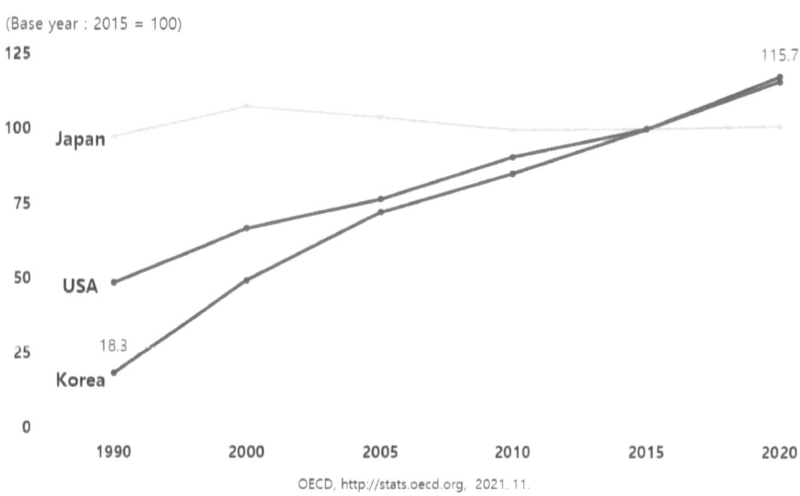

Figure 3-1 *Hourly wage index*

Figure 3-1 is an international comparison of the hourly wage index in the private sector, focusing on Korea, Japan, and the United States. Although the wage levels are different for each country, comparing the degree of change by year is meaningful. Comparing the cases of the three countries, based on 2015, the wage levels in Korea rose from 18.3 to an index of 100 over the past 25 years, while Japan's change was negligible, moving from 97.4 to 100. The United States changed from 48.5 to 100 and increased to 117.4 over the next five years. Korea also rose similarly to 115.7 during the same period. In contrast, Japan's change was almost non-existent, at 101.0. In terms of the speed of dynamism, Korea and Japan are entirely different. Korea has rapidly risen since the comparison was first started in 1990, the United States has a similar trend but at a slower pace, and Japan has shown little change, remaining almost stagnant. The hourly wage index in the manufacturing sector shows a similar trend.

Another comparison method is the purchasing power of wages expressed in dollars. In 1990, Japanese workers' purchasing power was three times that of Korean workers, while US workers' purchasing power was more than four times higher. By 2020, Korea's purchasing power of wage had surpassed both Japan and the United States. Although France was ahead of Korea in 2020, it was a tremendous reversal since it was more than four times ahead 25 years ago. This clearly demonstrates how rapidly the Korean economy has changed.

2) Weekly working hours of total employees

Korea has been infamous for its long working hours. Of course, it is undeniable that achieving today's prosperity through working longer than others had its merit. In many OECD countries, especially European ones, weekly working hours have remained almost unchanged or decreased slightly by less than 3 hours over the past 25 years. In contrast, Korea has seen a decrease of over 12 hours, from 52.9 hours to 40.2 hours. It is another confirmation of the speed of change.

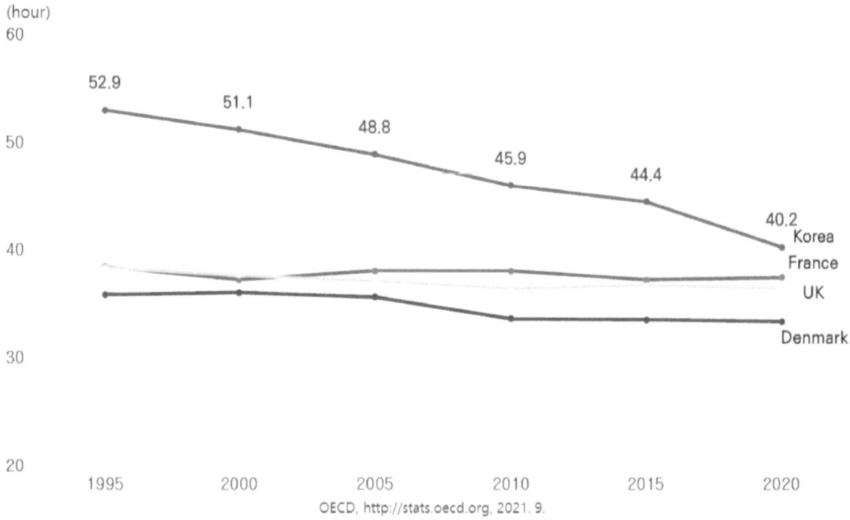

Figure 3-2 *Weekly Working Hours Trend: Total Employed Worker*

3) Level of pension benefit expenditure of old-ages

Old-age pension is one of the main indicators representing the welfare level of a country. In absolute terms, Korea's level was incomparably low to that of other OECD countries in the past. Compared to a generation later, the levels in advanced countries have increased by a few percent, while Korea's has increased by several folds. In 1985, when the comparison began, there was no such pension system in Korea, while advanced countries were already spending around 5-10% of their GDP. In the following 30 years, the OECD average increased from 6.2% to 8.2%, while Korea's increased from 0% to 3.2%. Although the absolute level is still far below that of advanced countries, the catch-up speed is unprecedented. This means that, in terms of welfare levels, Korea was once a poor country that could not even compare to advanced countries. However, now it has caught up considerably and continues to narrow the gap at a rapid pace. It is not easy to separately increase the expenditure share of a sector in GDP.

4) Level of unemployment benefit expenditure

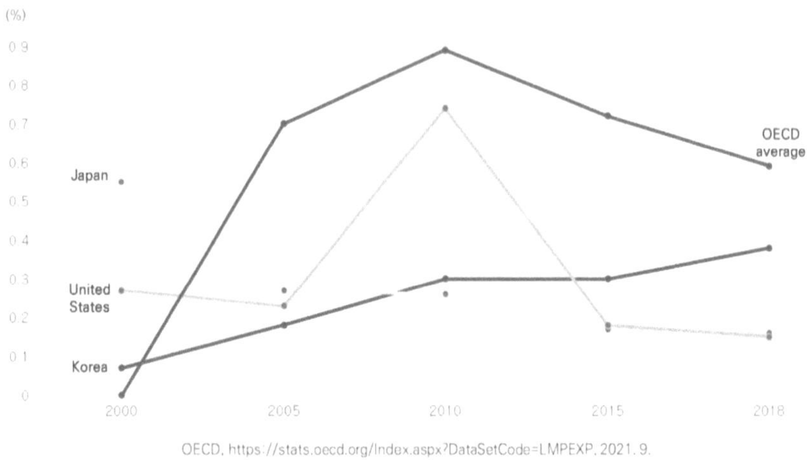

Figure 3-3 *Unemployment Benefit Expenditure Level*

The increase in unemployment benefit expenditure level is even more dramatic than that of old-age pension. In Korea, the share of GDP spent on these benefits was only 0.07% in 2000, after the implementation of the system. Eighteen years later, it rose to 0.38%, while Japan, which had a share of 0.55% in 2000, saw its share gradually decrease. Korea's rapid increase led it to overtake Japan and the United States in the 2010s. Of course, this figure is not always good when it is high, as it could be better for it to decrease due to improvement in economic and employment conditions. However, the point to consider here is the speed of Korea's change, which demonstrates its ability to handle expenditures.

Though it may be a repeated expression, in many cases, Korea has already reached a similar level to advanced countries in various sectors, both nominal and in real terms. The focus of interest here is the speed of change. As opposed to individuals or individual organizations, there has been no instance in world history where a country has made such rapid progress within a period of a single generation. The challenge now will be sustainability.

(2) Comparison of Health-Related Statistics

Next, we will compare Korea(ns) with other foreign countries, especially

OECD countries, using the data from 'Health at a Glance' published by the OECD in December 2021. The point to emphasize again is not to view the comparison in terms of advantage or disadvantage, for better or worse, but to see how and to what extent Korea(ns) has different characteristics compared to other countries(people) on average or as individuals, and the extent and speed of the timeline.

1) Life-span expectancy

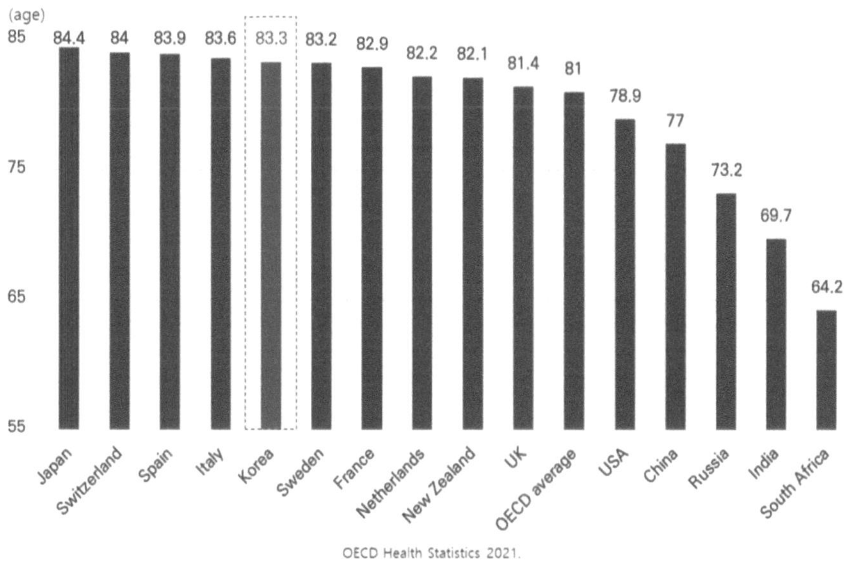

Figure 3-4 *Average Life-Span Expectancy (2019)*

Looking back at the changes in life expectancy for newborns over the past half-century, Korea was at a level comparable to middle-income countries until 1970, but by 2019, she had leapfrogged to the leading group. This is mainly due to the rapid rise in economic and medical levels. It is clear that Korea has a relatively higher level of life-span compared to other OECD countries.

2) Depression symptoms related to COVID-19

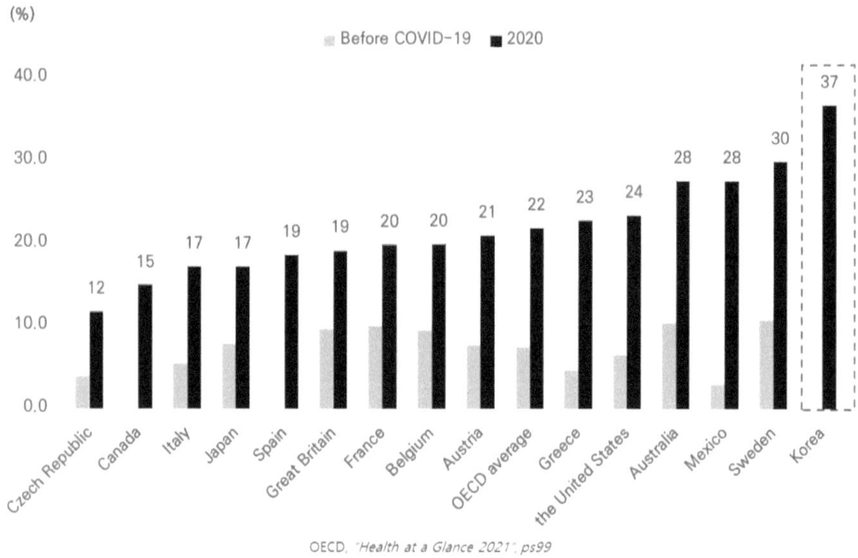

Figure 3-5 *Prevalence Estimates of Depression Symptoms Before and After COVID-19*

On the other hand, Figure 3-5 clearly reveals another distinct characteristic of Koreans. The prevalence of depression or depressive symptoms in adults can be compared between countries before and after the COVID-19 pandemic. In Korea, there were few symptoms before 2020, but the response to COVID-19 was much greater than other countries in 2020. This is evidence that Koreans are the most sensitive among OECD countries to this pandemic. Regardless of desirability, it demonstrates another unique characteristic and difference of Koreans by global comparison.

3) Self-assessment on health status

Related to the previous section, as shown in Figure 3-6, Korean adults tend to think that their health status is much worse or pessimistic compared to their counterparts in other countries, regardless of the income group they belong to. In this case, Japan also shows a similar tendency, but Korea is more extreme. People belonging to the higher income group in OECD countries generally have a positive view on their own health status, but in Korea, less than half of those in the higher income group feel that their health is average or on the good side. This is also an apparent difference.

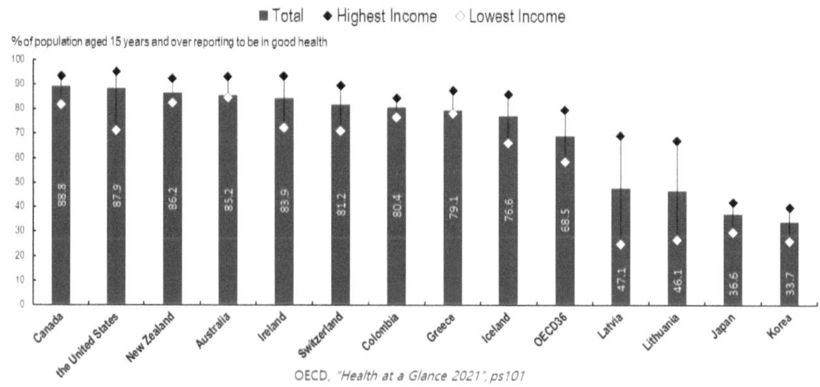

Figure 3-6 *Proportion of Adults Rating Their Health as 'Good' or 'Very Good'*

4) Number of doctor-patient consultations

Perhaps as a result, Korea is far ahead in terms of the number of face-to-face doctor consultations per person per year. As seen in Figure 3-7, Korea has significantly more consultations than Japan, who is next in line. It is more than twice the average of the 34 OECD countries. Naturally, the number of consultations per doctor per year in Korea is also unmatched, ranking first. In 2019, the average number of consultations in Korea was 6,989, while the average for the other 33 OECD countries was 2,122. The number of non-face-to-face consultations is not comparable, due to regulations related to healthcare. This issue will be discussed separately.

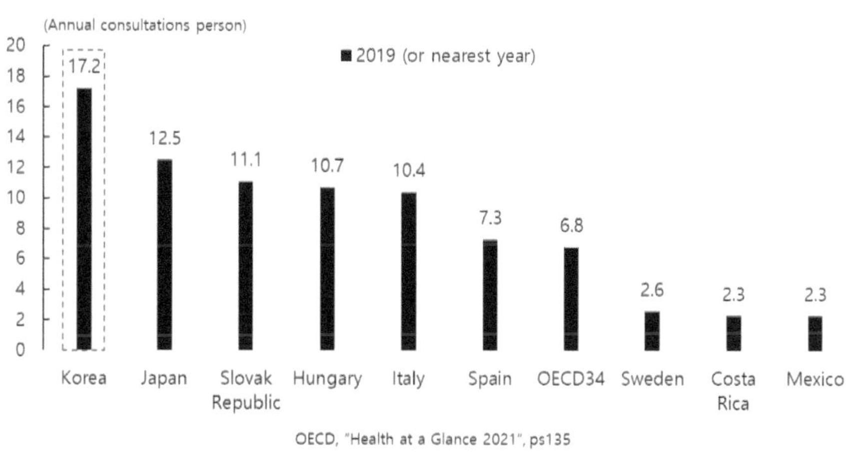

Figure 3-7 *Number of Doctor Consultations per Person per Year*

5) Length of hospital stay and death in hospital

Koreans are also unique in terms of the length of hospital stay and its changing trend. As shown in Figure 3-8, the average length of hospital stays of Koreans in 2019 was 18.0 days, about 2.4 times higher than the OECD average of 7.6 days for 38 countries. An even more significant characteristic is that the average length of stay decreased for almost all countries, especially OECD countries, after 2009, but only Korea saw a clear increase. The extent and direction of change in long-term care services for the elderly, aged 65 and older also shows similar aspects. The proportion of deaths in hospitals in Korea is also the highest among 22 OECD countries at 77% in 2021. Like the aforementioned features, while other countries have been seeing a decreasing trend in this proportion since 2009, Korea has been rapidly increasing.

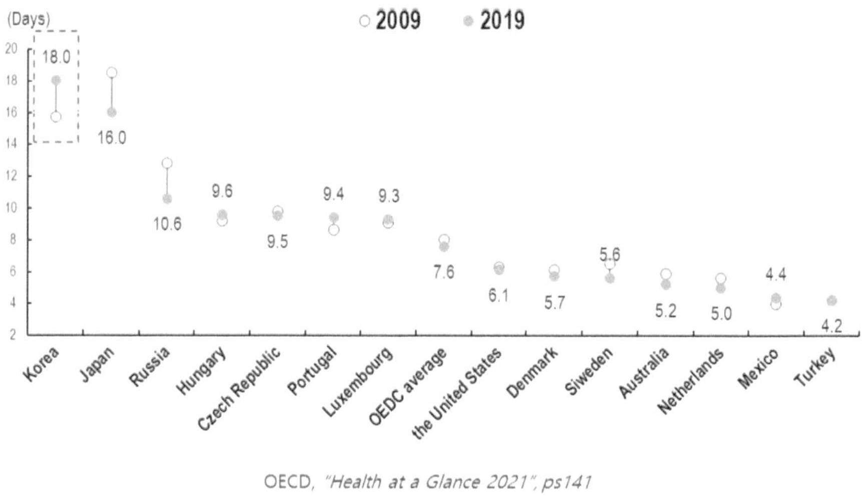

Figure 3-8 *Average Length of Hospital Stay (2009, 2019)*

6) Vaccination rate for the elderly

Korea is also the clear leader in the influenza vaccination rate (86%), which has increased significantly since 2009, going in the opposite direction of other OECD countries. Korea is also among the top countries for antibiotic prescription rate. This can be seen as a characteristic of having more interest and power of execution in one's health. In the case of COVID-19, although the government failed to secure vaccines early on, the vaccination rate, in spite of a late start, quickly reached the top tier globally.

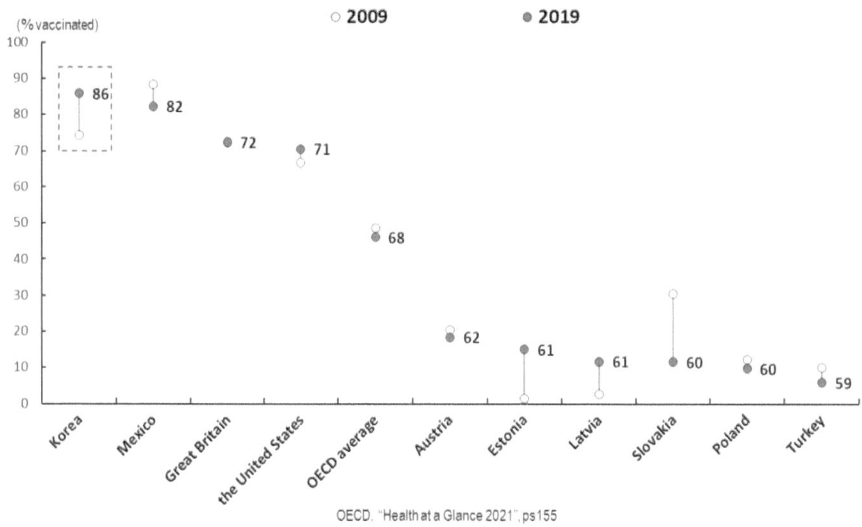

Figure 3-9 *Proportion of Population Aged 65 and Older Who Received Influenza Vaccination*

7) Health-related expenditure

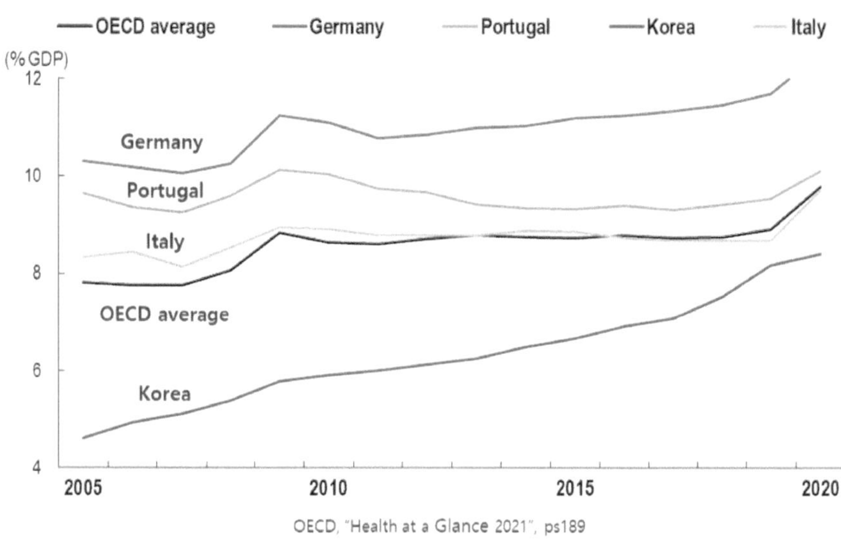

Figure 3-10 *Share of Healthcare Expenditure as a Percentage of GDP*

As of 2020, the share of health-related expenditure as a percentage of GDP is still lower compared to the average of 22 OECD countries, but the trend has changed significantly since 2005. As shown in Figure 3-10, health-related expenditure borne by the government is still below the average. However, the rate of change (increase) is the highest.

8) Two future predictions

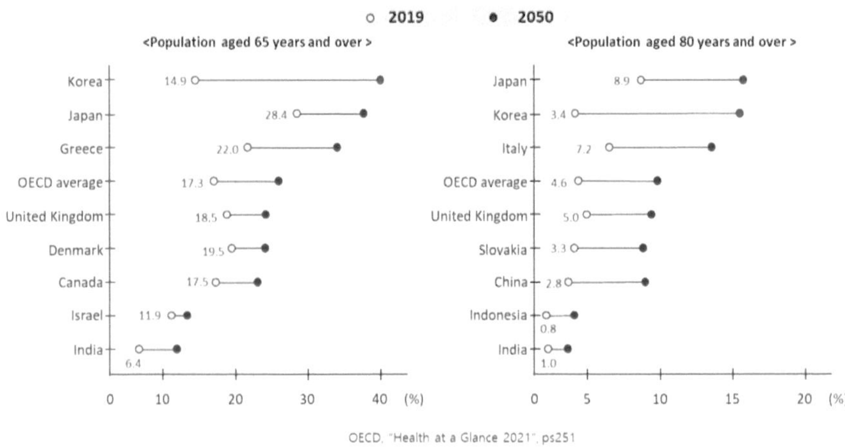

Figure 3-11 *Proportion of Population Aged 65 and Over and 80 and Over (2019, 2050)*

Considering the current pace of change and future prediction, Korea has many areas where she is clearly ahead. First, a 2050 prediction for the proportion of the elderly population aged 65 and over, and 80 and over, Korea is undoubtedly at the forefront, alongside Japan. The graph in Figure 3-11 clearly shows the speed at which Korea is moving, without a need to compare with other countries.

Another indicator is the predicted incidents of Alzheimer. Although it is not desirable, Korea shows a distinctly fast increase of dementia cases by 2050. This is another piece of evidence that Korea is clearly different in terms of the degree and nature of change in many areas compared to many other countries, and that it will continue to accelerate in the future.

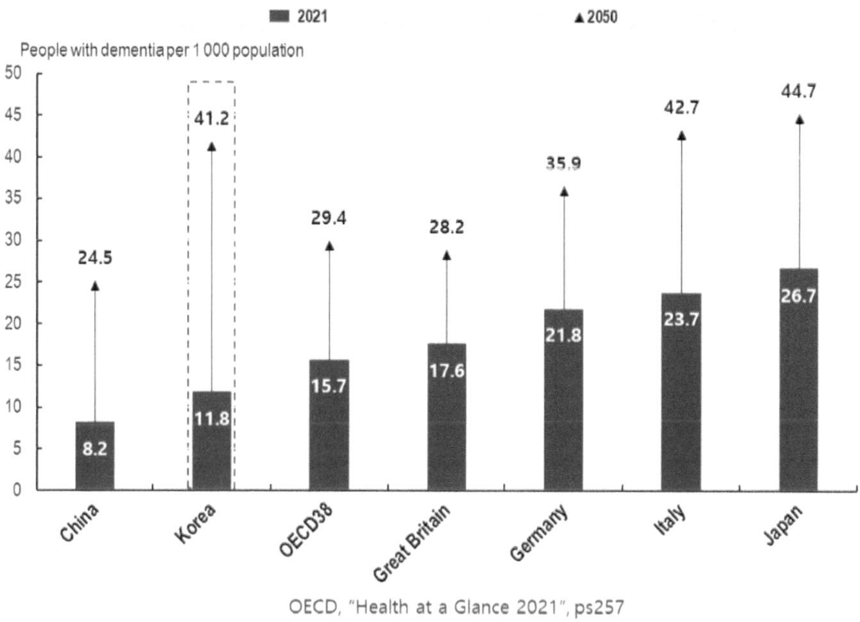

Figure 3-12 *Estimate on Dementia Prevalence (2021 and 2050)*

Once again, the emphasis is not on revealing the strength or weakness of Korea (and Koreans) through international comparison, but on reconfirming the fact that Korea has a relatively faster pace of change compared to other countries, especially economically advanced countries (developed countries), and that Korea quickly reached a similar level in many areas where she initially lagged behind. It is another piece of evidence that shows that Korea is truly unique with many areas that display surprising speed, regardless of desirability.

The OECD's 2021 report, "Inclusive Growth Review of Korea - Creating Opportunities for All," points out various aspects of the Korean economy and society that have not been addressed yet during this rapid growth and change. Now is the appropriate time to seek wisdom and listen carefully for rapid improvement on areas that are relatively lacking.

An Experience of Speed - Korea (2): Korean Life up to the 1970s

One cannot truly understand the past they have not experienced firsthand. Up until the 1960s, Korea was a very poor country where most citizens could not even afford three meals a day. The succeeding generations cannot truly know or feel this hardship, expressed in the term Borigogae(Spring hunger: food shortage before barley harvest). Even in cities, at that time, people had to use water drawn from wells for cooking and daily life instead of tap water, and there were no proper sewage systems or flush toilets. Collecting human wastes was a significant business, and if toilet papers existed, they were considered a luxury item. In the cities, coal briquettes (19-holed briquette) were used for cooking and heating, but it was also common to use firewood or charcoal. Briquette was used for room heating and deaths by carbon monoxide gas from it were frequent. The first pledge of the 1961 military coup was to solve the people's livelihood difficulties, which many people inwardly sympathized with at the time. In short, it was an incredibly challenging and exhausting time to live.

As expected, the level of education, culture, and art was also similar. In terms of education, one had to learn from the United States, European countries or Japan, which was already advanced. Obtaining foreign books or materials was expensive and difficult. Even if they were obtained, there was still the problem of language proficiency. This was because English proficiency was lacking after the Japanese colonial period. Therefore, obtaining and utilizing Japanese books, which were of a superior level at the time, was considered cutting-edge. Possessing hard-to-find Japanese books or materials made it possible to provide excellent lectures or classes. The materials were exclusive to the professors and teachers, and there were no proper textbooks written in Korean. Of course, there were no photocopiers or related functions at that time.

Culture and art were in the same situation. Novels, songs, movies, and all other areas favored the superior, diverse, and outstanding products of Japan, the United States and European countries. Japanese items were outright banned and shunned due to the government policy and national sentiment. However, because of the practical demand stemming from the differences in academic level, bookstores selling Japanese books still existed.

However, not everything even in the United States was quickly introduced or institutionalized either. The application of dental insurance coverage didn't become widespread until the early 1980s, so the gap between the U.S. and Korea wasn't that significant. The author was grateful for having received extensive gum surgery, introduced lately, while employed at a US university.

Emigration to the United States and South America that began in the 1960s was also an attempt to improve competitiveness. Many Koreans emigrated to the United States in response to the country's open immigration policy. This can be seen as an active attempt to break through the harsh reality of the times. Those who chose to go to the United States primarily pursued better living conditions as well as respected professional careers (e.g., medical doctors) and most commonly sought better education for their children. Many of these immigrants already had jobs or some sort of wealth in Korea. It was a progressive choice to spread their wings in a better place.

That generation's settlement process in the United States was by no means easy, but it can be said that most of them successfully went through the process with their unique speed and competitiveness as a Korean.

At the time, the United States was undoubtedly a land of opportunity in every aspect compared to Korea. So people who moved their roots to a new country would be amazed by the development of their homeland within the span of their own generation or less than half a century. Now, many immigrants from the past visit Korea for medical treatment or dental care and send their children to Korean universities or graduate schools. The status of Korea has completely changed internationally, and this is an unprecedented case for any country in history. Some people are willing to return to Korea for their later years but because of real estate prices and other factors are not able to. It is likely that none of the immigrants at the time could have predicted that the country they left would develop and change so quickly within their lifetime. This is the result of Korean speed.

3-4 Korean Character that Drives Speed (First Consideration)

One of the reasons Korea was able to achieve unprecedented changes in this pace is the vision and capacity of a leader who awakened the nation's potential and led them to industrialization and economic development. In response, the nation's constituent (citizen) had the ability, will, and practicality to adapt and change. Various factors have influenced and interacted with one another but the foundation lies in the individual citizen's determination, competitiveness, and especially, their sense of speed. While other causes may exist to make this rapid growth possible, it was ultimately the visible and sometimes non-visible leadership that properly directed all elements and competitive factors towards the ability to yield results.

As the astonishing economic growth materialized in a relatively short period, its impact spread to society, culture, arts, sports, and all other fields, and began to flourish at a pace not slower than that of industry and economy. That's why it is not awkward to use the prefix 'K-' to many sectors and phenomena in Korea at present. As evidenced in the examples listed above, the speed of change in Korea over the past half-century or less is unprecedented in the past or present of any country and society, and unlikely in the future. Recognizing this properly, is the right direction and task to maintain advantages while correcting or minimizing disadvantages and side effects.

In addition to the innate ability, two other personality traits of Koreans that contribute to a sense of speed are exceptional motivation for achievement and desire for upward social status. Korean enthusiasm for children's education is recognized and admired by the world, a noteworthy aspect of culture but is considered exorbitant at present. One of the most difficult and unsuccessful areas of Korea's economic policy around 2020 was estate policy, especially with the price of apartments. The apartment price issue has been one of the fundamental causes of education related problems, since apartment locations determine which school district the child will attend. The exceptional passion for children's education inevitably becomes more intense with the rapid decrease in the number of children.

The desire for upward social mobility can be explained in the same dimension. "Perhaps there is no other place with a desire for social mobility as strong as Korean society. People are never satisfied with modest achievements and always want to climb higher. That's why the competition is the fiercest in the world, and society is extremely dynamic. As this starts to stagnate, the immediate outcry of 'Hell Joseon!' erupts."[57] "There are

[57] Park Hoon, 'From Servitude to Nobility, That Long Journey' (Written by Kwon

no other people as passionate as us when they get into something. If the environment is provided, results will follow".[58] It is hard to hold back a competitive nature.

At the same time, we must point out the egalitarian aspect of the culture. The traditional saying, 'If your cousin buys a rice paddy, your belly aches,' is a typical example. The term, 'neighborhood cousin' represents a characteristic of Koreans expressing the village community, but at the same time, it reflects the competitive psychology that they cannot properly acknowledge the growth or changes of their co-struggling neighbors. Therefore, it is necessary to pay attention to the evaluation of a naturalized Chinese-Korean who said, "The (Korean)system is capitalist, but the mentality is communist".[59]

The changes in hobbies and leisure activities are also fast-paced, with golf being one example. As seen in Figures 3-13 the Korean golf population has grown rapidly, exceeding 11 million in 2021, about 31.5% of the population aged 20-70 years old, and even more surprising is the explosive increase of female golfers. Until the early 2000s, golf was considered an extravagant sport, primarily for affluent middle aged males. To this day membership golf courses still charge a considerable amount of special consumption tax (a kind of leisure tax) in addition to the regular green fee for each use.

Looking at the current composition of golf course users, it is thriving with females of all ages, especially young women.[60] It was not easy to find female golfers on the golf course even in the early 2000s. Such change is also without global precedent.

The biggest driving force behind this phenomenon is the success of Korean female golfers in the LPGA. Since the 2000s, Korea has firmly secured second place in the world of women's golf based on official tournament results. It's astounding considering the short history of golf in Korea, especially the entrance of female professional golfers. There is no other expla-

---

Nae-Hyun), Book Review, Chosun Ilbo, January 19th, 2019, A17, Book 152

58 Interview with Dr. Shin Hee-sub, Why section, Chosun Ilbo, February 14th-15th 2009, B2

59 Kim Tae-hoon's News-sniper, Chosun Ilbo, 'Chen Ran, Brutal Korea, Quirky Koreans' (Quoted from a Book Review), Chosun Ilbo, , February 15th ,2019, A2

60 One day in December 2021, at a membership golf course restaurant in Busan, the author noticed that more than two-thirds of the patrons during lunchtime were female customers.

nation besides K-speed.

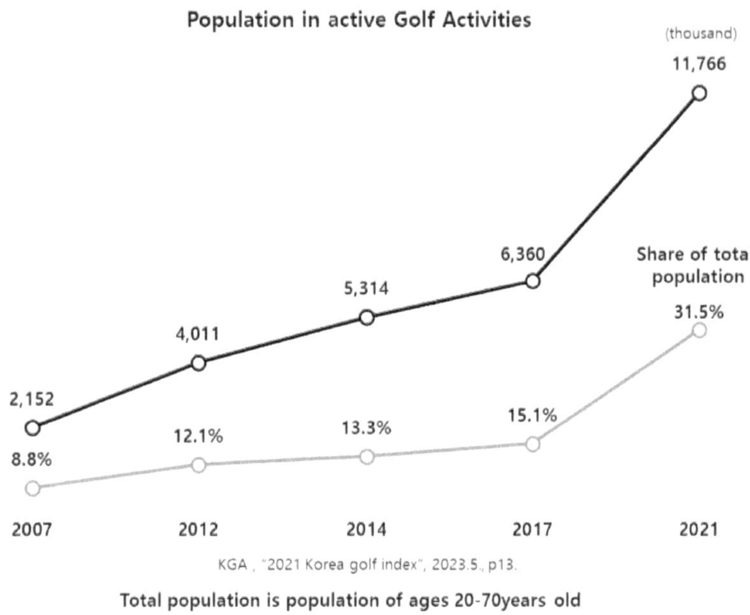

Figure 3-13 *Population in Active Golf Activities*

Global golf brands evaluate the Korean golf club market as the third-largest, following the United States and Japan. Golf, a sport in itself with a long history, became popularized and widely fashionable in Korea only since the 2000s, and not even a single generation (30 years) has passed yet. Despite this, Korean golfers change their drivers every six months on average, fairway woods every year, irons every 1.5 years, and putters every two years. Golf clubs are relatively expensive durable consumer goods and reflect the desire to do better and stay ahead of others. Considering the characteristics of Koreans described so far, it is not surprising.

There are pros and cons in everything, so being too fast can also be problematic and cause side effects. As the old saying in Korea goes, 'overdoing is worse than under doing', there could be many cases where being too excessive can cause problems. The current states in Korea may be seen as an example of not being able to properly control or adjust the aftermath of rapid growth and thus resulting in dangerous outcomes. It is possible to disregard excessiveness in the beginning, but it may have unfavorable consequences. As a fire catches quickly and burns with hope, it can extinguish quickly as well.

Chapter 4

K-Speed in Business, Industry, and Everyday Life

A country's macroeconomic performance is strongly influenced by the individual management performance. Competitiveness is the first factor that determines success or failure in management. As previously explained, competition inherently involves speed. Therefore, the success or failure of management is essentially determined by speed. This speed is a core element of innovation and improvement in all areas, such as decision-making, management planning, organizational operation and improvement, product planning, manufacturing, various services, sales, and management administration. In this case, the meaning of speed is to produce or process faster, cheaper, and better than others. As examined in various forms in this book, the process of economic competition was not particularly noticeable and progressed very slowly before the modern era, making it difficult to detect specifically over a long period of time. However, since the Industrial Revolution, the speed has gradually increased, and its application and scope have expanded. At this point, the degree of acceleration has become so rapid that it is overwhelming for all economic agents to properly recognize or perceive changes in a timely manner.

Of course, in this case, speed also means the pace of transformation and change. Over the years, frequent reversals or contradictions of past standard, practice, or lesson are happening in the transformation of industries, products, and business operations. For example, hardware companies are turning into software companies or vice versa, and the boundaries of industry classifications are disappearing as convergence is expanding. This is because more than any factor technology enables transformation.

In the past, the Go game term 'a big horse never dies' was quite persuasive in economy and management. This meant that if a company were very large, it would not easily collapse due to its size, even in the face of difficulties or sudden changes in management, economy, or unexpected situations. Moreover, the government and society tended to help those large companies because their collapse could result in serious consequences or side effects on the economy, such as over-all production, distribution, and employment situation. There have been numerous examples of this in both Korea and other advanced countries. Although this meaning differs from economies of scale found in economic theory, there was a dimension to which large-scale companies had an advantage for survival.

In terms of countermeasure, having a certain scale allowed companies to adapt more flexibly to market change, which was an advantage for larger companies. However, as the economy has become globalized and competition has expanded worldwide, solving domestic difficulties alone is no longer sufficient. The speed of competition, of course, is the main reason. Moreover, with the rapid spread of information and communication network such as internet and smartphones, the meaning of distance, time, and location have virtually disappeared, and the economies of speed[61] is becoming more important than the economies of scale.

4-1 Decision-Making Speed in Management - Global Trend

In the modern economic environment, the success or failure of a new business venture, transformation from the current position, or starting a business from scratch depends on the direction and decision-making speed. Of course, there are countless factors to consider, such as circumstance, situation, personal capability, and preparation, but the most important

[61] The term 'economy of speed' is not officially included in economics textbooks. The concept was once used to describe the utility of using concrete surface finishes in architecture (Sang-hyun Lee et al., Finite Element Method (FEM) Analysis Study for Evaluating the Carbonation Inhibition Performance of Concrete Surface Finishes, Journal of the Architectural Institute of Korea Structure & Construction Vol. 23 No. 9, 2007, pp. 151-158). The concept of the 'economy of speed' is starting to be used in business management to convey that it's more effective to rapidly transform than to grow in size ('The 'Economy of Scale' Goes, the 'Economy of Speed' Rises', Weekly DongA, Issue 267, January 11, 2001). For instance, the decision of AT&T in the United States to buy cable TV companies for 100 billion dollars to preempt the IMT-2000 market, (which was once called the dream market of communication and was the largest telecom company in the world) was an attempt to preempt through massive cost allocation. This wrong decision led AT&T to break up into four parts. It was a miscalculation of communication technology and consumer behavior, as well as the consequence of ignoring the economy of speed. Jae-yong Song, "Smart Management", 21st Century Books, also emphasizes the economy of speed.

factor that determines the outcome is speed, which is widely supported by empirical and academic evidence. In the infinitely competitive global market environment, it is clear that the speed at which one enters, exits, or transforms faster than anyone else, including potential competitors, is the most important factor in competition. There is a concept called 'survival of the fittest' that describes the ecosystem, including companies, and one of the crucial factors is the rapid change.

Just as the effect of the first move in a Go game greatly influences the outcome of the game, companies that start, launch, and change first have been winning in many cases since the mid-20th century, becoming an unspoken law. This applies to the best-performing companies in the world or even a single division within those companies. Of course, starting first or pre-empting does not guarantee success if they cannot sustain the speed afterwards. This is because the principle of acceleration, which outpaces all competitors by adding speed to speed, applies.

Paul Rogers, global head of the organization division at Bain & Company, described the decision-making process in a company as follows: "'fast' means making decisions faster than competitors, 'right' means looking back after some time and realizing that past decisions were excellent, and 'efficient' means not spending more cost and effort on decision-making than necessary."[62]Companies with slower decision-making speed than their competitors lose opportunities altogether. He argues that "companies with faster decision-making have a 5% higher sales growth rate." "Companies like Google and eBay do not make the mistake of missing opportunities by spending too much time on preliminary analysis, even if half of their decisions are right and the rest need to be corrected later," he emphasized.

Bill Graber, who led decision-making as a core executive at GE for 26 years, stressed the importance and significance of speed, saying, "GE didn't make better decisions than other organizations, they just made faster decisions."[63] Of course, as in the case of GE, rapid speed does not always guarantee better results in the end, as that company has proven. However, if the company had remained unchanged, it would likely have disappeared

---

[62] Quoted from an interview article in Chosun Ilbo on July 2nd-3rd, 2011. The content below also comes from the same interview.

[63] Chosun Ilbo, February 19th-20th, 2011

already. Quick decision-making is a factor that determines the success or failure of a company.

Of recent success or failure stories among global and Korean companies, who have either failed or succeeded by moving first with an idea or new product or companies who made significant gains by moving first despite the risk of failure or loss of vested interests, the core element is speed.

The speed mentioned above is determined by the decision-making process and the role of the final decision-maker. Even when decision-making occurs systematically, there must be a final decision-maker. All decisions come with the possibility of failure and consequences. This might be an irreversible failure, a partial or total loss, but success can also bring rewards and new opportunities beyond expectation. For decision-makers in this era, speed is absolutely necessary, albeit painful.

Commonalities among the world's super-giant companies such as Microsoft, Apple, Google, Facebook, Amazon, and Alibaba, who emerged like small comets at the end of the 20th century or in the 21st century, are the founders' excellent idea and entrepreneurial spirit, along with their quick move to preempt the market. This means that if they hadn't kick offed when they did, someone else would have appeared and enjoyed the prosperity and profits of today.

Another example of successful speed management worldwide is Amazon, founded by Jeff Bezos, which has grown into a global powerhouse in a very short period of time. Starting with mail-order book sales, Amazon now reaches the forefront of space development. The most prominent feature of Amazon is its relentless change and transformation, with speed being its core competitiveness. "All of Amazon's flagship services have been created and continue to evolve under the 'ultra-speed' philosophy... A 0.1-second slowdown in the loading of an internet page results in a 1% worse customer response."[64] Bezos' management philosophy is 'speed-centric organization theory'. He believes that the most appropriate team size for innovation is 6-10 people who can be fed with two large-sized pizzas, and he operates his organization accordingly.

---

[64] Lee In-Uk, Weekly Biz, Chosun Ilbo, August 25th-26th, 2012, C3

Another point worth emphasizing is that these global super-giant companies continue to innovate, transform, and diversify in various ways. In other words, they don't just stay in their successful fields but continue to undergo self-transformation, diversification, sales, acquisitions, and mergers for structural adjustment. In this process, the speed of decision-making is likely to be the most critical factor.

Photography has been an inseparable companion in human life since the invention of the camera. A contrasting example exists in the case of Kodak and Fuji Film, which held the first and second position in the world for camera film manufacturing. Kodak developed a digital camera that didn't require film but hesitated to commercialize it due to its reliance on film sales. As a result, Kodak disappeared from the camera market. In contrast, Fuji survived by transforming itself into a manufacturer of cosmetics, medical equipment, and pharmaceuticals, instead of giving up its main business. The importance of decision-making speed is evident here. Fuji's chairman, Shigetaka Komori, who executed the transformation, said "dominating the market should not be considered a divine right."[65] Cisco also developed 'Zoom' earlier but hesitated and missed a crucial opportunity. The commonality in these cases is the entirely rational fear and apprehension that their new product would kill or erode their existing products or markets.

A condensed statement of the importance of speed management is illustrated in the following newspaper article title: "In the age of imitation, release new products ahead of others, even if it kills your own products...."[66] The dilemma of leading companies is to what extent they are willing to take the risk of constant innovation that might result in the destruction of their own market. A concrete example is Nokia, which was the world's number one cell phone manufacturer since the introduction of mobile phones. However, as smartphones changed the landscape of the mobile phone market, Nokia could not let go of its attachment to mid-to-low-priced phones and failed to release new products, ultimately being pushed out of the mobile phone market. This was due to its attachment to the operating system it had invested billions of dollars in over the first decade. Nokia failed to recognize its own experience of transforming from a lumber-based

[65] CEO Inside, Maeil Business, January 24th, 2019
[66] Maeil Business, December 7th, 2018, C3

industry to a mobile phone manufacturer. It also failed to remember the trajectory of the MP3, which was the harbinger of mobile communication right before mobile phones. However, it is important to remember that Nokia's speed of transformation into a telecommunication infrastructure powerhouse after selling its core mobile phone business saved it from disappearing from the stage.

4-2 Speed in Korean Enterprise Management- Speed Management

The logic explained above is universally applicable without exception. The Korean industrial and corporate development story so far is an explanatory model for the logic that latecomers despite every disadvantage have the opportunity for fearless challenge. As is well known, the majority of Korea's major industries such as steel, shipbuilding, automobile, machine, electronics, aerospace and semiconductor manufacturing jumped into a market with no capital or technological capability which could have been considered reckless decisions. Success is not guaranteed just by following into reckless pursuit. Such decisions were made and executed by entrepreneurship, decision-making speed, and the support of industrial policy at the time.

Currently, Samsung Electronics is not only the number one company in Korea, but also ranks top-tier in the world in semiconductor sales. The core of the myth-like story of how Samsung Electronics started in the semiconductor business is the founder's quick decision-making, and also the speed of Koreans in defying expectations. In the early days of Korea's industrialization in the 1980s, Samsung's Chairman Lee Byung-chul made the decision to start the semiconductor business, and his successor actively responded to the turning points in the industry, leading to its current success. Another example is Hyundai's founder, Chung Ju-young, entering the automobile and shipbuilding industries. Hyundai, which had no experience or foundation in either shipbuilding or automobile manufacturing, entered the automotive manufacturing and shipbuilding industries as a result of the owner's decision-making speed. Korea's industrialization can be assessed as being achieved by the bold and quick decision of owners, along with the government's industrial policies. The possibility of risk associated with quick decisions can increase the speed of failure. Thus, we must also acknowledge the advantage of having a corporate governance structure that inevitably bears responsibility for failure.

Professor Song Jae-yong of Seoul National University, who analyzed the success factors of Samsung Electronics, explains that Samsung's "massive organization with a much faster decision-making and execution speed compared to overseas competitors, diversified yet maximizing the expertise of individual businesses, and the Samsung-style paradoxical management system that harmonizes American strategic management and Japanese on-site management" is the reason for overcoming the global economic crisis and expanding further.[67]

The semiconductor business, not only in the production process but also as a product itself, requires advanced technology for speed and substantially aggressive and preemptive investment, so the speed of investment decision-making and execution determines success or failure. In contrast, Japan, which was initially the strongest country in semiconductors, missed the investment timing due to its unique 'company-wide consensus' procedure. We can see in this case, even if the investment is not reckless, the possibility of failure always exists.

There are various studies and arguments about the relationship between decision-making speed in companies and corporate governance, but it is believed that a simpler decision-making structure results in faster decision and stronger driving force. There have been many controversies and mixed evaluations about the Korean chaebol(conglomerate) system, but at least the advantage of fast and bold decision-making is evident. The semiconductor, automobile, shipbuilding, steel and telecommunication industries, which are currently supporting the Korean economy, are the result of bold and rapid decision-making by founders, and the same logic goes for future transformation and change. The corporate governance structure in the early stage of Korean industrialization was a necessary condition for rapid industrialization. Of course, the relationship between decision-making speed, investment execution, and corporate ownership structure should be discussed separately as an academic topic.

This phenomenon may also signify a paradigm shift in corporate manage-

[67] Song Jae-yong, 'Smart Management', 21st Century Books, 2021

ment. For reference, up until the current speed era, a powerful lesson in life-goal management and business management principle was 'don't look sideways and dig one well.' This principle indeed demonstrated great force and results for a long time. It means focusing on what you do well and enhancing competitiveness in that area and until recently, this approach was maintained and successfully applied in various fields. However, now the advice is to change and find opportunities faster than others in the context of diverse connections and adjustments. Whether to abandon the advantage of the 'digging one well' approach is undoubtedly a challenging task.

A trend we may hope for is the fast transfer of the advantage of speed and competitiveness from traditional manufacturing to new areas such as cutting-edge digital-related industry, culture, arts, and entertainment. This discussion is covered in Chapter 5 and 6.

As one of the analytical frameworks frequently used in this book, speed or agility is undoubtedly an absolutely necessary condition for founding, growing, and transforming in corporate management, especially in all decision-making processes. Numerous studies and cases in the world prove this. One of the most successful factors in Korea's rapid economic growth is the speed of decision-making, and empirical research points out the agility in responding to changes in the execution process and circumstances.

Speed is a necessary condition but not a sufficient condition for successful management. Sufficient condition is the ability and insight of the top management and support from the management system. Such ability and judgment are naturally supported by collective intelligence, but ultimately, it is the responsibility of the top executive who creates and manages the organization. Therefore, both success and failure depend on the decision-maker like the success of military operation relies on their commander.

4-3 Meaning of Competition – Survival

Regardless of whether it is desirable, the average lifespan of companies competing in the capitalist market economy continues to shorten. It is due to the speed of competition. Not only individual businesses or small and medium-sized enterprises but even large corporations with a solid brand base, technology and financial power or global corporations and corporate groups, may see their rankings change or be absorbed, merged or disappear entirely within a short period. Therefore, the logic that companies who survive in the fiercely competitive market become the winners holds true.

Furthermore, even companies that survive or continue to grow are constantly changing. This is fundamentally different from the past. In most cases, the survivors can be called geniuses of transformation in terms of industrial category, product, and diversification. The idea of staying in one place as a growth spot is an outdated concept and is becoming an expired lesson. It is a clear lesson that companies who are slow to change and transform will decline. This is a clear change in the management paradigm.

In the case of the United States, which has a long history of dominating the world economy, only 80 out of the top 500 companies survived during the 50 years from the late 20th century to the beginning of the 21st century.[68] The content and speed of such changes are accelerating as time goes by. The trend of change is very clear globally as well. The tables below summarize the rankings of companies in the world, the United States and Korea, using the fluctuations in the top 10 of the respective top 500 companies compiled annually by Fortune magazine.

[68] Chosun Ilbo, December 22nd, 2007

Company Name (Industry)

Ranking	2000	2010	2022
1	• GM (Automotive)	• Walmart (distribution)	• Walmart (Distribution)
2	• Walmart (distribution)	• ExxonMobil (Energy)	• Amazon (Online Shopping)
3	• ExxonMobil (Energy)	• Chevron (oil)	• Apple (Internet, IT)
4	• Ford (automotive)	• GE (Electrical, Home Appliances)	• CVS Health (Healthcare)
5	• GE (Electrical,Home Appliances)	• BOA (Finance)	• UnitedHealth (Healthcare)
6	• IBM (computer)	• ConocoPhillips (Energy)	• ExxonMobil (Energy)
7	• Citigroup (Finance)	• AT&T (Telecommunications)	• Berkshire Hathaway (Investment)
8	• AT&T (Telecommunications)	• Ford (automotive)	• Alphabet (IT)
9	• Philip Morris (tobacco)	• JPMorgan Chase (Finance)	• McKesson (Pharmaceuticals)
10	• Boeing (Aviation)	• HP (Computer)	• AmerisourceBergen(Healthcare)

Fortune Global 500 (by revenue)

Table 4-1: *Changes in the Ranking of Top 10 US Companies (By Revenue)*

Summarizing the changes that can be read in the table above, in the recent 20 years, 1) industries have shifted from traditional manufacturing to internet, IT-related, finance, energy, and service related industries. More recently, on and offline distribution, health and pharmaceutical-related industries have rapidly emerged as growing industries. There is clearly something to learn from the United States.

Company Name (Industry)

Ranking	2000	2010	2022
1	• Microsoft (Information technology)	• Petrochina (Oil and gas)	• Apple (Internet, IT)
2	• GE (Electrical,Home Appliances)	• ExxonMobil (Energy)	• Microsoft (Information technology)
3	• NTT Docomo (Telecommunications)	• Microsoft (Information technology)	• Saudi Aramco(Oil and gas)
4	• Cisco Systems (Networking hardware, Networking software)	• ICBC (Financial services)	• Alphabet INC (Software and IT)
5	• Walmart (Distribution)	• Walmart (distribution)	• Amazon (Distribution)
6	• Intel (Semiconductor and Semiconductor equipment)	• China Construction Bank (Financial services)	• Tesla (Automotive)
7	• Nippon Telegraph and Telephone (Telecommunications)	• BHP Billiton (Metals and Mining)	• Berkshire Hathaway (Consumer Goods Conglomerates)
8	• ExxonMobil (Energy)	• HSBC(Financial services)	• NVIDIA (Semiconductors & Semiconductor Equipment)
9	• Lucent Technologies (Telecommunications equipment)	• Petrobras (Oil and gas)	• META (Software & IT Services)
10	• Deutsche Telekom (Telecommunications)	• Apple (Internet, IT)	• TSMC (Semiconductors)

David Hunkar, "The Largest Companies By Market Value Change Over Time", topforeignstocks.com, May 2021
PWC ,"Global Top 100 companies - by market capitalisation", May 2022

Table 4-2: *Changes in the Ranking of Top 10 Global Companies (By Revenue)*

2) In terms of international characteristics, the rise of China is particularly noticeable. As of 2022, Table 4-2, above shows that Chinese companies accounted for four of the top 10 companies in terms of total revenue, and also three ranked within the top five. The scale effect and fast growth rate of sales revenue explain China's rapid rise. On the other hand, the leading position of Japanese companies that emerged globally in manufacturing until the end of the 20th century has relatively shrunk; the degree and speed of change is clearer when compared to the case of the United States.

Company Name (Industry)

Ranking	2000	2010	2022
1	• Microsoft (Information technology)	• Petrochina (Oil and gas)	• Apple (Internet, IT)
2	• GE (Electrical,Home Appliances)	• ExxonMobil (Energy)	• Microsoft (Information technology)
3	• NTT Docomo (Telecommunications)	• Microsoft (Information technology)	• Saudi Aramco(Oil and gas)
4	• Cisco Systems (Networking hardware, Networking software)	• ICBC (Financial services)	• Alphabet INC (Software and IT)
5	• Walmart (Distribution)	• Walmart (distribution)	• Amazon (Distribution)
6	• Intel (Semiconductor and Semiconductor equipment)	• China Construction Bank (Financial services)	• Tesla (Automotive)
7	• Nippon Telegraph and Telephone (Telecommunications)	• BHP Billiton (Metals and Mining)	• Berkshire Hathaway (Consumer Goods Conglomerates)
8	• ExxonMobil (Energy)	• HSBC(Financial services)	• NVIDIA (Semiconductors & Semiconductor Equipment)
9	• Lucent Technologies (Telecommunications equipment)	• Petrobras (Oil and gas)	• META (Software & IT Services)
10	• Deutsche Telekom (Telecommunications)	• Apple (Internet, IT)	• TSMC (Semiconductors)

David Hunkar, "The Largest Companies By Market Value Change Over Time", topforeignstocks.com, May 2021
PWC ,"Global Top 100 companies - by market capitalisation", May 2022

Table 4-3 *Changes in the Ranking of Top 10 Global Companies (By Market Capitalization)*

In terms of market value instead of current revenue the story becomes different as shown in Table 4-3. Investors are interested in the future rather than the present performance of firms. Of course, the prospect of future activity always changes even year by year.

3) While it may be difficult for globally-scaled companies to readily change their status or rankings, the relative pace of transformation and change in the United States and the world is particularly striking, allowing for speculation on the future trend of change worldwide. In this context, looking at Korea's changes over the past 20 years (Table 4-4), it is worth noting that the relative speed and advantages of K-speed are not so evident.

4) To avoid misunderstanding it should be made clear that the companies that disappeared from these tables have not gone bankrupt or vanished; most of them still remain in the top 500 or 1,000 groups within their countries or globally. Their rankings have changed because their growth rates have relatively declined. Of course, if the timeline were a little longer, there

would be many cases where companies have disappeared from the list, and this pace is accelerating.

5) In another aspect, when comparing the total market value that reflects not only the company's performance up to now but also the growth potential in the future, the change in industrial structure and the rise and fall of companies become more pronounced and rapid. This judgment presents a completely different picture from the current performance (sales) shown in the previous table. Traditional industries such as manufacturing, finance, and energy were strong until the early 2000s, recognized as promising industries and favored by investors, but these nouns were changed in no time.

In other words, when looking at the top 10 global companies in 2022 based on market capitalization (Table 4-3), which represents the future value and growth of the company, three internet or internet related companies are ranked within top five places. Most companies are start-ups that have emerged in the past three decades. It is a rate of change that has never been imagined or experienced in human history up to the 20th century. In 2022, the rise of electric vehicles like Tesla are emerging and changing the landscape again. It is a paradigm change in industrial structure and a shift in industry itself.

6) This paradigm change can be compared to the case of Korea. As shown in Table 4-4, the top 10 companies based on total revenue in 2000 consisted of eight manufacturing-related companies and one finance-related company and one electric power plant company. Even in 2022, the structure is similar with minimal member change which is in contrast with the United States case. The face of K-speed cannot be found.

(Company Name)

Ranking	2000	2010	2022
1	• SK	• Samsung Electronics	• Samsung Electronics
2	• Hyundai	• LG	• Hyundai Motor Company
3	• Samsung	• Hyundai Motor Company	• SK
4	• Samsung Electronics	• SK	• LG Electronics
5	• Hyundai Motor Company	• POSCO	• POSCO
6	• Daewoo	• GS	• KIA
7	• Samsung Life Insurance	• Korea Electric Power Corporation (KEPCO)	• KEPCO
8	• LG Corporation	• Samsung Life Insurance	• Hanwha
9	• LG Electronics	• Hanwha	• LG Chem
10	• Korea Electric Power Corporation (KEPCO)	• Hyundai Heavy Industries	• SK hynix

Fortune Global 500 (by revenue)

Table 4-4 *Changes in the Ranking of Top 10 Korean Companies (By Revenue)*

7) The aspect emphasizing future performance shows a little different picture (Table 4-5). In 2010, in terms of market capitalization, the top 10 was not much different from the sales composition. Twelve years later, in 2022, there are still seven manufacturing-related companies, but the composition has changed, and one of them is a biopharmaceutical company related to non-traditional industries. Finance and insurance-related companies have been pushed back, and start-ups like Naver and Kakao, which are related to IT technology, have entered the market. Compared to the United States and the world, the degree of change is not fast, but the direction can be evaluated as similar. In the case of KOSDAQ (equivalent to NASDAQ of the USA), which includes many venture companies, the speed and content of such changes are much more pronounced.

(Company Name)

Ranking	2000	2010	2022
1	• Samsung Electronics	• Samsung Electronics	• Samsung Electronics
2	• SK Telecom	• POSCO	• LG Energy Solution
3	• Korea Telecommunications Corporation	• Hyundai Motor Company	• Samsung Biologics
4	• KEPCO	• Korea Shipbuilding & Marine Engineering Co.	• SK hynix
5	• Pohang Steel	• Hyundai Mobis	• LG Chem
6	• Hantong Freetel	• LG Chem	• Samsung SDI
7	• Kookmin Bank	• Shinhan Financial Holdings	• Hyundai Motor Company
8	• Tobacco Ginseng Corporation	• KB Financial Holdings	• NAVER
9	• Kia Motors	• Samsung Life Insurance	• Kia Motors
10	• Housing Bank	• Kia Motors	• Kakao

Korea Exchange , 2022,12. (by market cap)

Table 4-5 *Changes in the Ranking of Top 10 Korean Companies (By Market Capitalization)*

8) When comparing Korea and foreign countries, especially the United States, in terms of survival, change and transformation, an interesting result is found. 'Korea of speed' is slow in terms of corporation change and its relative position change in the market. When you look at rankings based on revenue and market capitalization on a 10-year basis, the top 10 companies in the United States change quickly and continue to be replaced, while Korea's rate of change is relatively slow and stable. It may not be pleasant news for the parties involved, but compared to the changing appearance and speed of global industries and companies, the transformation speed of Korea's industrial structure is unexpectedly conservative. While considering Korea's relative economic and market size, it may not necessarily be required to be similar to foreign cases, but Korea is already an open economic system with corporate activities that are globalized. This is something to think about. Competition in the free market is fierce and ruthless.

9) Samsung Electronics, in the early stage of business, raised the neces-

sary funds through the sale, repurchase, and resale of its hard-disc-driver(HDD) business, which was one of its initial businesses, to emerge as a world-leading semiconductor manufacturer. The key factor was speed and timing. The appearance, content, and various rankings of companies around the world are rapidly changing. The first cause of this change is technology. No matter how big and strong one may be, if they cannot stay ahead or catch-up in technological change, they will be pushed back or ultimately become extinct, as history has shown.

10) The survival rate of Fortune 500 companies between 1990 and 2010, a period of 20 years, is only 24%. During the same period, the survival rate of the top 100 Korean companies based on sales is 30%. If we extend the period to 45 years from 1965, the survival rate drops to 12%[69]. Around the same time, the 50-year survival rate of Fortune 500 companies in the United States is 16%[70]. The message here is that the speed of change is accelerating.

In 2015, John Chambers, chairman of CISCO, claimed, "40% of the companies that exist now will disappear within 10 years... In order to survive, they must quickly capture the rapidly changing market, innovate, and rediscover their businesses."[71] In other words, he emphasized 'change to survive' and presented the two paths of 'destroy or be destroyed.' The keyword here also is the speed of change.

11) Examining an interview with the same CISCO CEO[72] reveals many implications. "The competitive advantage lies not in size but in speed. CISCO anticipated market changes like a fast fish and responded proactively." One management method to execute this is 'shark tail' management, which involves faster product development, smaller organizational size, and more ideas[73]. A specific example is IBM, which eliminated market research and implemented changes by placing designers on site.

Management scholar Clayton Christensen argues that companies always face two challenges: Sustaining innovation for product quality improve-

[69] The Korea Economic Daily May 22nd, 2013
[70] Chosun Biz, Chosun Ilbo, December 22nd-23rd, 2007
[71] JoongAng Ilbo June 10th, 2015
[72] Chosun Ilbo, December 20th-21rst, 2014
[73] Maeil Business, January 5th, 2016

ment; and Disruptive innovation to shed existing product or method[74]. The purpose of these two challenges is to survive in the market.

The core of these cases is speed. If a company is slower than its competitors or fails to seize the right timing, all efforts and attempts will be in vain. We have seen how important speed in decision-making is for a company's survival, and as statistically shown, the speed of change is gradually accelerating.

12) Traditional companies are being pushed down or disappearing from the rankings due to the emergence of new companies or industries. A prime example is the rise of unicorns, with a company value of over US$ one billion, or decacorns, with over US$ ten billion. According to a foreign statistical report, Korea ranked 10th in the world unicorn company rankings with 11 unicorns, behind China (2nd) and India (3rd), while Japan ranked 13th.[75] The Korea Ministry of SMEs and Startups reported 18 unicorns, different from the above report.

4-4 Meaning of Productivity - Another Expression of Speed

Until recently, productivity in Korea was often narrowly perceived as a concept mainly related to the manufacturing industry. For example, productivity was usefully applied when comparing the output volume of manufacturing workers per unit of time or cost per unit of production. Both methods are ultimately related to speed. Given the relatively high proportion of the manufacturing sector in the country's industrial structure, this was natural. However, now the weight of the tertiary industry, also known as the service industry, has significantly increased in all aspects, including industrial structure, output, employment and trade. Furthermore, the service industry, including finance, has been fully liberalized, making it even more urgent to improve productivity in the service industry under international competition.

Since the late 1990s, the Korean approach, while technologically lagging, emphasizing speed, began to shine when developing various software to be incorporated into management or games to be released on the market.

---

[74] Chosun Ilbo, Issue 26717, reprinted
[75] Maeil Business, February 16th, 2022, A1, A4

As an example, in the case of video games, the Japanese approach involved meticulous planning, review, and preparation, thus taking more than three to four months to launch the initial product. In contrast, the Korean approach quickly launches a somewhat rough product within a month, and then continuously corrects problems that arise in the market over the next few months, eventually resulting in an almost perfect product. This allowed Korean products to outpace Japanese products that underwent longer but more meticulous initial preparation.

It is widely known that the release timing is sometimes an even more critical factor in determining success or failure in the global game market than the content itself. If a game with a similar level and content is launched and succeeds first, other similar games practically become obsolete, regardless of development cost and time. In other words, if you can't preempt the market, you are destined to be a latecomer. The preemptive effect is the speed itself.

There is also this expression: "... The vigorous energy and 'quickly-quickly' culture of our people, called Dynamic Korea, is a source of economic vitality that differentiates us from Japan's manual culture... Our dynamism and 'quickly-quickly' culture will not only disallow the (so-called) lost 20 years (of Japan) but will also not be able to endure that long period."[76] Of course, it is necessary to examine whether this 'quickly-quickly' is acceleration, constant or deceleration.

The manual method had been a significant advantage that made Japan what it is today, but it is not necessarily effective anymore. "PwC consultants point out that meticulous manuals are the strength of Japanese companies, but their weakness is the lack of flexibility. In contrast, Samsung is praised for quickly reading market trends and adjusting R&D speed while observing market conditions."[77]

It may not be easy to generalize this phenomenon in all sectors. For example, it may be difficult to apply this principle directly to a manufacturing that requires the utmost precision, but it can serve as an example

---

[76] Interview with Ha Young-gu, Chairman of the Bankers Association, JoongAng Ilbo, August 11th, 2016

[77] Maeil Business, May 19th-20th, 2012

indicating that speed at least is an absolute competitive advantage in the ICT-related field too.

China's Xiaomi, once recognized as a low-cost smartphone manufacturer, quickly emerged as a world-class IT company, thanks to its speed. "Xiaomi's operating system is updated every week. This 'unbelievable' speed race is possible thanks to a 100,000-person development team."[78] This can be a case similar to the releasing speed of games in Korea and Japan described above. If you continue to improve at a competitive price, albeit slightly lacking or insufficient initially, you can soon catch up.

Of course, there are side effects to the speed race. As the title of an old newspaper article stated, "R&D talent in Korea is leaving due to the 'quickly-quickly' and 'just do as you're told' mentality."[79] Hastiness can cause losses and ruin the work entirely. The side effects and downsides of speed will be discussed in a later chapter.

Productivity in some sectors of Korea's manufacturing industry is beginning to lag behind worldwide. It means that the advantage of the 'economies of speed' has disappeared or is disappearing. Since speed is undoubtedly a relative concept, falling behind in productivity per unit of time or cost signifies that the advantage of speed is no longer available. This can be directly confirmed at the level of individual companies and observed through changes in economic growth rate or export amount at the macroeconomic level, indicating that there are warning signs already in the Korean economy.

The opportunity cost of saved time continues to rise. This is because the value of leisure time increases proportionally with the time saved by using products or services that save time, regardless of whether the technology and functions are developed domestically or imported from abroad. Consequently, the value of leisure activities increases, and people are willing to invest in their preferred leisure activities at higher prices. We can easily find the reason why the cost of high standard cultural and artistic performances are becoming increasingly expensive in Korea and worldwide.

---

[78] Chosun Ilbo, October 22nd, 2015
[79] Chosun Ilbo, July 28th, 2016

4-5 Distribution and Delivery Industry, Changes in Consumer Lifestyle and K-Speed

Speed is, of course, a relative concept. There may be countries, companies, or social systems that are faster than Korea(ns), and faster competitors may emerge. However, as continuously expressed throughout this book, it cannot be denied that human speed, including the living environment aspect, has many intrinsic and genetic factors. Especially comparing Korea with other countries, there may be instances where the applied term should not be, 'not doing it' but instead 'not being able to do it.' This characteristic will be discussed in detail in Chapter 6 from the perspective of Koreans' genetic and sociocultural aspect.

Over the past 30 years, the service industry has undergone significant and fast changes in Korean industrial structure, particularly in the sectors related to distribution.

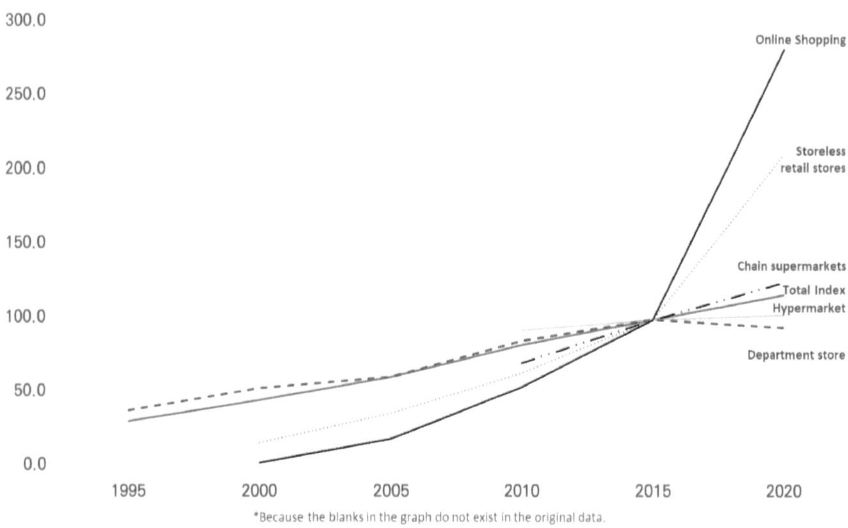

Figure 4-1 *Domestic Retail Sales Index by Type in Korea (2015 = 100)*

The nature and speed of change can be clearly felt when looking at Figure 4-1. The ups and downs of each sector vary greatly due to the increase in income and changes in consumer preference. Comparing before and after the base year of 2015 statistics from the Korea Statistics Office, the industry that is breaking away from the overall trend and growing rapidly is non-store (non-face-to-face) retail, and although relatively weaker, the fast-growing industry is convenience stores, especially chain convenience stores. Notably, the graph does not show the rise of passenger car retail.

On the other hand, department stores, large supermarkets, specialty retail stores, and general supermarkets are gradually declining. This is a result of losing market share to delivery-related business and convenience stores. All works and industries have ups and downs, which may be natural, but the point to note here is the speed. If this trend continues, the absolute and relative decline of department stores in Korea is inevitable.

The most characteristic change in these results is the change in consumption patterns and the corresponding change and speed in the distribution and service industries. Of course, the causal relationship between these two factors can also change. The first step in consumption is to order and purchase the target goods or services. Throughout human history, people have lived by going to markets or stores (department stores or others), looking around, picking and buying, or exchanging (ancient market transactions) for items they need but do not produce themselves. This method has been the basis since the beginning of human history. There were door-to-door sales in remote and inaccessible areas regardless of the East or West, but the basic transaction and consumption were in the market (including orders).

Historically, as time gradually became relatively valuable and as transportation and postal systems developed, the delivery system evolved. However, due to considerations such as cost, reliability, and delivery time, it did not develop into a commonplace aspect of consumer life. For instance, pizza delivery (Domino's Pizza), which centered around American university campuses, emerged in the 20th century, but this method did not spread to other sectors or industries. This can be easily understood when considered in terms of opportunity cost and transaction cost.

Regardless of any causal or chronological relationship as to whether changes in rapid consumption behavior influence changes in delivery methods due to online systems or vice versa, these two factors are mutually influencing each other. They are growing, developing, and changing the fastest in many places around the world, especially in Korea. As a result, there are forecasts that as of 2021, while offline store sales are twice that of online, with the ongoing decline in offline store sales, they will be overtaken by online in three years.[80] This is a speed hitherto unimaginable, exclusive to Korea.

Leading, inducing, or supporting these changes is, of course, IT and digital technology. Such technologies, which have speed, convenience, timeliness, and economy, are co-evolving as they change Korean consumption habits and behavior, and the functions and roles of the distribution industry. Hence, 'time' is developing into a form that is traded in the market like a tangible commodity.

(1) Evolution and Speed of Delivery Services

When examined more closely, because consumption and logistics involve transaction costs and opportunity costs, we can speculate that delivery services likely existed from the primitive age. Institutionalized delivery services started with the use of manpower dependent on foot, and can be traced back to the establishment of deliveries using horses or cows, stage-coaches, postal systems, and vessels traversing rivers and seas. Private and personal delivery services would have been in use long before that. Means of communication using animals like pigeons or beacon fires can also be categorized in the same group, considering they are for the delivery of information.

The commercial delivery service as we know it today evolved from the concept of quick service, starting from pedestrian document couriers in Wall Street, New York, to motorcycle courier services in Japan, and rapidly developed and spread worldwide. For a considerable period after the 20th century, United Parcel Service, the unrivaled presence in postal delivery via the US national postal system, and DHL, a private delivery company, dominated the US and global delivery service. Their strong competitive edge likely came from their advantage in air transportation and their proprietary logistics system.

Subsequently, with the advent of a new era of telecommunications, Amazon, now the world's largest online retailer, dominated as one of the strongest in e-commerce, starting from book delivery. Alibaba in China, utilizing events

---

[80] Leaders' Economy, May 31st, 2021, page 5

like the Singles' Day, emerged as the new center of the global e-commerce industry. These are just one of many new types of startups and numerous success stories.

Historically, traditional logistics methods in distribution have evolved into today's delivery systems - this is a given. However, as of 2022, the delivery services that are sweeping the world are less an extended continuation from the past, but rather are establishing themselves as a new industrial sector. Now, online markets, centered around e-commerce, are quickly eroding traditional offline markets.[81] Technologies using AI, 3D, and VR are supplementing the weaknesses of conventional online markets, leading to swifter reversal of positions than expected. Therefore, online distribution and delivery services are transforming into closely intertwined and complementary roles, much like two sides of the same coin.

In the sale of goods online, factors like product quality, variety, price competitiveness, marketing, and payment method all contribute to competitiveness. However, the most powerful competitive tool is the delivery time. Initially, delivery times were significantly reduced from a considerable period after placing an order to 2-3 days or longer, and then further shortened to within 24 hours with the emergence of so-called 'rocket delivery' as a new competitive tool. This trend of shortening delivery time is also taking place outside of Korea. Coupang, a leading Korean company, started this trend and it is only natural for competitors to follow suit. Coupang continues to expand its market share and enhance its competitiveness despite recording large-scale losses in 2021, which cannot be dismissed as a reckless approach. The company's direct listing on the New York Stock Exchange also signifies recognition of its potential.

Coupang's next move involves not only mediating transactions and deliveries but also directly purchasing products to reduce transaction cost and time, enabling same-day or early morning deliveries. This approach requires the establishment of large-scale logistics centers in key areas and significant investment, inevitably leading to structural change in the distribution industry.

---

[81] There are statistics indicating that Americans spent $100 billion online during the shopping season at the end of 2017, and the proportion of online sales surpassed 10% of total retail sales. Chosun Economy, January 17th, 2018, B7

In this light, the Korean delivery market may eventually be divided and dominated by a few large corporations. In the long term, this raises issues related to industrial policy and consumer welfare that need to be addressed. However, from a competitive standpoint, survival is the path to victory, and the economies of speed inevitably demands the economies of scale. This aspect can be regarded as a characteristic of modern service industries and requires diverse analyses and reviews.

Coupang's business model, similar to Amazon's, has expanded from dominating the retail market through direct purchasing to providing fulfillment service. It is difficult to predict the next stage of change. Korean Coupang, owned by American Coupang LLC, highlights the need to recognize that domestic online distribution businesses are already connected and competing globally.

As previously pointed out, it is essential to pay attention to the changing patterns and trends in industrial structure. In the past, delivery, shipping, or logistics were considered subsidiary functions of distribution. However, delivery services have now evolved to the point where they can potentially dominate and even influence the manufacturing and production of goods. The speed at which the direction changes will be crucial. In fact, if Kakao Mobility (taxi service) and T Map (navigation system) are recognized as negotiating parties with the substitute driver union, they would become the largest employers in Korea.[82]

The most decisive factor that has rapidly spread online shopping, delivery service, and courier service is the rapid development of communication means. Using the terms introduced earlier, the time and effort spent going to a store, choosing the desired item, and placing an order, in other words, the transaction cost and opportunity cost, are now significantly reduced in real-time, with little to no time and effort required. In the days when there were no phones, orders had to be placed in person at the seller's location, rendering delivery largely meaningless. Comparing this with receiving catalogs, newspapers, or flyers through the mail or advertising and then ordering by mail or telephone before waiting for delivery, the difference is incomparable. Therefore, the development of communication means has played a decisive role in changing distribution and consumption methods.

[82] Maeil Business, November 10th, 2021, A20.

The growth of Korea's delivery app market by tenfold in the past five years is evidence of this.

(2) Changes in Transaction and Consumer Behavior

1) The rapid shift from direct, face-to-face method to indirect, non-face-to-face method. Of course, the virtual space allows for browsing, reviewing, and testing without physically touching the product, so these methods are not entirely separate. However, compared to the past mail-order method based on printed catalogs, the new method has evolved significantly.

2) Big data and artificial intelligence have created an era where 'the seller knows me better than I know myself,' where sellers choose and provide products based on a consumer's preferences and desires without any deliberation. This means the emergence of the so-called subscription economy. This phenomenon could lead to the voluntary subjugation of humans to artificial intelligence, beyond the dimension of convenience and transaction cost. AI styling on fashion online malls falls into the same category. By trusting and relying on the AI, users may ultimately become subjugated. Some large supermarkets employ professional pickers to select ingredients on behalf of customers. This method saves opportunity and transaction costs in a different way, as big data and AI inform the picker of the customer's preference and taste in advance.

3) If goods or services I want or need on a regular basis are provided without me having to order, or go shopping for them, and they are supplied at the appropriate time, it would be an amazing service and a great help in daily life. The idea of Say's law that 'supply creates demand', initially a compelling argument in the development of Economics but later losing traction, has made a full comeback after more than 200 years. It is a method where proactive, tailor-made supply is backed by demand. Of course, the main premise is payment ability or, in other words, economic capability of consumers.

4) Moreover, even in direct purchases or sales, face-to-face transactions are gradually disappearing or declining, with the introduction and acceleration of unstaffed stores. This is an inevitable choice for cost-saving for sellers, and as a result, there are various benefits for buyers as well, so it

will inevitably evolve further. Security technology is rapidly advancing, making expansion possible and economically inevitable, but it may also result in a form of self-exploitation. This issue is more urgent for sellers or suppliers than for consumers or buyers. While consumers have individual judgment and choice, suppliers must compete and ultimately survive, so they must respond and adapt more quickly than competitors. Such changes and innovations often lead to increased consumption.

5) Various sharing services naturally become a form of subscription service, and in the case of automobiles, they continue to evolve in methods such as vehicle-specific and period-based leasing. Services that lease expensive art pieces for a period of time, allowing them to be switched out, can also be considered part of the same category. The difference between permanent ownership or ownership for a certain period and the social or personal evaluation of value increase or decrease over time will determine the development of these services.

6) This could bring about changes in the traditional marital lifestyle and the division of roles with spouses. Some of the functions that were previously performed separately by husbands and wives are now being replaced by different methods. These changes may already be directly and indirectly influencing factors such as the rise in marriage age, the increase in single-person households, and the rise in divorce rate.

7) Korea is not the originator of subscription service. However, this approach is still in development and application stages, so as in other cases, it is possible to compete both domestically and internationally based on related technologies, swiftly and innovatively. The focus of interest here is whether the Korean-style (K-) online shopping and subscription service model will go beyond the domestic market and become a global standard. It goes without saying that the source of its competitiveness and distinctiveness is speed.

(3) Rapid Growth of the Delivery industry

The delivery industry in Korea, which is growing at the fastest rate, provides a striking example.

1) All kinds of methods are used to deliver faster. In particular, they diversify competitive means, such as 'one order at a time, to shorten the time between ordering and delivery. Delivery drivers are in a battle against time by nature, so they take risks themselves. Delivery times are becoming increasingly competitive, with services like rocket delivery within 24 hours after an order, dawn delivery for fresh groceries ordered the night before, and ultra-fast delivery within 15 minutes of ordering for nearby locations. As a result, consumers may find it less time-consuming and cheaper than going to the store and purchasing the items themselves, increasing the growth potential for these services.

2) Competition evolves continuously. In addition to the original food delivery, various items are now delivered together, and the service has naturally evolved from delivering cooked food to delivering raw ingredients too. Despite the sensitive nature of delivering fresh ingredients, which are different from general products and directly related to consumer preference and freshness, the service is expanding.

3) For reference, Korea's fresh food dawn delivery is an uncharted territory that even Amazon in the United States failed to succeed in. Amazon had already started a service called Amazon Fresh in 2007, which delivered fresh groceries right to the doorstep for a $299 annual fee but had to discontinue it without fully implementing it. In October 2017, they introduced In-Home Delivery, which delivers items inside the home, but it didn't receive much attention due to security issues. Some ideas and their real-world applications are in different dimensions.[83] This approach might be successful only in Korea.

4) Since ingredients are related to cooking, delivery speed and arrival timing are crucial competitive factors. Since morning is the busiest time of a day for everyone, delivering fresh ingredients to the customer's doorstep at dawn would be more competitive. Among various factors that adapt to this situation, the last order time and the delivery speed for timely arrival are crucial. Competing with orders placed before midnight the previous day and the next day's dawn delivery is both natural and possible in Korea.

5) Market Kurly in Korea is a leading player in the fresh food dawn delivery

---

83 http://www.sisajournal.com April 4th, 2019

market, and it is experiencing a typical rapid growth curve without exception. Naturally, other large companies and supermarkets are also jumping into this market. This is another example of the dramatic changes in distribution and consumption. Market Kurly and other companies like SSG.com are also preparing to go public on the capital market.

In the dawn delivery market, which mainly delivers fresh ingredients, it has now evolved to deliver items such as sandwiches and other breakfast essentials. This trend may be related to the changing demographics of Korea, particularly the increasing number of single-person households, leading to a tendency to rely solely on eating out or delivery for all meals. The fact that 'eating jajangmyeon (noodle food) delivered to the Han River beach' has made it onto some foreigners' bucket list illustrates that Korea is indeed a delivery powerhouse.

6) Online businesses have begun to combine with offline methods to manage inventory. As of the end of 2021, among the three major dawn delivery companies – Market Kurly, SSG.com, and Oasis – only Oasis recorded a profit. This is because they handle excess inventory from dawn deliveries by discounting and selling them at local cooperative stores. This method is called the 'ambidextrous strategy' and can be thought of in terms of the economies of speed.[84] It is essentially no different from existing supermarkets utilizing delivery methods.

7) The most crucial element in physical preparation for faster delivery competition is infrastructure such as logistics location and facilities. Relying solely on securing conventional logistics warehouses will not suffice to meet the competitive edge of reducing delivery time. Existing supermarkets are also utilized, and based on economic principles, shared logistics such as fulfillment service rather than a single company's logistics are used for certain areas. This involves using gas stations as well as convenience stores located throughout the region. This method has become realistically feasible because big data accumulates information that allows for demand prediction in advance.

CJ Logistics' e-fulfillment service opened a mega hub center in Gonjiam, Gyeonggi Province, in 2018. The center, which spans floors 2 to 4, is compa-

---

[84] Chosun Ilbo December 30th, 2021, B4

rable in size to 16 international standard soccer fields, and the total length of conveyor belt is 43 km. E-commerce orders from contracted companies are packed and sent to the center's lower-floor terminal, then transferred to the consumer's local server terminal for courier delivery. With this system, orders placed before midnight can be delivered the next day. It is a business model aimed at meeting the needs of speed and cost saving.[85] Other distribution giants have also begun to participate in this business. While Korea is not the first to adopt such a method, it is an example of quickly following suit and advancing with better approaches. This progress is possible because the country's socioeconomic conditions support it. Large platform companies have started to own their own fulfillment facilities.

8) In addition to conventional delivery riders, various methods are being employed to save time and cost, such as neighborhood walking deliveries centered around convenience stores and utilizing Yakult beverage ladies who sell the drinks on a motorized cart. Robots and drones are also being used both domestically and internationally, and if deemed competitive, the speed of Korea's adoption will be swift.

Memories of Food Delivery

In fact, Korea can be argued to have pioneered commercial food delivery. There are records of top Seoul restaurants providing food delivery services during the Japanese occupation (1910-1945), and Chinese-style restaurants have been offering delivery services (using metal tiffin carrier, called as an iron bag) for all Koreans to experience up to the 1990s.

In the past, Chinese-style restaurants made jajangmyeon (noodle food) from scratch, starting with the dough and then making the noodles, followed by cooking. This process took a considerable amount of time. Since there were hardly any suitable dating spots at the time, Chinese-style restaurants were considered one of the best options. Thus, even if people placed orders in person, it was more time-efficient to have the food delivered after it was prepared. It was a good method for both producers and consumers.

Of course, other Korean restaurants also tried to offer delivery services similar to Chinese-style restaurants, but they were not very successful. A notable

85 Maeil Business, August 5th,2020, A18

example is the delivery service for lunchtime meals for merchants in traditional markets who couldn't leave their stalls. This old-fashioned delivery service, where food was carried on the head, should also be recorded. The method of reducing opportunity cost and transaction cost had been developed a long time ago. At the same time, the preference for soup and broth-based dishes in Korean table settings may have influenced the preference for delivery over lunch boxes. Of course, one could argue that delivering lunch and snacks to farming sites from home in the early days is the origin of Korean-style delivery.

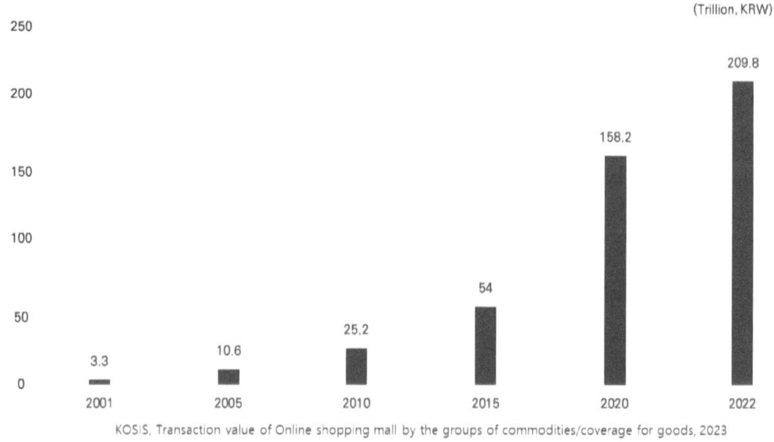

Figure 4-2 *Changes in On-line Shopping*

9) The growth of online shopping in Korea has been rapid in recent years as shown in the above Figure 4-2. Although it has been accelerated by digitalization, it has also been driven by the compatibility with daily habits. According to Korea Statistics Office data (20 Years of Online Shopping in Statistics), online shopping increased by 48 times from 2001 to 2022, with food and grocery items increasing nearly five times as much. Much of this growth is due to online food orders and delivery.

10) The eating habits of Koreans are also related to speed. According to data released by the Korea Statistics Office, the average time spent on meals in 2014 was 1 hour and 20 minutes, with less than 30 minutes per meal.[86] Additionally, the time spent preparing meals has been decreasing, making

---

[86] In the 2019 National Health and Nutrition Survey, the percentage of people eating out was 31.7%, a 6.5% increase from the previous year.

food delivery a representative method to save both preparation time and effort while also reducing the time spent traveling to and from restaurants.[87] The delivery app market, which allows users to install delivery apps on their smartphones and receive the food at a touch of a button anytime, anywhere in urban areas, is growing rapidly.[88] In addition, as the coronavirus pandemic has made non-face-to-face contact more commonplace, food delivery increased even more.

The food delivery market is all about speed. Initially, food delivery was handled by the restaurants themselves, but now almost all use delivery agencies. Delivery workers' income depends on the number of deliveries they make, and their use of motorcycles has raised concern about their safety and traffic violations. For delivery drivers, time is indeed money (speed is competitiveness), so they take risks while speeding on the road day and night.

This speed is not limited to the time spent on the road. To stay ahead of the competition and accept delivery orders (calls) first, some delivery workers possessed two mobile phones. The competition is determined by speed, so every possible means and method are explored. Furthermore, to save delivery time and increase competitiveness, delivery app operators now monitor real-time traffic conditions and provide optimal routes to multiple delivery destinations, improving delivery productivity.

(4) Changes in Industry and Industrial Structure

The distribution industry, which includes delivery, has a long history in the world's and Korean industrial structure, but it is essentially transforming into a new form.

---

[87] Food delivery is a business with considerable history. After Korea's liberation from Japan, Chinese-style restaurants introduced delivery services early on, delivering food in so-called 'iron cases'. Of course, it was a round-trip service where the staff would return to collect the empty dishes and payment after the meal was finished. In an era when phones were scarce, customers had to go to the restaurant to place orders directly. Labor was abundant and wages were low, so it was a feasible method. As telephones became widespread and bicycles came into use, the delivery range naturally expanded, and with the introduction of disposable dishes, deliveries were reduced to one way trips, including payment collection. With motorcycles becoming a widely used mode of transportation, delivery services became more extensive and universal.

[88] JoongAng Ilbo, October 6th, 2015

1) As of March 2021, the market capitalization of Coupang, which went public on the New York Stock Exchange, was KRW 100.4 trillion (around US$ 84 billion), equivalent to seven times the combined market value of Shinsegae department store, E-Mart, Hyundai Department Store, and Lotte Shopping, which are four largest departments and shopping markets in Korea. If we include other specialized big delivery companies like Baedal Minjok and Market Kurly, the changes in the Korean distribution industry and its domestic and international status can be clearly felt. Market capitalization is an indicator that reflects investors' expectation and prediction, hinting at the potential speed of future changes.

2) Naturally, existing department stores and supermarkets must respond sensitively to these changes. Well-known department stores have not only installed ready-to-eat food stores but also started food and beverage delivery service. They have even begun subscription services that deliver a selection of side dishes once a week. The three major telecommunication companies in Korea, which are in completely different industries, may not ignore these changes and are known to transform their business into a subscription-based model that provides various services for a fixed monthly fee. Consequently, department stores and existing supermarkets will have no choice but to struggle and seek transformation in the face of changes brought about by platform-based distribution.

3) A representative example of changes and transformations in the existing distribution industry is the function and role of convenience stores. In the past, convenience stores were the so-called 'hole in the wall(corner)-stores' found in every neighborhood. Now, some of them have transformed into the center of offline distribution, offering grocery shopping, electronics products selling, parcel delivery, and insurance application. As mentioned earlier, their role has expanded to include serving as a delivery service hub, partnering with Naver and Kakao for payments and sales, insurance application, and handling customer complaints for telecommunication companies, all by leveraging their convenient location and accessibility. Of course, the ownership structure, dominated by large corporations instead of individuals, and the systematic operation methods that provide efficiency-advantage must also be considered.

4) One point that should be emphasized even more than the functional

advantages is the number of convenience stores. As of the end of 2020, there were 47,884 convenience stores, meaning one store for every 1,082 people. In urban areas, there is practically a convenience store as soon as you step outside your home. Although Japan, where convenience stores developed earlier than Korea, has more stores at 55,924, there is only one store for every 2,253 people, making Korea twice as dense.[89] Following the precedent set by Japan, there is also the possibility that the scope of convenience stores will expand to include not only the function of social infrastructure, such as public agency work delegation but also the function of lifestyle services. It will be a continuous series of transformation beyond expectations.

5) The phenomenon of online distribution surpassing offline is also occurring in the United States, with Amazon's sales overtaking Walmart, the largest US distributor, in the first half of 2021.[90] In terms of sales scale, China's Alibaba is twice the size of Amazon, making it the largest online distributor in the world. The trend and speed of change are also of interest here.

(5) Changes in Workplace and Innovations Brought by Speed

Naturally, the proportion of delivery-related sectors is increasing in terms of employment and job opportunities in the nation's industrial sector, while the proportion of direct or face-to-face distribution industries is decreasing.

1) According to a survey conducted by Chosun Ilbo from March 2020 to March 2021, the top two companies in terms of the increased number of National Pension subscribers among the top 20 are Coupang-related companies, with Market Kurly ranking fourth after Samsung Electronics[91]. The proportion of these three delivery-related companies is 50.8%, more than half. Among the top 20 companies, there are only three manufacturing companies, with a combined proportion of just 16.6%. There was virtually no change in the number of National Pension subscribers among the 103 companies with more than 5,000 subscribers during 2020. This is one aspect of the changes in the industrial structure of Korea from an employment perspective, and more attention should be paid to the speed of change.

---

[89] Chosun Ilbo May 17th, 2021, A6
[90] Chosun Economy, August 19th, 2021, B2
[91] Chosun Ilbo, June 1rst, 2020, A6

2) According to an analysis by the Korea Labor Institute, as of 2020, an estimated 114,000 workers are involved in delivery and transportation businesses using platforms. This number is projected to reach 200,000 a year when including part-time workers who are not full-time employees. This increase in the number of workers reflects the growth of the market size. Depending on how the data is compiled, the number could be much higher if simply calculated based on delivery personnel employed by each company.[92] Such changes naturally affect related industries, positively impacting the scooter and electric bicycle industries in the first place.

3) According to a 2021 survey by the Korea Employment Information Service, approximately 220,000 people, or 0.8% of the employed population aged 15 to 69 in Korea, are working full-time or part-time in the platform industry. If classified as an industry, the platform industry has grown rapidly to the point where it is undoubtedly one of Korea's growing industries.

4) The transformation in the distribution and delivery industry has led to the emergence of the gig economy, where people work only during convenient hours. This significant experimental change is altering the traditional meaning and content of employment and labor, with Korea at one of the forefronts.

5) While it is obvious that big data increases the efficiency of delivery companies, it also helps individual delivery riders. The startup Mesh Korea's 'Broong' service is an app that uses big data to optimize individual delivery routes, avoid overlapping assignments, and consider parking methods, increasing motorcycle delivery drivers' income by an average of 40%.[93]

6) Korean platform companies are expanding into the growing Southeast Asian market, riding the wave of the Korean Wave(Hallyu). For example, Lineman, which has entered Thailand, is the local number one delivery platform.[94] In addition to the influence of various Korean Wave factors, Korean-style competitiveness in convenience and payment processing speed is contributing to their success.

Another noteworthy phenomenon is that older generations in Korea, other than millennials and Generation Z, are participating in the early morning

---

[92] Maeil Economy Focus 21, Maeil Business, August 27th, 2021, A32
[93] Big Data Changing the World, Maeil Business, November 6th,2019, A4
[94] K-Platform's Southeast Asia Strategy, Maeil Business, April 28th, 2020

delivery market. The OPAL (Old People with Active Lives) generation, aged 50-60, is also adapting to this digital platform-based lifestyle. While the COVID-19 situation has accelerated this trend, the widespread adoption of non-face-to-face purchasing and consumption methods is becoming a part of everyday life, clearly demonstrating K- speed.

With various factors such as technology, social structure, speed of change, adaptability, and a densely populated nation on a relatively small territory, Korea can confidently assert that she will never fall behind, and lead in the delivery and distribution industry. As mentioned several times, one more specific area where Korea can catch up and lead with its unique competitiveness is the online delivery industry, which is one essence of K-speed.

To emphasize once again, Korea is undoubtedly a first-mover in the logistics delivery and food delivery industries. Even if not the first pioneer, Korea can be seen as a case where she moves faster and more innovatively in similar conditions. It is also a clear case of having more competitiveness when starting under similar conditions.

4-6 Analysis of Korean Competitiveness in Distribution and Service Industry

At this stage, we should consider the following questions: Why does the competitiveness of Korean industries and Koreans stand out more in distribution and consumption? How can Korea move faster than countries that are economically and culturally more advanced or those that compete with Korea in various aspects? Furthermore, it is necessary to discuss why many developing countries cannot follow the same path as Korea.

First, it is about the condition. Without the proper conditions, even if there is a willingness and desire, an actual execution can be difficult. The first specific item is the support of economic power. There must be purchasing power to buy and sell. With sufficient demand and supply, the distribution and consumption market can develop. In the digital age, the major consumer market has become significantly different from previous predictions, as the 'economies of scale' has become a competitive necessity. Producing, procuring, and supplying goods more cheaply and quickly requires large-scale investment. Moreover, a necessary condition for bulk purchase and small sales is the reduction of unit cost by the economies of scale.

Korea, which has grown rapidly within a short period of time, may not have a market size as large as China or the United States, but it can be said that Korea has a market size that can realize economies of scale in online-related distribution. In the open world economy, it is not easy to survive and grow with the competitiveness within a small country boundary.

Second, it is the support of infrastructure. There should be favorable conditions in terms of communication infrastructure, such as the internet, the universal distribution of PCs and mobile phones, the expansion of transportation infrastructure through road, rail and air networks, and the availability of various vehicles such as motorcycles and bicycles. At the same time, a relatively smaller land area and a high urbanization rate reduce the unit transaction cost. Realization of credit society is another factor for the development of this non-face-to-face transaction.

Third is the speed of market and consumer response. As emphasized repeatedly, speed can only be measured relatively. Therefore, a report by international comparison can be a useful reference for the response speed and actual consumer price adjustment speed in Korea and the Korean market regarding exchange rate fluctuations in the service and distribution of shoes and clothing[95]. That is, Korea is unrivaled in reflecting exchange rate fluctuation quickly, but she reflects that change in the actual selling price relatively slower by international comparison. This means that fluctuations (shocks) appear very quickly, but the adjustment speed is comparatively slow. This is likely because the competition in the open service market is intense, and the competition is speed itself.

It is well known that Korea plays the role of a testbed for various new products worldwide. The country has a relatively high national income and a large population compared to its land area, providing perfect market conditions for experiment. Furthermore, with world-class IT infrastructure, Korea has optimal conditions for observing market reaction to new products due to her fast communication speed.

Fourth, it is the change in lifestyle. In the past, when there was more time available, going to the market or shopping was a pleasure and a major part

---

[95] OECD, Measuring Competition in Service Market with Pass-Through Speed of Adjustment, OECD Trade Policy Paper vol. 258. 2021

of social activity. Until recently, even if people did not buy anything, they found satisfaction (utility, in economic terms) in just looking around, as evidenced by the phrase 'window shopping.' In the modern world, filled with various convenient and time-saving machines and tools, it is paradoxical that everyone has become busier, and time has become more precious. As income rises, the opportunity cost of time increases to an incomparable level, and the time and effort spent on shopping and selecting items could be considered as a considerable transaction cost. Consequently, consumers (actors) make choices regardless of their awareness or consciousness. Choosing a more enjoyable and satisfying activity, even if it means idling, could be more valuable to an individual. Going to a restaurant to eat can also be explained in the same context.

In situations like the pandemic, where face-to-face contact is impossible or discouraged, contactless transactions and lifestyles are necessary, making methods like delivery and subscription services more suitable. The act of buying time is naturally settling into the economy and daily life. Epidemics are accelerating these lifestyle changes.

The above explanations become necessary conditions for Korea to have a competitive advantage in the digital economic environment and related consumer life. Any country with similar conditions can have a competitive foundation. However, a sufficient condition is also necessary, which is the 'speed' that characterizes Korea and Koreans.

Taking delivery as an example, the commercial start of the delivery business began early in Europe, the United States, and Japan, and it continues today. However, Korea is unrivaled in the speed of development and dissemination. In terms of expansion to other countries, Korean speed provides a definite competitive advantage also.

4-7 Pros and Cons of the Delivery Service Development and Speed

Consumers make rational decisions and changes in their behavior mainly by the advantages in transaction cost, if convenience and satisfaction compared to cost are relatively higher. Suppliers, on the other hand, change themselves to stay ahead of consumers' changing preferences and win the competition, resulting in faster change. This phenomenon is happening in every country worldwide and is an unstoppable trend.

Nothing in this world is absolutely beneficial. The rapid growth of this industry inevitably brings side effects too. The increase in motorcycles leads to a rapid increase in accidents. After platforms dominate the market, consumers face limited choices, essentially resembling a monopolistic market, leading to paradoxical situations where consumers pay more for the same product due to advertising, delivery, and delivery booking fees. This is a common phenomenon in a monopolistic market.

As the delivery industry develops rapidly, so do the problems related to the environment. There is a report that the plastic waste generated by one person in Korea per year is 88kg, ranking the third after the United States and the United Kingdom.[96] Countries with larger populations will have even bigger problems. In 2017, the number of courier shipments in China was reported at 20.7 billion. According to the report, if the cardboard boxes used for delivery were spread out, they would cover an area of approximately 9 million square kilometers, enough to cover the entire China. The length of the tape used for packaging in 2015 was 17 billion meters, enough to circle the Earth 425 times. A food delivery app company that receives 10 million orders a day consumes 600,000 square meters of plastic bags daily, equivalent to the area of 84 soccer fields.[97] Korea is no exception, albeit on a different scale. This aspect also needs to be considered from the perspective of speed.

China began its significant economic development later than Korea, which has allowed observers to look back on Korea's past. Moreover, since China's development took place more recently, it can be said that the pace of change in various aspects has been even faster than Korea. The following story box describes some memorable moments from the author's visits to China for approximately 20 years from 1990 to 2010.

---

[96] National Academy of Sciences, Engineering, and Medicine (NASEM), USA, Chosun Ilbo, December 3rd, 2021, A1

[97] Chosun Economy, November 1st, 2017, B7

An Experience of Speed: Traveling in China in Early 1990s

In terms of the pace of change, China's transformation could be considered even faster than Korea's. Since the adoption of the reform and opening-up policy in 1978, the changes have been more rapid in some respects compared to Korea, which started almost 20 years earlier.

Before opening up, China was a closed socialist society, along with the Soviet Union's Iron Curtain, known as the Bamboo Curtain. At that time, it was the Cold War era between the United States and Europe, and the Soviet Union, so China was even more closed off to countries allied with the West. It was not until Korea established diplomatic relations with China in 1992 that exchanges between the two countries took place, enabling firsthand experiences in China.

In the summer of 1990, before the establishment of diplomatic relations, I had the opportunity to attend a seminar on the development of the Tumen River (a river dividing North Korea and China), hosted by the East-West Center in Hawaii. I traveled to Beijing, then to Jilin through Chang Chun, and after the event, all participants visited Mount Paektu (known as Changbai Mountain in China). Since it was before the establishment of diplomatic relations, I obtained a separate visa on a blank sheet, not in my passport.

The immigration procedure at that time was relatively complicated, and baggage inspections were slow and thorough. However, these processes improved rapidly, and 20 years later, they had completely changed, becoming relatively faster in terms of digitalization and automation. It was a level that surpassed Korean pace.

In 1990, the streets of Beijing could be described as a sea of bicycles. Since bicycles were the primary mode of transportation, the sight of lines of bicycles riding or waiting for signals was truly astonishing. Many residents wore People's Style clothing, and women were no exception. While taking a walk around the hotel in the morning, I observed people buying their breakfast from street vendors or taking it home. I was particularly intrigued by the fact that some food items cost as little as 10 Jia (a unit of currency equal to one-hundredth of a Yuan).

In many ways, it was still a time when the socialist system was maintained, leading to unexpected events. For example, I heard that airplane seats reserved in advance were often unilaterally canceled or flight schedules changed without notice. Since there were no direct flights between Seoul and Beijing at the time, a Korean colleague who had to return to Seoul via Tokyo had his reservation unilaterally canceled and had to go to Shanghai to catch a connecting flight to Tokyo.

Before the system completely changed, hotel staff rarely received tips. I remember the awkward and blushing face of a staff member when I followed Western custom and gave tips after staying at a nice hotel. The coffee provided at the hotel's Chinese buffet-style breakfast was so tasteless that it was difficult to drink. Locals typically stayed at local inns called guesthouses which reminded me of old Korean boarding houses from the exterior observation.

Many tourist attractions charged different admission fees for domestic and foreign visitors, with foreigners paying about ten times more. However, the cost of living was relatively cheap compared to the exchange rates at the time, so even paying more wasn't considered expensive to foreigners. Public restrooms were so poor that they were reminiscent of those in Korea in the 1950s, causing great inconvenience. I heard that they started constructing restrooms exclusively for foreigners. In 1991, when I visited our sister university, Nankai University in Tianjin, I had an embarrassing experience using a public restroom when I suddenly had a stomach ache while exploring the city's famous shopping streets. The toilet stalls were completely open in the front and on the sides. An unexpected situation forced me to enter the stall before the university staff accompanying me could buy toilet paper, and I had to wait in agony for a long time since he couldn't find any place to buy it.

After the official event in Changchun, I had the chance to visit Mount Paektu. The road to Mount Paektu from Yanji was under major expansion due to the growing number of tourists. The road was treacherous, and modern construction equipment was scarce. I heard that the construction workers mainly came from Shandong Province and lived together on-site.

In 1990, I was a visiting researcher at the East-West Center in Hawaii, and I had several opportunities to interact with a delegation from China's Ministry of Agriculture who visited the center. Their visit, led by a government director officer, aimed to seek help in processing China's census data using computers. The delegation was humble and serious. Through them, I could imagine how our Korean seniors must have behaved during their foreign trips *in the difficult times after the Korean War. At the time, the price of breakfast at the university cafeteria was less than $3, but none of the delegation members came to eat. They probably had simple meals in their rooms.*

Since they were a delegation invited by the U.S. government, they had many invitations to lunch and dinner, so they likely saved a significant amount of money on meal expenses, which would have been a considerable sum by Chinese standards at the time. As I recall, our seniors also used to save on expenses during their foreign trips, bringing back wristwatches, radios, or cameras, which were greatly appreciated and envied at that time. One more thing to remember is when I stopped by Beijing the following year, I asked the English interpreter of the delegation to Hawaii for guidance. After completing the guidance and on the way back, he carefully took the plastic bag we had used for shopping. It must have been a valuable item back then. It is a piece of evidence that allows one to imagine a glimpse of China's tremendous changes and development speed.

About 10 years later, the China I visited was in the midst of transforming into a completely different appearance. The rate of change in China was faster than that of Korea during that period, and almost everything, including streets, clothing, buildings, cars, people's behavior and thought patterns, attitudes towards foreign visitors, and price levels, had changed or was changing rapidly. As the President of the Busan Development Institute, I once visited the Shanghai Municipal Office. The director of the Shanghai Municipal People's Government Development Research Institute who also served as a communist party official at the time had set China's entry to the WTO as his personal and organizational goal and was actively pursuing it. After joining the WTO, China grew and changed even more rapidly.

Since the establishment of diplomatic relations with Korea in 1992, so many people have come and gone and had affluent experiences that there is no need to explain the changes and appearances of the recent 20 years separately. However, comparing the speed of change in China with that of Korea would be an interesting topic. Personally, I feel that China is no less rapid in the speed of change than Korea. In some areas or parts, China's changing speed is even faster. For example, China's first Special Economic Zone, Shenzhen increased its population by 460 times, its GDP by 4,660 times, and its area by 4.9 times after designation.

The delivery industry has rapidly grown recently and is inherently part of the gig economy because of its characters, making it inevitably very competitive. Therefore, it can be pointed out that workers in this industry have difficulty being protected by laws or regulations. Whenever a new industry or business emerges, unprecedented problems always arise, and it is extremely difficult for laws or regulations to keep up with the pace. Time and speed are directly related to the income of delivery workers, which increases the probability of traffic accidents and raises issues related to overall social safety.

On the other hand, the delivery system, means, and speed play a significant role as well. Dividing orders by region and transporting them to delivery hubs (logistics warehouses) using mass transportation means such as trains, ships, and trucks, and then dividing the delivery destinations again from those hubs, significantly reduces transaction cost, processing time, and delivery stages and time required. However, in this case, economies of scale play a decisive role, and a certain level of size is necessary to be competitive. We can understand the structure, characteristics, and growth process of the delivery distribution industry, which needs to rapidly transform and grow from small-scale startups to super-large companies to have a definite competitiveness.

In the early days of the last century's digitization age, there were many analyses and forecasts that the development of related IT technologies would make the market more competitive and improve consumer's welfare and the industrial ecosystem. Ironically, the development of digital technology and industry has concentrated the market dominance of leading companies in terms of competitiveness. Both domestically and globally, telecommunications, digital, and online distribution industries become virtually oligopolistic markets despite laws, systems, or national policies that do not protect specific companies or block competitors' market entry.

The acceleration of speed being a competitive advantage is the same both domestically and internationally. At the 2020 World Knowledge Forum, in Seoul, Alibaba Vice President Huo Wei declared, "COVID-19 has changed everything. In the distribution industry, if you cannot establish a response system within 30 minutes, you now have to worry about survival."[98] This

[98] Maeil Business, September 18th, 2020, A1

30 minutes also refers to delivery reaching the consumer. It may sound exaggerated, but it is an expression that reflects the reality of competition.

Even large and bulky products, which were transported by train or ship in the past, are now increasingly demanding rapid delivery.[99] As a result, air freight transport is inevitably increasing due to the influence of speed. This is another evidence of the increasing economic value of speed. Amazon offers a service called 'Amazon Prime,' which provides free shipping within two days across the United States for an annual fee of $99, and the number of members is rapidly increasing. To cover the vast US continent in just two days, air transport is the primary means. The economies of scale and scope mentioned earlier are the main weapons to realize the economies of speed and bring about a paradigm shift in the industry. Of course, the precondition for this is the telecommunication revolution.

The primary means of transportation for food delivery, convenience store delivery, postal service, and traditional quick service is motorcycle or equivalent. Considering urban traffic conditions and operating costs, it is hard to imagine delivery services without motorcycles. However, the new method being tried in Korea is to use convenience stores scattered nationwide as short-distance delivery hubs and have people deliver on foot within a certain distance. This is because several large companies own the convenience store business. In this case, convenience stores serve as small logistics centers. This method is named 'Eco-friendly, Healthy Delivery Service' as local residents deliver orders to neighboring residents. The method of increasing delivery speed and minimizing cost continues to evolve. Of course, the next step will inevitably be the rapid introduction of robot or drone deliveries instead of human deliveries.

This method has evolved to allow customers to order single items from convenience stores near their homes and receive the items within an hour, as well as meal kits and other goods. It has also evolved into a subscription service model that regularly delivers items such as laundry, artwork, and decorative items tailored to individual tastes. These changes are driven by the growing number of single-person households and the preference for non-face-to-face transactions. The essence of K-speed lies in continuous innovation, adaptation, and quick response to change.

---

[99] Chosun Economy January 17th, 2018, B7

4-8 Speed in Medical and Health Services

One of the most important factors that made Korea a leading country in plastic surgery and attracted foreign medical tourists is, of course, surgical technology, but speed is also a significant factor. Korean plastic surgeons typically complete breast augmentation surgery using silicone implants within an hour, while Western surgeons can take up to three hours. Rapid and precise surgical techniques of Korean doctors are highly regarded. The development of 'filler' plastic surgery where collagen substances are injected into the body to enhance nose and fill-in hollow cheeks, or 'one shot' plastic surgery has also played an important role in attracting foreign cosmetic clients.[100]

In many cases, speed plays a crucial role in saving lives in medical procedures, especially in emergency treatments. This is particularly true for heart and brain failures, where first aid and intervention are often required. An experience of a French doctor who worked in a Korean hospital demonstrates the importance of speed. The doctor was amazed by the number of patients and the speed at which the Korean medical staff worked. Korea has competitive advantages in heart surgery, cancer surgery, and advanced health examinations. The one-stop medical system that completes examination and simple treatment within 1-2 days is necessary.[101]

The experience of the above French doctor is impressive. "I came to a Korean university hospital because I was told I could see a variety of vascular patients, and there really were a lot. In France, I see about 10 patients in the morning, but in Korea, I see 50-60 in two hours. I could not have imagined it. The number of patients I saw in the last two months was more than I've seen in my entire life. Either way, encountering a variety of patients was a good experience from a doctor's perspective... The most surprising thing in Korea was the amount and speed of work. When I was on the cardiothoracic surgery team, I could only sleep for two hours a day. We perform more than two heart surgeries every day and also perform emergency surgeries at night. I even rode on a police motorcycle to fetch the heart of a brain-dead patient for transplantation. The Korean system is very 'efficient'... Heart surgery, cancer surgery,

---

[100] Chosun Ilbo, March 7th,2011

[101] Chosun Ilbo, December 6th, 2007

advanced health screenings, etc. Korea definitely has competitiveness." However, the question that arises here is whether this practice is still continuing to this day.

Furthermore, speed is being implemented in other areas of medicine, such as the development of a fast-track program that completes cancer diagnosis and surgery within seven days.[102] While there may be concerns about medical reliability and misdiagnosis risks, this program is not something that can be implemented in every country. Of course, the side effects and costs associated with such rapid treatment fall on the patients[103].

4-9 Digital Technology and Digital Government

(1) Digital Technology

The Fourth Industrial Revolution is associated with digital technology. Without understanding and utilizing digital technology, it is impossible to comprehend or explain today's science, industry, and daily life. Digital technology is, as emphasized several times earlier, the foundation of competitiveness and competitiveness itself. This technology has already been incorporated and evolving rapidly in all areas of industry and economy as well as in daily life, institution, culture, and cognitive structure. The term digital transformation encapsulates all these concepts. Under the current circumstances, Korea has relatively favorable conditions for digital transformation since she stands on a similar starting line.

Interestingly, digital technology manifests itself concretely as tools or roles that increase the speed of products or functions, that reduce time, or make things smaller and more convenient. The direction of technological advancement has reached a stage where artificial intelligence independently executes tasks previously performed by humans or machines.

---

[102] Chosun Ilbo, May 22nd, 2013

[103] In relation to medical services, the challenges facing Korea will become more severe in the future. Speed is money. However, since medical practices are strictly regulated by the health insurance system in Korea, it is impossible to institutionalize the so-called, fast track. In other words, it is fundamentally impossible to provide or receive better services even if one can pay more money. Wealthy people choose to go abroad to receive better quality services.

Extending this trend will inevitably lead to a stage where humans or systems receive commands or directives. Organizations or groups that fail to embrace or keep up with digital technology will lose competitiveness, making this technology indispensable for survival. The speed change in communication, which can be considered the core of digital technology, demonstrates the frightening acceleration of this technology. Under such circumstances, a new relationship between digitally advanced countries and dependent countries is bound to emerge.

Initially, digital technology primarily served to increase speed in fields such as communication. However, it quickly evolved to combine or converge with existing technologies in a very short time, and now it has evolved to the point where distinguishing industries or fields is even meaningless. This change has been in full swing since the early 21st century, and it is amazing that many people are accepting and utilizing these changes without a sense of rejection or alienation. It is as if the primitive age and modern times coexist and thrive on together. By extending this logic, it could also be used to describe the current generations of elderly and young people in Korea. Those who cannot properly use or utilize digital devices or means can be aptly referred to as digital primitives.

The change in industrial structure due to digital technology has become vivid evidence. In the case of companies, in 2007, only Microsoft was a digital-related company among the top 10 companies by market capitalization worldwide. However, as of 2022, Apple, Microsoft, Alphabet (Google), Amazon, Tesla, Meta (Facebook), and Nvidia are included. In 2016, there were five companies: Apple, Alphabet (Google), Microsoft, Amazon, and Facebook. This is not because traditional manufacturers like GE and GM or large banks have necessarily shrunk, but because digital companies are growing faster. Amazon, a company that started as an online bookstore using the internet in 1995, is transforming into a new company that has become a powerhouse in artificial intelligence technology combined with digital technology. Tesla has created the foundation for making electric cars autonomously driven smartphones and is expanding as a leader in private space travel.

In discussing the digital age in relation to competitiveness, Korea must make faster and more innovative changes in all areas related to digital technology in order to lead the world economy or maintain the current status and position. In the process, how to utilize the speed of Korean competitiveness becomes crucial. Specifically, either she will lead in digital technology or closely follow it by applying digital technology to increase speed in various aspects.

In an age where automobiles powered by internal combustion engines, a symbol of the industrialization era, still dominate, flying cars may seem like a distant future. Electric cars, hydrogen cars, and autonomous-driven cars, which are currently in full swing, may come next. Saying again, when flying cars are commercialized, the sky will have to be used like today's roads, so traffic systems and rules will be completely different. There may be a new lane concept introduced in the sky and a new signaling system will have to be adopted. As wearable robots advance, autonomous personal flying vehicles using concepts like chairs may emerge. The gradual shift from the concept of car ownership to sharing is also due to digital technology.

However, most of these changes are involved with the giant digital companies mentioned earlier, directly or indirectly. These companies can expand and transform quickly by buying technology or ideas rather than trying to develop or apply them on their own, using enormous financial resources.[104] This is another example of the changing growth paradigm of companies and industries in the digital age.

Applying foreign models to Korea, it is possible to imagine that internet companies like Naver or Kakao in Korea lead the change or giant companies like Samsung Electronics or SK transform and lead the change. However, it is difficult to say how realistic such a plan is. For example, it requires revolutionary imagination for Naver or Kakao to partner with innovative global companies and attempt an autonomous flying car business.

---

[104] It is worth noting that there are reports raising issues about the negative behavior of these dinosaur-like internet companies and the impact they have on the industrial ecosystem.

(2) Digital Government

country	UN E-Government Development Index 2020 (0-1 scale)	ITU Development Index 2017 (0- 10 scale)	WB Digital Adoption Index 2016 (0-1 scale)	Cisco Digital Readiness Index 2019 (0-25 scale)	Network Readiness Index 2020 (1-100 scale)
average	0.82	7.58	0.73	16.33	67.92
Republic of Korea	0.96	8.85	0.86	18.22	74.60
Denmark	0.98	8.71	0.79	18.98	82.19
Germany	0.85	8.39	0.84	17.85	77.48
United States	0.93	8.18	0.75	19.03	78.91
Singapore	0.92	8.05	0.87	20.26	81.39
United Kingdom	0.94	8.65	0.76	17.86	76.27
Japan	0.90	8.43	0.83	17.69	73.54
Canada	0.84	7.77	0.69	17.33	74.92
Australia	0.94	8.24	0.71	17.89	75.09

George Ingram and Meagan Dooley, Digital government Foundations for global development and democracy, 2021.12, P61

Table 4-5 *Composite Digital Government Index - Recent High Income Countries*

One fact that we are not aware of is the speed of digitalization in Korea, including government administrative services. The speed of digitalization of the Korean government is far ahead in the world. Korea ranks second, on par with Denmark, in the "e-Government" ranking among high-income countries based on the UN's 2020 standards. Other agencies' evaluations based on different criteria and methods are the same or similar. This is the result of Korea's speed, ahead of other factors. The recent high-income country comparable to Korea is Singapore, another East Asian city-state, while most of the other countries are long-standing advanced countries.

The Ministry of Public Administration and Safety of the Korean government developed a new address system based on digital technology reflecting the international standard and it goes abroad for adoption for many foreign governments. In terms of e-government, Korea is recognized as the leader in various fields.

In 2021, the Japanese government faced a problem when it sought to provide disaster relief funds to children under 18, as the cost of issuing coupons for execution was estimated at 100 billion Yen (about US$ 1 billion).[105] This is the price to pay for not implementing digital administration in time, and it represents the 'cost of speed' that must be paid even by developed countries if they are relatively slower.

105 Chosun Ilbo, December 9th, 2021 A16

4-10 Innovation Cycle and Speed of Competition

It is conceivable that humans have been relentlessly attempting innovation and improvement since the beginning of time. For example, one can speculate that human history itself has been a continuous process of innovation and improvement, such as using stones as tools, refining them to be more useful, and creating tools by combining them with other materials. Even when innovation occurred, the propagation speed was slow, so there was a significant time difference in imitation or application. Therefore, innovation cycles were long and the speed was slow.

The changes experienced by the author over the past 70 years have been introduced in boxes under the title 'Experience of Speed-Korea (1), (2)'. Among them, the accelerated change in Korea is vividly portrayed. Ignoring or forgetting what one has experienced, neither individuals nor countries can guarantee future success and better achievement. Time is continuous and does not flow differently by scope.

In the context above, the speed and cycle of innovation, which signifies today's technological change, have become incomparably faster and shorter. The recent change could be seen as a discrete change rather than a continuous one. In other words, it is more appropriate to express it as a sudden jump (quantum jump) rather than a continuum of change.[106]

In the case of companies, if they fail to respond appropriately to the shortened innovation cycle, their survival itself may be threatened. This innovation cycle not only applies to the company's products and industries but also has the same meaning as the company's transformation speed. Until the 20th century, a company belonging to a certain industry was classified as a lengthy associate to that industry, but now that classification method is inappropriate.

For example, it is not possible to classify Amazon, which started with online book sales, as a book sales company. It can only be classified as the world's largest conglomerate leading the forefront of the Fourth Industrial

[106] Broadly speaking, while the shift from the First to the Second, Third, or Fourth Industrial Revolution could be seen as leaps, many of the technological changes currently being experienced by humankind would be equivalent to quantum jumps.

Revolution. Chinese online distribution companies like Alibaba are trying to transform into leaders of the 4th industrial revolution with huge financial power. The speed of technological convergence and softening makes the traditional concept of industrial classification meaningless. It becomes difficult to answer where Amazon belongs to in the Korean industrial classification system.

The reason is simple. It's because you can't survive if you don't change. The common point of companies that have grown into the world's leading companies in a short time, such as Google, Alibaba, and Amazon is that they started with ideas and technology, not huge capital. Therefore, even large and well-established companies face the real and potential risks of being overtaken or becoming extinct by new ideas and technologies if they do not change. Convergence is not limited to technology but also appears as industrial convergence (industrial mix) in companies. In other words, innovative companies need to cover business areas spanning all industrial sectors to properly respond to changes, and survive.

This means that innovation cycles have become very short and will become even shorter in the future. Also, innovation is changing beyond the dimension applied to one industry, crossing multiple industries. From such a perspective, when looking at the change cycle of Korean industry and companies, it can be seen that they do not meet the global trend. As seen in Table 4-1 and others, in the case of the United States, the rankings of almost all leading companies have changed in the last 10 years.

On the contrary, Korea shows relatively less fluctuation in ranking, which generates more concern than positive aspects. Although Samsung Electronics is a leading company recognized worldwide and is continuously innovating and diversifying to become a better company, it is not always a desirable phenomenon from the perspective of global trends. It is impossible not to worry when imagining how Samsung would respond when Chinese semiconductor companies soon catch up.

It would be an ironic situation if Korea's industries and companies, which have rapidly increased their competitiveness after industrialization, can no longer compete with foreign competitors due to their lagging speed. Reasons could include corporate complacency, lack of agility due to bloated size, regulation-oriented industrial policies, and unfavorable domestic and international economic conditions. However, in the global competitive environment, it is certain that there will never be separate consideration for such circumstances.

The following story box shows an example of a giant country which lagged behind in changes in various fields except military technology and the interim result by the 20th century.

An Experience of Speed: Traveling in Russia in Early 1990s

After the establishment of diplomatic relations between Korea and Russia, I visited Russia three times, all for official business or research-related invitations, and I only visited Far Eastern Russia. Even if my experiences are fragmented, sharing them could be beneficial.

Until the Cold War era of the 1980s, Russia was one of the two superpowers of the world, competing on par with the United States in military power, including nuclear weaponry, especially in the field of strategic weapons. It was a technological powerhouse that stunned the world by launching the first human lunar exploration satellite.

My first visit was in 1991 for a project being carried out by a research institute in Japan for the publication of the Far Eastern Russia Economic Yearbook. The publication of the book was difficult to carry out independently, so it was a task carried out with the help of Japan. To summarize my visit in a single word, it was a series of experiences of enormous imbalances. There were disparities in hardware and software, macro and microeconomics, demand and supply, facade and reality, system and actuality.

In Khabarovsk, where the main government of Far Eastern Russia is located, there was only one hotel for foreigners, and despite the facilities being subpar, the cost for one night was a whopping 200 dollars. Considering the exchange rate and local prices at the time, it was an exorbitant fee, but foreign visitors had no choice.

Even though the communist system had already collapsed, old customs and systems were still in place. Plainclothes security guards (police) controlled the entrance of the hotel, and monitors were on duty 24 hours a day on each floor. The hotel room did not have a proper hot water supply, and shampoo, soap, and toilet paper were so inferior that I was reluctant to use them. When I visited again the next year, the hot water supply issue was still present, but the shower amenities were fully stocked - it was a set product from Amore Pacific Cosmetics (a Korean company)

Despite being a country that launched satellites, the car manufacturing was not up to par, so the main vehicles were imported used cars from Japan and Korea. It was a dangerous situation as vehicles from the two countries, which have different driver's seat positions, were operating together in the same area. Most of the buses were used buses from Korea, and they still had the Korean destination signs with numbers and Korean advertisements attached to them.

The rigidity of the system was particularly severe in Russia. The flight to Seoul departed around 8 a.m., but the hotel restaurant wasn't open until 8 a.m., so there was no chance of having breakfast on the day of departure. There were no restaurants or convenience stores near the hotel, and at that time, airport stores and restaurants were not open either. When the hotel restaurant opened, most of the servers themselves sat down and started eating first. If they brought the wrong food and it was pointed out, the servers sometimes got angry.

Just like the past regime, city buses and boats sailing the river were free, thus punctuality and service quality were not even a topic of discussion. Hard labor was often carried out by North Korean workers locally. I saw some workers who spoke Korean fixing up the front yard of the hotel. I offered to treat them to dinner that evening to a person who appeared to be their supervisor. After asking me to wait and consulting someone, he came back and refused. I estimated it would have cost around 100 dollars to treat dozens of compatriots to dinner at a local restaurant.

For the heating in the entire city, three hot-water boiling factories were operated and thus the city was surrounded with heavy and thin iron pipes. I asked the guide if one factory was out of order and what would happen. The answer was that you have to wait until it is fixed in the midst of Siberian cold.

No significant changes were found on my second visit the following year. This time, with the help of an American participant, I hired a car and a guide for 5 dollars for a local experience, with one condition attached: to have lunch at the guide's home. The young driver, whose parents all worked at a local foreign consulate office, gave us a tour of his university and took us to his home for a simple Russian-style lunch. It was a well-off home by local standards, and I remember seeing many canned goods stacked in the kitchen. When I wanted to go to the bathroom, they gave me a flashlight. The toilet was flush-free, and it had to be manually filled with water.

The English-speaking guide was a middle-aged lady who was teaching at a local university, and she was dignified and exceptionally well-dressed, like a typical Russian woman. At the end of the tour, when I expressed a desire to see her home, she took us to her neighborhood, but ultimately did not show me the inside of her house. From the outside, it looked like a large wooden panel house.

I visited the Russian Orthodox Church, which was once the state religion, and the exterior and interior were impressive. One memory that still remains is seeing a lady who was cleaning the church, standing and conversing respectfully with a young priest. I had never seen a believer talking so humbly and seriously with a clergyman in my entire life.

About 20 years later, I visited Khabarovsk, Vladivostok, and China. Compared to my previous visit, they showed signs of improvement and change in various aspects, but it was a slow pace compared to the changes in Korea and China. My experience crossing the border of the Russian region is described in another story box.

Changing a once rigid system and culture is genuinely difficult, and the pace of change is not fast. As for China, which operates its politics and economy separately, it is still a subject of observation, and we should wait to see the result of the experiment.

Chapter 5

K-Culture and K-Speed

As detailed in Chapter 7 on the realization condition and generalization possibilities of K-speed, the rapid economic growth has brought about new phenomena in culture, art, sports, food and many other sectors, along with political and social changes such as democratization to Korea. These cultural phenomena are named Hallyu (Korean Wave), and the prefix K is attached in various sectors related to these phenomena as K-00. This process, particularly the speed of change and development, is a unique case unprecedented by other late coming or competing countries. Not only in pop music, classic music, movies, web toons, dramas, games, beauty, and food, etc., but also in the education market and services which are often brought up as a problematic issue within Korea, has emerged anew as K-edu. The most notable aspect here is the speed of change. As mentioned several times before, the K-00 phenomenon across various fields has burst out in a short period of time, with most of the changes spreading worldwide, within less than twenty years. It is necessary to point out that the formation and growth of Hallyu have, in turn, brought about significant and unexpected changes in Korea's economy and industrial structure as well.

5-1 Korean Wave (Hallyu) and Changes in Korean Economic and Industrial Structure

Hallyu has already become a major industrial impact factor on the Korean economy. Statistically, the sales of K-content related industries amounted to KRW (Korean Won)126.7 trillion (US$ 105.5 billion) in 2019, compared to KRW 107.6 trillion for petrochemicals and KRW129.4 trillion for semiconductors in the same year. The number of related employees also increased from 620,000 in 2015 to 682,000 in 2019.[107] In terms of economic effects, the production-inducing effect (co-efficient) of the manufacturing industry is 1.89, while the cultural content industry is 1.97. In the value-added-inducing effect, the manufacturing industry is 0.64, but the cultural content industry is

[107] Maeil Business, June 23rd, 2021, A1

0.83, which is significantly higher, allowing for comparison of their proportions and contributions to the Korean economy. Dissemination of Hallyu has become wider and larger these days and has an important impact on the Korean economy in export, value added and employment in other fields.

These changes naturally occurred within a generation. Korea was initially a chronic deficit country in cultural and service trade. However, since 2014, the personal and cultural services payment sector has continuously recorded surplus in service trade statistics, indicating that there is now more to sell than to import in the fields of culture and leisure services.

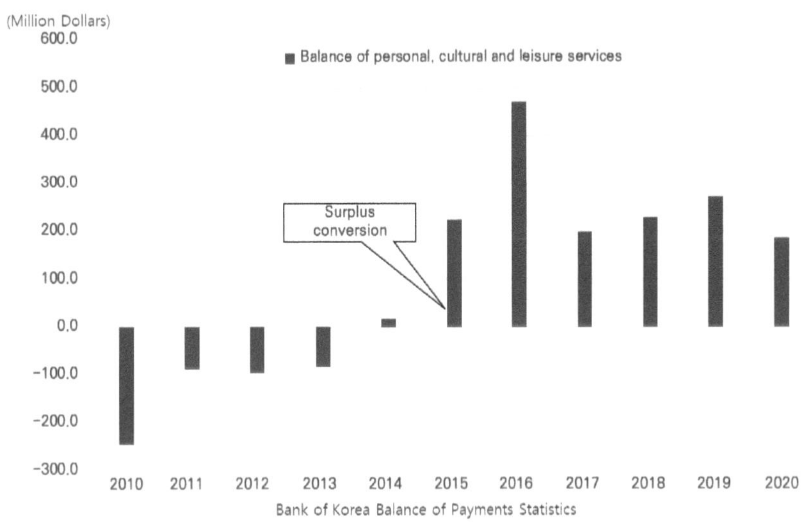

Figure 5-1 *Culture-related Service Trade Balance in Korea*

A British magazine (Monocle) rated Korea's soft power as the second in the world, following Germany.[108] Although not an official evaluation, the rating is worth noting and reminds Koreans of the remarkable speed of change in their country. This is even more so because it is not the manufacturing industry, which has driven growth for a long time since the early days of industrialization, but the culture and service industries. This is an example of how the transformation of Korea's industrial structure is viewed from the outside. World-renowned cellist Yo-Yo Ma said, "Korean culture currently possesses the ability to express the dreams held by not only Korean but also

108 Maeil Business, November 28th, 2020, A22

the entire Asian and global generations, which always amazes me."[109] At the time Yo-Yo Ma made his debut on the American stage, Korea was still experiencing difficulties and challenges economically and culturally.

The beginning and development of Hallyu must emphasize the confluence of various conditions and situations, particularly the digital age, but those are secondary factors, and the essence lies in the speed of Korea (and Koreans). This content of this phenomenon will be briefly examined by dividing them into a few categories.

5-2 Speed of Korean Wave Formation and Its Dissemination Process

After liberation from Japanese colonization and the Korean War, everything was scarce in Korea, and people were busy making a living, so naturally importing, imitating, or replicating culture and art from developed countries was the best option up to the late 20th century. Korean tradition and culture were generally perceived as dull or old-fashioned compared to the new culture imported from economically powerful foreign countries. This perception was further compounded by the historical experiences of national failure and colonization, causing Korean culture to be pushed to the back seat. For a considerable time after the liberation, foreign, especially American, cultural influence affected all aspects of society and daily life.

On the other hand, under the oppressive government, some newly introduced or attempted trends were labeled as decadent culture and became targets for government regulation and crackdown. For example, men with extremely long hair were forcibly shaved in the street, and women's preferred short skirt lengths were limited to a few centimeters above the knee, even measured with a ruler by police in Myeongdong, Seoul, Korea's busiest district at the time. This historical fact is difficult to understand for the current generation. American pop songs were popular on university campuses, while Korean popular music took a back seat. Japanese culture, which inevitably had considerable competitiveness at that time, was strictly banned for political reasons. These unimaginable and impossible events happened until the early 1980s, not because of a lack of creative thinking

[109] Chosun Ilbo, October 21rst, A18

or mindset, but because copying or imitating was cheap, easy, convenient, and sold well, thus allowing people to make a living.

As the economy grew and people's basic needs were met, cultural and artistic desires became prominent, faster, and more diverse, and the domestic market was properly formed. Conditions were established for Koreans to exhibit their unique 'enthusiasm' and 'talent.' From then on, the focus shifted from importing, imitating, and replicating to creativity, innovation, and export, and a corporate structure and management concept gradually took hold, backed by capital. The advent of the digital age, represented by timely mobile technology, opened up real-time communication and exchange pathways that extended beyond Korea to the world.

In culture, arts, entertainment, and sports, the atmosphere changed to the point where parents actively provided full support and encouragement for their children to develop their talents and abilities from an early age on. This was a complete reversal from the previous mindset of strictly prohibiting and discouraging those activities. This change can be exemplified by connecting the new start of Korean women's golf with Se-ri Pak, which has been referred to as the 'Se-ri Pak phenomenon.' This was the result of a rational outlook and quick judgment based on changing values in Korea and the outside world. Of course, this was possible because the individuals involved had the 'talent' and 'aptitude' in their respective fields. However, the speed of change in those developments is faster than in any other country or case. That may be described as adaptability.

The Korean Wave can be divided into several phases: Korean Wave 1.0 started in the late 1990s when Korean dramas gained popularity in China, who was experiencing rapid economic growth through opening up, and earned the name 'Korean Wave (Hallyu).'[110] Korean Wave 2.0 began when K-pop idol groups gained popularity in Japan in the early 2000s, marking a reversal from the invasion of Japanese culture to that of Korean culture. Until then, the Korean Wave had mainly remained in the Asian sphere, such as China and Japan. Following this, in Southeast Asia, specifically ASEAN, the Korean Wave started to form a new market by combining with the millennial generation.[111]

---

[110] Statistics Korea, Window of Statistics 19, Winter Edition, 2019
[111] Evolution of the Korean Wave, Maeil Business, July 30th, 2019

In 2012, Psy's 'Gangnam Style' dance and song spread throughout the world, marking the beginning of the K-pop era. It can be seen as the entrance to the Korean Wave 3.0 era. Around this time, idol groups such as BTS emerged and showed explosive popularity and achievements on global platforms like YouTube and the American Billboard charts, proving that their influence would be long-lasting, contrary to initial concerns. In conjunction with this, various other Korean sectors, such as movies and dramas like 'Squid Game,' also emerged as K-dramas, mutually exerting a positive influence. Now, there are opinions that the Korean Wave will settle as a global cultural phenomenon and genre (sector), similar to Latin pop.[112] In other words, it means that Korea has become an important transmitter of culture, rather than just a recipient of foreign culture.[113] 2020 and onwards, could be classified as the era of the New Korean Wave. The globalization of the Korean Wave and its related industries are also on the rise.

Here, we should pay attention to how the Korean Wave has followed various Korean products, including electronic products, which have swept across the world. In other words, the Korean Wave is not a simple coincidence. Therefore, a convergent phenomenon is now emerging where Korean products and technologies benefit from the Korean Wave also. At this point, what everyone should consider and develop are measures for sustaining this wave.

Another factor is the realization of this saying 'the most Korean means the most global.' In that case, flavors and styles unique to Korea can gain more certain global competitiveness. The popularity of performance 'The Tiger is Descending' which mixes traditional Korean clothing and musical sound with modern dance, is one example of this. Some argue against this concept, but it is also difficult to explain the phenomenon of the Korean drama 'Squid Game' becoming the world's number one in viewership on the Netflix platform in the second half of 2021. However, generalizing this proposition may be risky or inappropriate.

Eva Chow (Korean name Jeon Hee-kyung), a Korean-American whom the New York Times called the 'Queen of LA Culture,' described the reason

---

112 Infinite Evolution of K-pop - Candid Talk by Professors Lee Jang-Woo and Lee Kyu-Tak, Maeil Business Newspaper January 18th, 2021, A32

113 Interview with Lee Eo-Ryung, Chosun Ilbo, February 12th, 2020. 2. 12

for the current success of K-culture in the US as feeling like a "cultural volcanic eruption".[114] Following the logic explained earlier, not just one or two fields, but all fields are beginning to bloom, bear fruit, or harvest, albeit with some time lag. In the following, we will explore a few sectors among the many fields that can be called the Korean Wave or K-00.

5-3 K-Pop

Represented by BTS, K-Pop has not only become culturally significant but has also taken on a large industrial weight. With over 100 million global Hallyu fans, it has become so industrialized that it has even coined a new term, 'Fandustry'(Fan+ Industry). BTS's global fan club, known as the 'Army' has become a powerful and influential market through their passionate support and purchasing power in concerts, social media, and merchandise. This is the meaning behind the term 'Fansumer' (Fan+ Consumer), which implies a force as strong and influential as an army. BTS has been invited three times to the General Assembly of United Nations as a speaker.

To provide some quantitative examples, the number of K-Pop-related tweets increased from 5 million in 2010 to 6.1 billion in 2020, more than 1,000-fold growth in just 10 years. Hive, the company that owns BTS (formerly Big Hit), was valued at around KRW 11.7 trillion in 2021 when it went public, while its value in 2012 was only about KRW 20 billion. The speed of this growth is astonishing. Including the other three publicly listed agencies (JYP, SM and YG), the market value exceeds KRW 16 trillion. Harvard Business School's Elberse and Woodham estimated the annual economic impact of BTS at $4.9 billion (about KRW 6 trillion).[115] BTS has become a massive enterprise. At the end of 2021, 200,000 people gathered for a BTS concert in Los Angeles. Quoting a news report, "The packed stadium echoed with the united voices of fans, known as the 'army,' regardless of race, nationality, gender, or age."[116]

Hive was selected among 100 most influential enterprises in the world in 2022. The BTS group appeared on the cover of TIME magazine. It was a

---

[114] Chosun Ilbo interview article December 27th, 2021, A30

[115] Anita Elberse and L Woodham, 'Big Hit Entertainment and Blockbuster Band BTS: K-Pop Goes Global', Case Study, Harvard Business Review, June 8th, 2020

[116] Hyo-Hye Kim, Maeil Business, November 30th, 2021, A33

groundbreaking event when McDonald's developed a BTS menu and sold it in 50 countries with great success. Products are developed and sold because of demand and popularity. The Hallyu wave has become a starting point for the commercialization of various other items, giving rise to the term 'Bangtan Economy.' Thirteen thousand applicants came for the audition of Hive in the US.

Not only BTS but other Korean idol groups also maintain popularity worldwide. At the Taiwan concert of Black Pink, one of the girl groups, five hundred thousand gathered. BTS stopped group activity from the second half of 2022. But the member's individual activity still maintains high popularity.

Regarding the sustainability of Hallyu, the unexpected longevity of BTS and other idol groups at the center of the wave is due to their internal innovative nature. In the case of BTS, members are directly involved in songwriting, rapping, choreography, and soundtracks, which allow for more innovative ideas.[117] The talent development system also plays a role. Their approach of communicating with fans through social media from the beginning is another form of innovation. This allows fans and stars to grow together and achieve synergy. Exporting the star development system abroad is the right direction for sustaining popularity and commercialization.

5-4 K-Drama

The Korean dramas, which paved the way for the Hallyu 1.0, is a case where the attributes of speed are demonstrated in various ways. Factors contributing to their success include the activity of actors who move between films and dramas, appearances by K-pop stars, and drama content that appeals to humanity. Unlike foreign dramas that have succeeded as series over many years, the planning of the short format of 12 to 24 episodes, which induces addiction by making viewers wait for the next episode, has emerged as a competitive aspect that showcases K-speed.[118] This is a case of strategic agility. Revising the script right up to the actual filming is a speed factor unique to Koreans that people from other countries would not attempt.

---

[117] Monde Diplomatique Newsletter, November 10th, 2020, Professor Hye-Jin Lee, Semyung University.

[118] Chosun Ilbo, January 30th, 2021, A4

The series 'Squid Game' also fulfills this strategic factor. It is highly possible to infer this agility to the movie 'Parasite' and BTS into this category. Using the same logic, this can be compared to the past when Korea was poor and struggling, and a trust in 'American-made' products evoked positive feelings. K-dramas, K-movies naturally conjure up confidence in Korean made works and products. This is a process instead of a one hit wonder coincidence.

Success in one field leads to success in other fields as well. Since 2020, the Korean drama craze is reignited among Japan's MZ generation, and the K-beauty wave is spreading, as reported.[119] This evokes a sense of rivalry, as until the last century, Japanese cosmetics were, along with European (French) and American-made products, the object of envy for Korean women. Korea's cosmetics export to Japan skyrocketed from $229 million in 2017 to $645 million in 2020. It's an astonishing reversal and an astonishing pace.

Digital industries, especially platforms like Netflix, have become catalysts for viewership and consumption, which should be noted. Rapid responses to content, consumer taste and consumption pattern change, and the reflection of the zeitgeist in addition can be seen as manifestations of K-wave.

Again, as a seemingly trivial but meaningful example of change, the competition rate for participating in an event where Korean Air in-flight meals were served in Japan was 20:1.[120] The change in the Japanese MZ generation, intertwined with the Korean Wave, could also serve as a clue for future prospects in Korea-Japan relation, which continues to be tense for political reasons.

5-5 K-Movies

The official entry and recognition of Korean movies on the world stage is also a very recent development. There were occasional achievements, such as winning awards at prestigious international film festivals, but these did not constitute a genuine debut and recognition on the world stage. The real beginning can be seen in 2020 when director Bong Joon-ho's 'Parasite' won four categories at the Academy Awards, including Best Picture and

---

119 Busan First Economy, June 23rd, 2021
120 Chosun Ilbo, November 16th, 2021, A1

Best Director, and also in 2021 when Youn Yuh-jung won Best Supporting Actress for her role in director Isaac Chung's "Minari(buttercup)." Although there is debate over whether "Minari" is a Korean movie, it can be classified as a US made K-movie. Many consider Bong Joon-ho's works to possess timeliness, mass appeal, uniqueness, and innovation. Now that the floodgates have opened in the film sector, it is expected that various solo and collaborative effects will continue to emerge.

The Korean film industry's resolute opposition to the 2007 reduction policy of the screen quota was an acknowledgment of their own lack of competitiveness against Hollywood movies.[121] The screen quota system is explained more in Section 9-7. However, in just over a decade, it has become a central axis of the Korean Wave and is now making global waves. This is thanks to K-speed and the synergistic effect across various sectors. One might wonder if the same result would have been achieved if the screen quota had not been reduced. It is worth emphasizing once again that it is not just movies but the mutual boosting of culture, art, and entertainment that is driven and supported by economic growth and K-speed.

5-6 K-Web toon, Web novel

The competitiveness of Korean web toons lies in their speed. Korean web toon artists work at a fast pace due to the intense competition in their environment. Like games and other fields, the production speed is a necessity for competitiveness and success is achieved through simultaneous factors based on this foundation.

Web toons and web novels not only represent their own genres but also contribute to the richness of content and the improvement of the quality of works derived from various original materials. The reverse path also naturally exists, as communication with consumers takes place in advance. Korea is also the most active in the format industry, which exports basic concepts, structures, and production methods of entertainment shows and dramas to be remade locally.[122] This is an example of the rapid recognition of artistic and commercial competitiveness.

---

[121] Director Bong Joon-ho is said to have been very active in opposing the reduction of screen quota at the time.

[122] Chosun Ilbo, June 25th, 2021, 'Ilsa Ileun' requoted

Web toons and web novels are not only experiencing rapid growth in their own markets but are also expanding into the global market at a fast pace. The domestic web toon market grew from KRW 150 billion in 2013 to KRW 1 trillion in 2020, representing another typical growing sector. The Web novel market is growing even faster, with a projection reaching KRW 1 trillion in 2021 from 10 billion in 2013.[123] These areas also generate intellectual property rights that spread to dramas, movies, and games, resulting in even greater synergistic effects. Two major Korean companies, Naver and Kakao, are securing and expanding platforms for these fields both domestically and abroad, which demonstrate the scale and expansiveness of this market. For instance, in September 2021, Naver acquired a web novel platform Moonpia, which started as an online community in 2002 and now has more than 47,000 registered authors. Both companies are actively acquiring foreign websites as well. This already constitutes an industry in its own right. As dramas and movies created from web toons and web novels achieve great success on OTT platforms, their prices (licensing rights) also increase. This is another example of economies of scope.

5-7 K-Games

One of the pioneers in the era of the Korean Wave, including K-pop, is the game industry. The reason why Korean games have become dominant in the global market is, in a phrase, competitiveness in speed. Although Korea was not the first country to develop various types of games, it has achieved its current position in the game industry because it quickly caught up and surpassed the original creators. Specifically, the spread of IT and the internet in Korea was relatively fast, and the PC-room culture developed early on, creating favorable conditions. The concentration and competitiveness of Koreans, as well as their unique imagination, undoubtedly contributed to enjoying and developing games.

A very important factor in the success of games is development speed, along with ideas and content. Preemptive effect and subsequent effect are essential conditions for success in games, and Korea overwhelms foreign competitors in development and release speeds, as explained before. Nexon Vice President Jung Sang-won said, "When meeting foreign developers...

[123] Chosun Ilbo, October 2nd, 2021, A17

they are amazed that while they take 5 to 6 years to complete one game, Korea has already released several follow-up series during that time."[124] Since speed is an essential attribute of games themselves, it is naturally a competitive factor in their production and distribution.

Games also play a significant role in expanding from one sector to multiple sectors (one-source-multi-use). This is a case where economies of scope, economies of scale, and economies of speed all work simultaneously.

The Korean ability to turn crisis into opportunity is also remarkable. In the early 2010s, when the Korean government imposed restrictions on late-night gaming for teenagers and the Chinese government deliberately denied permits for Korean games in retaliation for the THAAD deployment for the anti-missile defense system, Korea focused even more on expanding into the global markets. The export of game led by the top three game companies – Nexon, NC Soft, Netmarble – and the so-called new "big three" – Krafton, Smile gate, and Pearl Abyss – reached KRW 5 trillion ($ 4.2 billion) in 2020, with the new big three achieving 87% of their sales overseas.[125]

Although console and PC games were not developed or started by Korea but rather overseas, the time lag is not significant. Mobile games started 10 years later than Japan, but Korea quickly caught up. It has been rediscovered and reaffirmed that, in competition that starts with similar conditions or timing, Korea's speed and imagination can certainly provide a winning foundation.

The same explanation applies to e-sports. Although Korea did not develop or initiate e-sports, Korea has entered the market that the United States had dominated, and Korean e-sports games' presence has continued to grow. Additionally, the number of professional players and the scale of prize money have reached global levels. In other words, Korea's share in global esports prize rankings and winners is rapidly increasing. In March 2021, the finals of the '2021 PUBG Global Invitational,' a battleground game developed by Korea's Krafton, drew simultaneous connections from 10 million people in dozens of countries.[126]

---

[124] Maeil Business, January 25th, 2018
[125] Maeil Business, October 6th, 2020, A5
[126] Chosun Economy, June 8th, 2021, B3

While the United States dominates the PC game league, Korea is relatively more advantageous in mobile e-sports. Korea also excels in applications. Smile gate's game 'Crossfire', developed in 2007, was successful on its own, but it was developed as an e-sports game in 2013, founded as a global pro-league, and reportedly became a huge success as a 36-episode drama 'The King's Avatar' in China in 2020. A contract for the first movie adaptation of a domestic game was signed, and there are plans to build theme parks in Shanghai and Suzhou as offline business.[127] Changes are natural, but the speed of change cannot be the same for everyone.

The global expansion of K-content, such as K-pop, dramas, and games, created with the latest technology 5G, is naturally faster. Since Korea has a competitive edge in latest technology, its content can build up that strength, resulting in a synergy effect. The recent active overseas expansion of 5G content by the three major Korea telecommunication companies is an example of this.

5-8 Expansion and Growing Speed of K-Wave

In addition to the areas individually discussed above, there are more sectors that are actively expanding and influencing the world, such as animation, OTT industry, classic music and food (K-Food), etc.

The classical music genre is equally thriving as the K-pop industry. In the past, only a handful of musical talents surprised and moved the nation by winning a prize in an international competition despite an unsupportive background and environment. These days winning an international competition is no novelty. In most worldwide competitions such as the Tchaikovsky Competition, Queen Elisabeth Competition, Van Cliburn Competition, Chopin Competition and many others, finding a Korean winner's name is becoming a normal routine. Korean musicians are actively engaged in famous overseas orchestras, ensembles, choirs and other groups. You can easily find Korean names in the Vienna Boys Choir. Other genres such as musical theater, composition, ballet, dance, fine-arts and sports reflect this also. The point here is that these developments are not spontaneous events and show the development of the current Korean culture.

---

[127] Maeil Business, June 25th, 2021, A5

As mentioned before, these phenomena did not occur abruptly, but they are following the interaction of cultural software and atmosphere, thanks to the economic power led by the hardware and industrial sector. Furthermore, these phenomena should be understood as a process and result of mutual influence, rather than individual and isolated effort. The crossover field, which transcends both tradition and fashion, is also rapidly expanding, which is a noteworthy phenomenon.[128]

The same context applies to sports. While the Korean sports market has grown rapidly in many fields including baseball and soccer, the overseas expansion of talented individual players has become more active, reflecting the changing landscape. In the past, there was a term called the 'Se-Ri Pak Moment,' meaning if one person succeeds, several others follow, creating a boom in nurturing young female golf players from childhood. As a result, Korea has become a world-renowned powerhouse in women's golf, often surpassing even the golf powerhouse UK and the strongest nation, the United States. All of this has happened within just 20 years after the Se-Ri Pak phenomenon.

Along with professional golf, amateur golf is growing at an even faster rate, with the Korean golf population exceeding 6 million as shown in Figure 3-13. In the past, considering the cost and conditions, it was mainly focused on middle-aged or older male with economic affordability, but currently the number of women and younger generations is growing at a surprising speed. Various factors and reasons such as economic conditions can be found, but it is difficult to find any decisive reason other than K-speed.

The same applies to Korean food and ingredients that are welcomed and popular around the world. When the author was studying in the United States in the 1970s, Japan was making her mark worldwide. At that time, one of the most expensive and popular menu items in major cities was Japanese 'sushi'. It was a time when many Americans looked at Japan with awe. The author also remembers that traditional Japanese theater performances like Kabuki attracted considerable attention. It is reported that in the heart of London, Korean-style street toast is popular, with long lines forming.[129] Toast is originally a British food.

---

[128] Chosun Ilbo, September 16th, 2021, A16

[129] Seungyoon Kim, The world of taste, Chosun Ilbo, February 24th, 2022, A33

The spread of the Korean Wave inevitably leads to an increase in demand for the Korean language(Hangul) as means of communication. With over 100 million Hallyu fans worldwide, the Ministry of Education developed Korean language textbooks for elementary and secondary school students abroad. A total of 8 different types of textbooks have been developed, primarily utilizing lyrics and music videos from the popular band, BTS. The learning and promotion of Hangul is rapidly and seriously progressing worldwide, primarily due to the significant influence of K-pop.

Moreover, the number of King Sejong Institutes, which promote the Korean language, has increased 27 times from 3 countries in 2007 to 82 countries in 2021, with 235 institutes established. The number of learners has increased around 103 times from 76,000 to 7.4 million. It is said that there are 8 million Korean learners on Duolingo, a global language-learning app. Hangul courses appear during prime time on Vietnamese terrestrial TV, and the number of Korean language courses and students in prestigious universities in the United States and the United Kingdom are also increasing significantly.[130] The establishment of courses at universities is not merely a policy to respond to temporary increase in demand. In the past, Japanese culture spread significantly worldwide as Japan economically stood out, but its scope, speed, and extent are incomparable to the Korean Wave.

As mentioned in various parts of this book, for a long time, Japan was ahead of Korea in many aspects not only because of the history of colonization but also because she was so far ahead of Korea in various sectors that it was difficult even to catch up. However, in a very short period of time, Korea has almost caught up economically with Japan and is expected to overtake Japan in some macroeconomic indicators (such as per capita income) soon[131]. For the generation that has been around for a long time, this is a truly unbelievable turnaround.

This is not to say, in spite of the fact that the gap between Korea and Japan in terms of economic or hard power remains the same, Korea has suddenly overtaken Japan in soft power. Still at the hypothesis stage and not generalized, hard power and soft power may have a sequential order and albeit

---

[130] Chosun Ilbo, December 6th, 2021, A1, A14

[131] Nihon Keizai, December 16th, 2021-report quoted by Chosun Ilbo on December 17th, 2021

in difference of strength but are companions, especially in terms of sustainability.

There is a Korean proverb that 'if the daughter-in-law looks charming, the back of her head also looks pretty.' The continuous expansion of the Korean Wave can also be applied in the same context. In Korea, it was once a common perception that everything foreign was superior and better due to extreme poverty and poor living conditions. This has reversed. However, without change and innovation, this reversal can quickly become stale. The same applies to the economy and other industries.

Metaverse is rapidly emerging as a new method in communication, exchange and transactions, etc. As they start under almost the same conditions, Koreans can be competitive, especially in cases where they are prepared in digital-related fields. More than anything else, a non-obstructive institutional environment and a supportive atmosphere will be the factors for success. This is an opportunity for Korean speed to enable a new breakthrough.

Chapter 6

Cultural, Social and Anthropological Considerations of K-Speed

'Does the 'K-speed' really exist?' This question is a grand proposition that needs to be explored and proven through history, geography, sociology, anthropology, biology, and medicine, among other fields. Even aside from academic debates specific to each field, Korea in the past 20th century, and even more so post-liberation, could affirmatively answer this question. However, it is uncertain whether this would still be the case in the 21st century and beyond.

What kind of people are Koreans? What potential and flaws do they possess? There has been considerable research and discussion on these questions. Of course, the 'K-speed' could be a phenomenon that appears according to the ethnic identity and relative status of Koreans, so these studies should form the basis. However, this discussion aims to approach the attribute of speed possessed by Koreans in a slightly different way from previous approaches. That is, it aims to find an answer to the question above through several observable characteristics.

6-1 Physical Aspects

(1) Body Type

Firstly, there are characteristics of body type. Body types may be classified into Southern and Northern types around the globe, and in this case, Koreans belong to the Northern type with an oval face, flat back of the head, and a tall vertical forehead. In terms of talents, they belong to the 'intermediate type talent,' which is a mix of the northern type with a bit of the southern type. This is said to give them a competitive edge in ice sports where quick reflexes are absolutely necessary. The well-known ability of Koreans to bond and overcome hardship, and their familiarity with the 'Ppalli Ppalli' (quickly quickly) culture, are also attributed to these traits.

This observation is an attempt to explore any possible correlation between body type and speed.

As an interesting example, Professor Choi Chang-seok of Myongji University, Korea explains the difference in facial shape as the reason why Kim Yuna, who won the 2013 World Figure Skating Championship singles event, outranked Japan's Asada Mao, who finished third. Figure skating, which requires extensive use of back and leg muscles and strong mental strength, is a sport suited for the 'Northern typeface.' Kim Yuna's forehead, cheekbones, and chin all have typical Northern features, while Asada Mao has a face closer to the Southern type. He insisted that Kim Yuna possesses more 'Northern type' human genes, who primarily lived by hunting.[132] While it may be difficult to generalize, it is an interesting observation.

In other words, it is possible to think that we are physically quick due to the DNA and physique of the Korean race. However, it's not accurate to claim that every race with a northern type head shape will have a constitution or personality similar to Koreans. It is needless to say that people living in the North, where ice forms, would be better at ice sports than people living in the South, where ice is scarce or precious.

From another perspective, if one has a generally larger and bulkier physique, he or she would typically be stronger and more powerful, but his or her agility would be relatively lacking on average. It cannot be argued that agility in action is directly linked to speed of thought or judgment, but it is equally difficult to argue the opposite.

(2) Hand Dexterity and Agility

Physical speed refers to the quickness of feet, hands, or movements. The rapid economic growth achieved by Korea in the last century was a miraculous event unparalleled in the world. Upon analyzing the causes, in this context, we can prove that the physical and cultural attributes of Koreans supported this. For example, the main export items in the early days of Korean industrialization in the 1960s were products like wigs, sewn goods,

[132] Chosun Ilbo, People & News, March 18th, 2013

and running shoes. For these industries to be internationally competitive, they required not only cheap labor but also the agile and precise hand movements of female workers. Physically, Koreans' hands are, on average, smaller and less thick compared to Westerners, providing physical conditions that allow for quick and precise handling of products. It goes without saying that Korea had a comparative advantage in the assembly of high-precision electronic components and other areas during times when automation had not yet advanced.

Another example of quick hand movements can be seen in money counting. In the past, when there were no currency counting machines, bundles of money were placed between the thumb and forefinger of the left hand, and the money was counted quickly by flipping each note with the right thumb and forefinger. This was a speed that rivaled the speed of the money counting machines used in banks today. Even now, by watching various foreign banks and individuals count money one note at a time, we can infer just how fast and accurate our hand movements are. In the same dimension, the speed of the abacus, which is no longer used, was at a level that did not lag behind electronic calculators. The abacus was always used in banks and commercial transactions, and it was never slower than today's calculators for skilled professionals and was no less accurate. Mental arithmetic was taught alongside abacus instruction, and it was no less efficient or speedy than today's calculators. This is something that cannot be done if one does not have a physically quick hand movement.

This speed and precision are not just a thing of the past. At the Yeongdeok Chukdo Fishery Port's seafood processing center, in Gyeongbuk Province, the work of preparing squid is mainly done by women in their 60s to 80s, who can take out intestines of a squid in just three seconds, working faster than machines. They can process 600 squids per hour.[133] This is an inherent ability of Koreans. Perhaps most skilled Koreans can do it.

In the early 2021 film "Minari," which garnered attention in the global film industry, the protagonist's job, a Korean immigrant to the United States, was a chick sexer/tester, which also required delicate hand movements and was a popular job for early Korean immigrants in the United States after the 1960s.

---

[133] Why Section, Chosun Ilbo, December 19th-20th, 2015

Another example is the grafting of cacti, which requires delicate hand movements. On average, 1,500 to 1,600 grafts are made per day, with a grafting success rate of 70-90%. This success rate is more than double that of competitors in China and other countries with the same East Asian cultural background.[134] It's possible because they are Koreans.

In the 21st century, Korea is proud of its precise and sophisticated surgical techniques in medical technology. Foreign doctors admire the delicate hand movements and relative speed of Korean medical professionals.[135] Even in robotic surgery, which uses machines, delicate hand movements are still necessary. The Senior Vice President of Intuitive, a US company that manufactures and sells the most robotic surgical device 'Da Vinci,' said in an interview with the media that their development engineers study how to improve their surgical equipment by watching the surgical technique of skilled Korean surgeons with excellent hand movement.[136]

"Korean doctors are the best in the world in laparoscopic techniques and robotic surgery - surgeries that take two hours in Korea take American doctors four hours," say medical experts. They argue that the unique dexterity of Koreans and the 'quick-quick' spirit, a characteristic of Korean culture, serve as significant advantages in the overseas expansion of Korean hospitals. Minimizing patient discomfort by making as few incisions as possible and using endoscopes instead of scalpels is a trend in modern medicine, and Korean doctors with excellent hand skill have an innate international competitiveness in this field.[137]

This is another example of a medical procedure. Stroke patients must be given clot-dissolving treatment within three hours of onset to avoid sequelae - from October 2007 to December 2008, over 400 stroke patients who came to the emergency room of this hospital completed imaging tests within an average of 15 minutes and clot-dissolving treatment within an average of 45 minutes at Hallym University Sacred Heart Hospital. The American Stroke Association recommends completing imaging tests within

---

[134] Business Section, Chosun Ilbo , January 1rst, 2011

[135] As an example, plastic surgery requires agile and meticulous hand movement and Korean doctors are famous for this. An increase in income and general lifestyle attracts many foreign patients as well.

[136] Maeil Business, Date unsure, 2019. A20

[137] Chosun Ilbo, November 29th, 2010

25 minutes and administering clot-dissolving treatment within 60 minutes. The above mentioned hospital received an A rating in 9 categories in a stroke treatment appropriateness evaluation conducted by the Ministry of Health and Welfare and the Health Insurance Review & Assessment Service in 2008... The shorter the time it takes to administer clot-dissolving treatment, the better the treatment results for stroke patients, so efforts must be made to further streamline the process after patient transfer and arrival at the emergency room.[138]

It is an accepted fact that the United States is more medically advanced than Korea. The treatment times set by American hospitals or societies are based on the measurements derived from their own environments and experiences. Shortening the time beyond that standard is something that can be accomplished without issues only in Korea, where quick treatment is possible.

While the automation of airports worldwide is progressively reducing the difference, the speed of immigration processing at airports during international travel was unsurpassed in Korea. That is, the time taken at Korean airports for procedures where passports and visas are manually checked was significantly shorter than at any other international airport. From my experiences and observations while traveling around the world for a long time, it was apparent that, although immigration officials in every country do not intentionally delay the process, there was a distinct difference in the speed of processing compared to Korean airports.

(3) Chopstick Using Culture

There are only a few countries where chopsticks are mainly used for meals, such as Korea, China, Japan and some Southeast Asian countries. Among them, Koreans are the most adept at using chopsticks. Chinese chopsticks are thick and long, emphasizing their function of lifting or pushing food rather than picking up side dishes or objects. Japanese chopsticks allow for more refined manipulation compared to Chinese chopsticks, but wooden ones (waribashi) are not as thin or pointed at the ends, making it difficult to pick up small and delicate items. In contrast, Korean chopsticks are gener-

[138] Chosun Ilbo, August 25th, 2010

ally thin and pointed, making it possible to lift even tiny items like grains of rice. Koreans do not lift their rice bowls while eating like the Chinese or Japanese, perhaps because they can scoop up side dishes and rice without spilling. Until now, lifting rice bowls has been paradoxically labeled as a sign of table manners.

In the 1980s, when studies on the economic development of four Asian countries of Korea, Singapore, Taiwan, and Hong Kong (also known as the Four Asian dragons, Asian NICs or Asian NIEs) for rapid growth were popular, there was an active search for finding commonalities among these countries. One of the hypotheses suggested was that they belong to the Confucian or chopstick-using cultural sphere. It may be worth revisiting this idea.

The refined and fast finger movements might be related to the physical, physiological, or structural characteristics of the hand, but training plays a significant role as well. The continued use of chopsticks by generations would have improved precision and accuracy, allowing fingers and hands to perform other tasks quickly. This is one of the blessings inherited by the Korean people.

6-2 Personality and Ability Aspects

(1) Ability to Act Fast (1)

There is scarcely any research or data concerning whether the Korean people have traditionally possessed a relatively quicker disposition and constitution compared to other ethnicities or groups. However, a few examples can be cited to infer the culture or temperament of quickness.

1) A long time ago, a typical expression used by Koreans to describe the temperament of a Chinese person was 'manmandi' which can be interpreted as a comparison that suggests Koreans are not like the Chinese. In other words, when Koreans thought of Chinese people in the past, they imagined a slow pace of walking, talking and reacting to various tasks with clasped hands. Of course, this image is vastly different from the Chinese people we interact with or imagine today. Nonetheless, it may

be inferred that Koreans have been relatively more agile than the Chinese since ancient times.

2) An example that illustrates the characteristics of Koreans and Korean companies is a suggestion by a German company that has expanded into Korea. They recommend capitalizing on Korea's quickness to build it into a technological hub in Asia. "Korea has a truly unique market, possessing something different from Europe and even neighboring Asian countries.... We were extremely surprised to see that tasks that usually take 2-3 months in Europe were perfectly concluded within 10 days in Korea. Koreans have the advantage of being able to handle work faster than even the meticulous Japanese or the Chinese who still lack strategic thinking."[139] Though this comment is a bit dated, it appears to be a sharp observation from an outsider based on experience.

3) It is necessary to examine whether such traits existed in the past, either culturally or at the level of DNA. One example is as follows: "'Speed' is also our great heritage. During King Jeongjo (1752-1800)'s reign, Hwaseong was designed as a new city, expected to be completed in 10 years. But it was finished in just 2 years and 9 months. The potential for being an internet powerhouse didn't just fall from the sky. We cannot overlook the striving for first place, the competitive investment, the sophisticated 'fingertip culture' evident in chopstick use and the 'persistent affection for human life' that enables us to create great dramas."[140] This demonstrates the remarkable results achieved through the speed of work, supported by technology and ability. While there are certainly many examples of speedy construction in countries throughout history, the fact that this speed was achieved more than 200 years ago is an impressive record.

4)"Hanyang (Seoul) Fortress... covered around 18.2 km and was designed as an earthen wall on flat ground and a mountain fortress on hilly terrain. To complete this massive and urgent project during the agricultural off-season, 118,000 people from all over the country were mobilized in the first and second lunar months of 1396, completing most of the fortress

[139] Interview article with Gauze Bayer Korea CEO, Chosun Economy No. 27584

[140] "Koreans' agility for learning and quickness in anything", Chosun Ilbo, April 3rd, 2007. 04. 03

walls in 49 days. In the fall off-season, during the eighth and ninth lunar months, another 79,400 people were mobilized for 49 days to complete the Dongdaemun (East Gate) area that wasn't finished in the spring, as well as the four main gates and four small gates.... Considering the population of Seoul was around 100,000 at the time, it was an enormous construction project with 872 casualties."[141] Even if it was forced labor that mobilized many people and even if meticulous work plans were established, it is hard not to first consider the speed ability of the workers who were able to build over 18 km of fortress walls in just three months without any special construction equipment in the distant past.

5) One current example from contemporary Korea is the Korean drama production process, which is central to the Korean Wave currently. Regardless of the merits or drawbacks of the method, it's hard to imagine in any foreign country that the drama script for the day's shooting would be distributed right before filming and that filming would continue until the day before or right before the broadcast. In foreign countries, this is simply something that 'can't be done,' but in Korea, it's possible. And it's done because it's possible.

Of course, a work (product) that can be changed up to the last moment has higher competitiveness. One of the secrets behind the explosive popularity of Korean dramas like "My Love from the Star" and "Reply 1994" in China is the flexible scripts. Korean dramas are filmed while writing the script, reflecting the viewer's reactions - as mentioned by a Chinese movie director.[142] Two key features of successful Korean dramas are strategic agility and communication with consumers.[143] This is also a skill of Koreans. Rather than sticking to a predetermined path based on pre-planning and production like Japan, the ability to revise scripts and filming in response to consumer reactions requires not only intention but also practical feasibility.

6) As mentioned earlier, when we look at the competitiveness of airports, the time it takes to depart from Incheon Airport, which is transitioning to a digital airport, will be reduced from 51 minutes to 16 minutes by 2030.

---

141 www.chf.or.kr
142 Premium section, Chosun Ilbo, March 11th, 2014
143 Weekly Biz, Chosun Ilbo, April 24th-25th, C3

The arrival time will be 11 minutes, which is only 25-30% of the International Civil Aviation Organization's recommended standards (60-45 minutes). The number of lost baggage incidents is only 0.7 per 100,000 pieces, which is only 1/21 of the world average of 14.6.[144] Quick reflex and agile judgment are essential for an efficient immigration process and baggage handling. Even in developed countries, travelers often experience lost or delayed baggage.

In addition, the competitiveness of airport immigration and baggage handling is not only influenced by human factors but also by system and technology. In 2018, Incheon International Airport Terminal 2 reduced the entry and departure times by 5-10 minutes compared to Terminal 1 due to new facilities, and the baggage lines of both terminals are connected, allowing passengers to load their luggage even if they mistakenly go to the wrong terminal. Passport and fingerprint verification are done automatically, and customs declaration can be done through the customs app, making it possible to complete departure inspection in just 3 seconds. This astonishing change is driven by the speed, accuracy, and efficiency of the system rather than human intervention, demonstrating the power of K-speed, evident in areas beyond human capacity.

7) In 2008, there was an accident in Nepal involving the crash of a UN peacekeeping helicopter (PKO). The UN mission in Nepal (UNMIN) requested Korea to conduct genetic testing on all the deceased. With no suitable equipment in local hospitals and a 3-month waiting period if the testing was done in India, the Korean relief team that arrived first on the scene was asked to perform the testing.[145] This was not so much because of the slow pace abroad but because of the speed of Korea.

8) Korean statistics are another example of the ability and will to act quickly. Korean statistics are known for being fast and accurate. In particular, Korea is the only country that releases monthly import and export statistics on the first day of the following month.[146] The global business and financial sectors are said to use this indicator as a leading indicator, praising it for its role like a canary that senses danger in a coal mine and

---

144 Chosun Ilbo, July 15th, 2015
145 Chosun Ilbo, March 7th, 2008
146 Chosun Ilbo, April 22nd, 2011

alerts in advance. Most countries release this information with a lag of at least a month. It happens in Korea not because of differences in system or individual ability, but because it's possible in Korea. In the past, without computerization, everything was processed by hand—a clear testament to the capability and will to act quickly.

9) The COVID-19 pandemic spread simultaneously across the globe, and everyone faced difficulties without being fully prepared. In the initial stage of diagnosis, Korea received recognition for its outstanding performance including the 'drive-through examination' method. This is an example of the ability to make faster decisions and respond more effectively when faced with similar or identical situations. In this case, the speed of Korea surpassed that of other countries, which was an astonishing result. The development and practical application of these innovations should be noted for having been creatively achieved in the private sector. Although Korea's medical technology level and conditions haven't yet reached the stage where they can pioneer the development of vaccines and treatment drugs for this new disease, it's certain that we are demonstrating a pace that's catching up. However, the political and administrative judgment and ability, which lost the early opportunity for immunity and disease control by missing the timing to secure vaccines developed abroad, show a regrettable side of Korean society.

(2) Ability to Act Fast (2)

The essence of management is universal and consistent across time and space. It is difficult to think of sustaining successful management that deviates from this essence throughout history. However, the application of these principles has varied according to the era, region, culture, and race, and many cases have adapted differently to various situations. In other words, it's not the change of management principle but rather a difference in the application method and the result may vary depending on the environment and conditions. Continuing from the previous examples, let's discuss more about the Korean-style management related to speed, which has persisted until recently.

1) "The 'quickly, quickly' mentality is not an object of ridicule, but rather

a blessing bestowed upon the people of Korea. One foreign entrepreneur who has lived in Seoul for over 10 years said that Koreans' 'quickly, quickly' temperament represents ambition and desire sought by those who are unafraid of change.... The 428-kilometer Seoul-Busan Expressway was completed in a record short period of just 2 years and 5 months (1968. 2-1970. 7), an achievement made possible by the 'quickly-quickly' mindset.... Although some criticized it as a hastily made rag, it was the right answer for that time.... The 'quickly-quickly' approach seems to be in line with the wisdom of our mothers who, while peeling an apple, would give the peeled part to children before completion... Now, it is necessary to integrate the 'quickly-quickly' mindset, which has served as the foundation for Korea's economic growth, with laws, systems, and customs to develop it into a new system."[147]

The author of the book quoted above advocates a viewpoint that resonates with us. In other words, Koreans have an inherent and constitutional ability to work quickly. Thus, it is true that Korean society has been transforming by leveraging this advantage. Let's review a few more examples of the Koreans' work efficiency and drive for achievement.

2) The construction of the Gyeong-Bu Expressway, mentioned above, was an impossible plan considering Korea's industry, technology, and financial circumstances at the time. It was an excessive start, promising to accomplish the same length of highway construction at a quarter of the cost and in much less time than Japan, which had far better technology and experience at the time. But in reality, they achieved it in a short time.

The following is a summary of a newspaper report that described the construction situation of the tunnel which was the most difficult part of the entire project; "The goal was to build it cheaply, sturdily, and quickly, and the construction company, supervisors, and workers all went crazy. Hyundai Construction Co., which was responsible for the construction of that section, eventually gave up the cost calculation, and produced and supplied reinforced cement which is three times the price of ordinary cement, and everyone worked relentlessly around the clock. Satisfying one of the goals of 'cheap,' 'sturdy,' and 'quick' generated problems with the

[147] Hur Man Young, People Who Build up Peace, 2007, p101-103, partially quoted.

others. When the goals clashed, 'quick' was usually prioritized."[148] It was possible because they were Korean.

3) Speed alone is not enough; sophisticated technology must also be supported for success. Another example is the admiration of Boeing and Airbus officials for the work at the Korean Air Aerospace Division Tech Center in Busan. "At one side of the factory, 5-6 engineers were working on finishing the raked wing tip. The raked wing tip is a structural component mounted at the end of an airplane wing, reducing air resistance during flight and saving fuel in the process. A company official said, "This part requires a high level of skill, and Boeing highly evaluates the sophisticated handiwork of Koreans in shaping it."[149]

4) Ability, speed, and a sense of mission must come together to produce excellent results. "There was a Scottish 'foul-tongued mentor' behind making Korean shipbuilding the world's number one. He was William John Duncan, who was in charge of technology at UASC (Arab Shipping) in the Middle East. In the late 1980s, when he was about to leave Korea completely, he often told his foreign friends, 'Look at those guys (Hyundai Heavy Industries). They've done what would take 100 years in the UK in just 3-4 years. Now, shipbuilding has to ask those guys.' Hyundai Heavy Industries, which learned technology from him, became the world's number one shipbuilder in 1983, and Korean shipbuilding surpassed Japan to become the world's number one shipbuilding country in 1999."[150]

5) This phenomenon also appears in other industrial sectors. "In the case of deep-sea fishing, Korea achieved the greatest results in the world's deep-sea fishing industry despite lack of equipment and technology, probably because of its speed."[151] Han Byung-gu, CEO of DHL Korea for 35 years, said, "We have grown 100 times and were recognized as one of the best local subsidiaries to overcome the 2008 global financial crisis. It's all thanks to Koreans' tendency to handle everything 'quickly.'"[152]

---

148 Chosun Ilbo, March 8th, 2015
149 Chosun Ilbo, September 8th, 2010
150 Chosun Ilbo, December 10th, 2011. partially quoted from the articles.
151 Hee Moon Park, presentation at the Innovative Thinking Forum, February 28th, 2013
152 Chosun Ilbo, December 4th, 2012

6) "It's rare for a country to develop its own outdoor materials and products in such a short period of time as Korea."[153] "In foreign countries, they are closely watching Korea's development of biosimilar (biopharmaceutical replicas) as it shortens the typical 10-year development period to 5 years."[154] "Has anyone ever seen an airport as fast and convenient as Incheon Airport? Our level of service is now surpassing that of advanced countries."[155]

7)There is another more surprising example: "I planned to have lunch at a nearby restaurant while waiting for my driver's license to be made at the Seoul License Examination Office... 'How long will it take?' The answer from the counter staff was, 'Please take a seat.' Exactly three minutes later, I heard my name being called... The Seoul License Examination Office reduced the need for waiting in line with lightning-fast administrative service. Bus stops with real-time arrival information service allowed passengers to sit and read newspapers instead of standing in line. The system has covered up the often-criticized genetic flaw of Koreans."[156] The aforementioned examples are not possible or achievable in any other country. In other words, they are possible in Korea, but not in foreign countries. It is a joint product of the system and the ability to process tasks quickly.

8)In other words, this fast processing speed, when combined with a system, has a synergy effect. No foreign countries, even more advanced than Korea, could catch up with the speed of Korean service as evidenced by the installation of home telephone or internet connection. People who had lived in the United States, the United Kingdom, and other advanced countries in the past would have experienced that it usually took 1-2 weeks to apply for a telephone or internet connection after moving-in. Until recently, Korea was able to provide connection service on the same day or the next day. It is not that the system of society or companies in those advanced countries are inferior or inefficient, but rather the individual's ability to process tasks and the competitive environment that made it possible. In other words, it is a result of a complex interaction of quick disposition, rapid hand and body movement abilities, organizational

---

[153] Chosun Ilbo, October 25th, 2012
[154] Chosun Ilbo, January 11th, 2014
[155] Chosun Ilbo, July 1rst, 2014
[156] Sunoo Jung, Chosun Ilbo, February 16th, 2011

systems and sociocultural characteristics. This is the competitive advantage we must not overlook and must preserve.

9) In the past, Koreans would often approach service counters and ask simple questions to staff members while they were assisting other customers. Simultaneous multitasking is possible for Koreans, but most foreigners find this impossible or unfamiliar. Now, the numbered ticket system in Korea is actually hindering efficiency, and the country is quickly following the inconvenient and inefficient ways of other countries.

As shown in the examples above, the driving force behind Korea's unprecedented and tremendous growth in a very short period should be seen as a combination of ability, will, speed, and a sense of mission towards work. However, we have to reserve judgment when asked if this is still the case. The admirable speed and sense of mission mentioned above may no longer be possible. The purpose of writing this book is to repeatedly discuss how to utilize this in a positive direction and guide it towards sustainable growth.

Since 2018, the Korean government has been suppressing or prohibiting these advantages or competitiveness that we have enjoyed so far through legal, institutional, or policy measures. For example, 52-hour workweek laws controlling working hours, sudden increases in minimum wage and wage regulations, working method control, punitive measures against management for construction or manufacturing site accidents, and the expansion of union influence. As a result, even if an individual or a group wants to exert their advantages, the system and regulations are blocking the motivation to do so. In particular, labor unions tend to emphasize standardization of work methods and working hours while promoting collective bargaining and struggle, which ultimately undermines their own competitiveness in terms of speed.

(3) Intelligence and Agility

The next proposition to consider is the relationship between the ability to act quickly and the brain. Generally, it is a natural phenomenon that clearer thinking and faster judgment come with a sharper brain. We commonly use expressions like 'quick-witted' in our everyday speech, emphasizing speed regardless of context or meaning. If we consider this speed to be related to swift actions or agility, we could argue that the agility of Koreans is associated with genetic factors, and in an extended sense, manifests as a cultural characteristic. There's no need to separately prove that a sharp brain and agile action have a high correlation.

1) In intelligence quotient (IQ) surveys by various global institutions or organizations, Koreans are always ranked first, second or third.[157] One interesting fact is that there is a clear correlation between the national income or economic development level and the average national IQ.[158] However, the ranking of national IQ and some indicators such as per capita income by country do not follow a strict correlation, meaning that they do not go hand in hand in a 1:1 manner.

2) The fact that Koreans rank among the top groups in the world in terms of Intelligence Quotient (IQ) might have enabled our unprecedented rapid growth in the world so far. However, there has been no academic research or claims thus far stating that a nation's high average IQ is an absolute factor in economic growth or development. A high IQ could greatly contribute to efficient or fast work, but after a certain point, it could potentially become a hindrance or obstacle. Despite having the highest IQ, the overall conditions and perseverance and consistency of individuals or organizations may have been lacking.

One interesting observation is that Israelis, who resemble Koreans in many ways and lead the world in technical skills, particularly in the field of startups, have a significantly lower average IQ than Koreans. What is reaffirmed here is that while a high IQ is a necessary condition, other supporting conditions need to be met for exceptional intelligence to be fully demonstrated. It should be noted that IQ statistics may vary depending on the entity measuring or compiling the statistics.

---

[157] www.damoadamoa.tistory.com, www.m.tip.net>question, February 13th, 2010
[158] Such surveys can be found in various sites. For example, http://m.blog.naver.com

rank	country	IQ	rank	country	IQ
1	Hong Kong	107	13	United Kingdom	100
2	Republic of Korea	106		Singapore	100
3	Japan	105	14	Poland	99
	North Korea	105		Spain	99
5	Taiwan	104	15	Iceland	98
6	Austria	102		Australia	98
	Netherlands	102		Denmark	98
	Germany	102		France	98
	Italy	102		Mongolia	98
10	Luxembourg	101		Norway	98
	Sweden	101		United States	98
	Switzerland	101	28	Canada	97
13	New Zealand	100	34	Russia	96
	Belgium	100	45	Israel	94
	China	100	47	Ireland	93

Richard Lynn, Intelligence and the Wealth and Poverty of Nations, 17p

Table 6-1 *World Average National IQ Scores*

3) An interesting fact is that, as seen in the table above, all countries currently referred to as developed nations with higher per capita income in the world belong to the group with relatively higher average IQ scores. There is no need to prove the causal relationship between these two variables, but it is evident that Korea possesses favorable conditions.

4) While the high intelligence and quickness of Koreans have been confirmed, not everything in this world can be good, so there is potential for smart minds to be used in negative ways. Sometimes, people can be fooled by their own cleverness. However, these instances may be the price to pay for the side effects of having a clever mind and speed. These aspects will be discussed later when addressing the side effects of speed.

5) Another related characteristic of Koreans is their 'Nunchi', which is an attribute of quickness that cannot be expressed in foreign languages. 'Spontaneous judgment' may be its interpretation or meaning. It is a logical conclusion that people with quick Nunchi excel in actions and responses. Even foreigners familiar with Koreans emphasize Korean 'Nunchi' to the point of mentioning it. 'Nunchi' is also related to observation skills.

Quickly realizing and judging a situation is a person's ability and attribute. If a person has quick Nunchi on average, their response and reaction speed will also be faster. Therefore, their ability to adapt to situations is relatively high. From another perspective, Koreans are also evaluated to be flexible and diligent.[159]

6) From this perspective, concerns and emotional reactions are also likely to be quick. In a survey conducted by a US public opinion research firm on more than 14,000 people from 14 countries, including the US, Germany, and Japan, regarding COVID-19, 89% of Koreans regarded the "spread of infectious diseases" as a serious threat, which was the highest among the surveyed countries.[160] As another piece of evidence, as seen in the various tables in Section 3 of Chapter 3, Koreans exhibit a relatively high sensitivity in response to various diseases compared to those in other advanced countries.

7) Due to their quickness, Koreans also display an impulsive nature. As a result, Koreans tend to be in an angry state. In a study on the "Resentment of Korean society" published by the Happiness Research Center at Seoul National University, 54% of the sample subjects were found to be in a state of psychological resentment. In other words, they were under stress or feeling angry. For comparison, the rate in Germany was about 2.5%.[161] While this could be seen as a fundamental aspect of the Korean character, the rapid pace inevitably forces comparisons to be made in front of one's own eyes.

8) A quick temperament can easily lead to impulsiveness and, on the other hand, quickly forgetting and moving on. The 'mad cow disease crisis' triggered by inaccurate reporting on imported US beef by a public broadcaster in 2008 plunged the entire country of Korea into severe confusion, anger, and anti-government protest, contributing to the recent political situation. Yet, in less than a decade, Korea has become the largest importer of US beef.[162] This can be seen as a case where some politicians and social activists at the time manipulated the Korean public's short lived response using an

---

159 Interview with Yohan In(Underwood), Mail Business, June 19th, 2017, A19
160 Chosun Ilbo, September 11th, 2020, A11
161 Myung Soon Yoo, Seoul National University Alumni Newspaper, Vol 490, January 19th, 2019
162 DongA Ilbo, January 11th, 2022

'anti-government denial' frame.

9) In the OECD's comparative national happiness index, the ranking of Koreans from 2018-2020 was 35th out of 37 countries. The suicide rate is twice the OECD average.[163] As shown clearly in Section 3-3-(2), this is another indicator reflecting the nature of not being easily satisfied and quickly becoming discouraged. Not only is the level relatively high, but the rate of reaching that level is also the fastest. Figure 6-1 shows another evidence that Koreans belong to the group of relatively less happy countries among developed countries. Among the relatively less happy group, Korea stands at the extreme point.

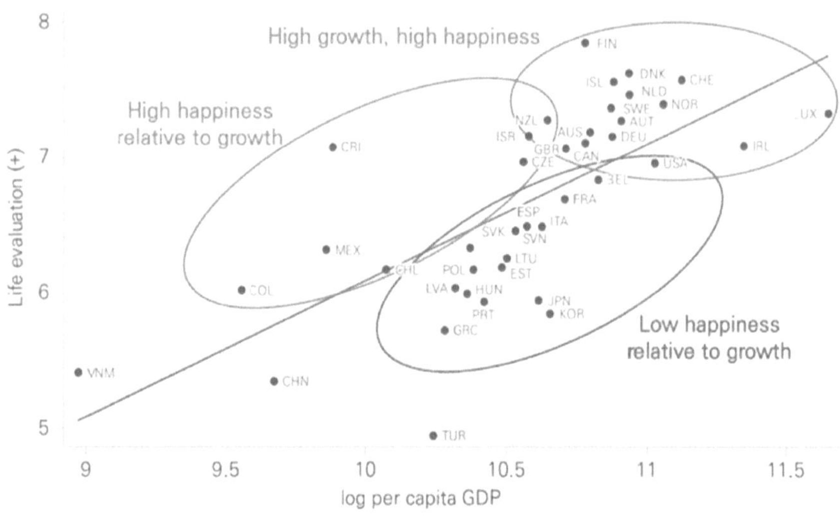

Figure 6-1 *Economic Growth and Gross National Happiness In Selected Countries. Source: Seonga Kim, Research in Brief, 2022-6, KIHASA, 2022, p2*

(4) Absorption and Dissemination Speed

In the speed of adopting and assimilating new and unprecedented things, Korea is undoubtedly leading the way. Koreans absorb western trends very quickly and transform them into more appealing forms as shown in various examples. As the economy and income have grown rapidly, all accompanying changes have been naturally quick to follow. Among numerous

[163] Chosun Ilbo, Reportage Korea, August 30th, 2021

examples, including the previously mentioned spread of apartment living, the dissemination of coffee beverage and coffee shop culture, the smartphone penetration rate and speed, car ownership rate and the increase in the proportion of imported cars, the rapid growth of the delivery industry, the growth rate of online shopping, the rapid global success of female professional golfers, and many more sectors showcase the astonishing speed of Korea. The overall transformation of Korea can serve as a global example of speed.

The fusion of art and culture that resonates with the world, commonly referred to as the Korean Wave (Hallyu), including K-pop, dramas, web toons, and films, also demonstrates the process and speed of absorption and propagation. The 'coin frenzy' in Korea related to cryptocurrency trading that swept the world around 2021 can also be attributed to Koreans' characteristics, regardless of its appropriateness.[164] That is a recent example reflecting Koreans' rapid immersion and speculative nature.

In a country like Korea, where the economy has grown rapidly, the concept of 'supply creates demand', mentioned several times in Say's law in Economics, becomes even more relevant. This is evidenced in the case of the 'speedy Korea' of today, where new products or services generate more new demand. The rapid proliferation of delivery services and the subscription economy can also be explained as additional examples. It means that newly developed or distributed products or services create demand that did not exist before and play a leading role in expanding the market.

As seen from the various examples and explanations given in this chapter, it can be asserted that Koreans are a people who have the qualities, abilities, reflexes, and will to act more quickly than others in many aspects, including physique, personality, history, and culture. The key question is how to lead these qualities and abilities in a desirable direction and maintain them in the future.

Such rapid speed since the 21st century could also be interpreted as having led to various forms of side effects in many sectors such as politics, economies, and society. Given that industrialization was followed immediately by

---

[164] 'Korea's share of coin issue is about 2% in the world but trading volume is around the 10% level' Maeil Business, April 23rd, 2021, A35

democratization, the friction and side effects that followed were probably inevitable. But if the speed was due to anthropological or ethnic cultural factors, the outcome would be unavoidable. Rather, acknowledging the inability to endure, devising proper methods and countermeasures will be a way to enhance or maintain competitiveness.

6-3 Korean Character that Drives Speed (Second Consideration)

One example of Korean traits that pursue both speed and efficiency is 'Bibimbap'. The practice of mixing various ingredients together in one bowl with rice is a highly unique Korean tradition, regardless of its origin. By blending most of the prepared food, the taste is enhanced while significantly reducing the time it takes to eat. Adding 'Gochujang', a hot pepper paste, without exception, also complements the Korean personality. Although it may seem like a simple idea, it is a creative culture unique to Korea, a natural outcome of pursuing speed. Nowadays, as Korea rapidly globalizes, the 'Bibigo' logo has been placed on the LA Lakers' uniforms through a sponsorship deal. In 2020, CJ CheilJedang's acquired brand "Bibigo" recorded global sales of KRW 1.85 trillion.[165]

This Bibimbap mixing technique was applied to an artistic work in 2020, receiving global attention with the performance by Lee-Nalchi band and Ambiguous Dance Company titled 'Tiger is descending'.[166] The seemingly mismatched combination of traditional costume, tracksuits, sunglasses, and traditional helmets, along with the fusion of synth-pop with traditional Pansori music, and the blending of traditional dance, freestyle dance, and modern dance, spread worldwide through YouTube. It is a fitting example of the globalization of the Bibimbap idea, and such ideas will continue to be developed and applied in the future.

This fast pace creates a 'fiery' character and constitution that is reflected in the palate. Spicy food can cause some pain and discomfort, but Koreans have transformed this sensation into a form of pleasure. The dietary habit of deliberately choosing and eating spicy peppers is becoming widespread. The same can be said about eating salty food. It is the unique

[165] Chosun Economy, September 23rd, 2021, B8
[166] Chosun Ilbo, November 8th, 2021, A8

Bibimbap (mixing) culture of Koreans that revolves around speed, spiciness, and saltiness.

The 21st century is often referred to as the age of creation, innovation, and convergence. Creation is the fruit of imagination. Innovation is about attempting change and pursuing speed, while convergence is a combination of imagination and creativity, resembling the principle of Bibimbap. These elements align well with the essential attributes of Korea and Koreans.

In the same vein, the characteristic of enduring and even enjoying heat is something that foreigners might not understand. An outsider might not understand the expression 'It's so refreshing' when entering a hot bath. Not only do Koreans enjoy the heat, they also do not hesitate to spectate it, as seen in the large crowds that gather to watch a fire scene.

Contrarily, there is another extreme of deliberately preparing and enjoying cold food. Foods like Dongchimi (radish water kimchi), cold noodles, and cold soup are enjoyed even in cold regions, which is rare among other ethnic groups. Imagine eating Pyongyang-style cold noodles in the severe cold of winter in the North, when heating was not proper. This is a phenomenon that other ethnic groups cannot understand. It could have been an unconscious way to control the fire in one's heart with cold food. This is evidence of a fast and urgent personality.

Every language has abbreviations. Long words or compound words are hard or difficult to pronounce, so there are abbreviations that only pronounce the first letter or only take the first part of a compound word. Although it's not systematically researched, there may be no language in the world that uses as many abbreviations or acronyms as recent Korean. Even within Korea, abbreviations that are almost incomprehensible are increasing daily for generations who do not frequently use YouTube or SNS. Even official media such as newspapers and broadcasts are increasingly using abbreviations. It is hard to explain this phenomenon except as a preference for speed from both the writer and the receiver.

Another characteristic of Koreans is the repetitive use of exaggerated adjectives in expressions to emphasize one's emotional state. The use of exaggerated expressions like 'so', 'extremely', 'tremendously', and 'incredibly' in daily life or creating new words to convey images quickly has led to a rapid change in language use. This can be seen as another aspect of the pursuit of speed.

It goes without saying that speed is emphasized and changes are rapid in consumption habits, patterns, trends, and other aspects. As an example, the CEO of Wanaco, owned by Calvin Klein, which can be considered the origin of jeans production and fashion, said, "The Korean market is overflowing with energy, and the jeans trend is the fastest."[167] The timeline of this quotation is out of date in terms of K-speed.

6-4 Determination and Ability to Accomplish

Completing tasks quickly requires both the motivation and will to do so, as well as the ability to accomplish tasks at a fast pace. Even if one has the motivation to work quickly, it is impossible without the ability, and conversely, even if one has the ability, they won't hurry unless they have the will to do so. Nations that possess both of these traits are not well known in the world, and it's rare to find such persistence historically.

The Korean diaspora of the past century is a historical aspect and evidence of the will and ability for speed that the Korean people possess in their attempts to overcome their hard situation. The numerous hardships and adversities that the Korean nation has faced over the past 100 years and the process of overcoming them are remarkable evidence. It's deeply related to genetic traits that our ancestors who had to leave for Manchuria and Far East Russia, either voluntarily or involuntarily, during the late Joseon era(1890s-) and the Japanese colonial era (1910-1945) overcame all difficulties and settled down and took root in those places. Especially, if Russia and China had not been communized, the sphere, status, and activities of the local Korean community would be significantly larger than now.

From that perspective, the forced and sudden displacement of 170,000 Koreans (also known as Koryo people) living in regions such as Sakhalin and the Far East Russia by the Soviet dictator Stalin in 1937 to Central Asia (Kazakhstan), a distance of 6,000 kilometers, and the ability to survive till the end and successfully take root locally is undoubtedly a product of a

---

[167] Chosun Ilbo, March 30th, 2012

special will and ability that other ethnic groups could not have demonstrated. The ability to adapt quickly to adverse environmental changes and conditions must have been the driving force to overcome hardships.

The early 1900s saw Koreans leaving for the United States by contract labor on sugar cane plantations in Hawaii, which is also an aspect of the rapid achievement motivation that has allowed the current Korean-American community to survive. Leaving a home that their ancestors lived in for generations and deciding to dive into an entirely unfamiliar and uncertain environment, along with overcoming all kinds of hardships and difficulties in the new country, speaks of their will and ability to adapt quickly. It's noteworthy that they chose to leave their homeland voluntarily, not through coercion but through invitation and recruitment. Even though the actual contract conditions were poor, similar to slavery on the farm, many remained in the local area or moved to the mainland U.S. to settle and establish their homes after the contract period ended.

The Oscar-winning movie 'Minari' in 2021, which captivated the world, is a story about the second generation of Korean immigrants after the Korean War, which began in earnest in the 1960s. The election of three Korean-American Federal Representatives in the 2020 U.S. Presidential election is not a coincidence.

The agricultural migration to South America from the 1960s and the movement of nurses and coal miners to Germany are more recent examples. If we speculate on why the host countries accepted or invited Koreans at that time, the answer is clear: they recognized the Koreans' ability for speed and their will to adapt. It is said that the primary task initially assigned to Korean nurses in Germany was handling corpses, which was undoubtedly a challenging working environment. In a country like Germany, they could not have gained recognition without working quickly and accurately. The same goes for miners. Recognizing the situation, overcoming it quickly, and not repeating the same mistake is a unique characteristic of the Korean people.

Even today, immigration and migrant labor from developing to developed countries continues, and it is expected to continue in the future. So now Korea is in the opposite situation, accepting migrant workers and immigrants. The situation has reversed in a very short time. However, the surprising results of quantitative scale and qualitative change achieved by Koreans during the last century (the 20th century) have never been seen before and probably will not appear again. It's not just because the situation and conditions are different now, it's about race and people.

Statistically, the largest number of people living outside their home country worldwide is Chinese, with an estimated over 60 million. Koreans, with about 7.5 million, are significantly fewer in number. However, when compared to the current population, about 4.3% of the total Chinese population is dispersed abroad, while about 15% of the Korean population has ventured overseas. The situation for the Korean people is incomparable in relative terms. Even when combining the populations of North and South Korea, the number exceeds 10%. This statistical comparison is something many Koreans themselves are unaware of or don't fully realize. It is not only due to the unfortunate history of the Korean people in the past but also the result of their active efforts to overcome difficult situations.

6-5 Most Distinct Achievement and Its Consequential Cost

Based on the logic and evidence presented so far, it can be argued that Koreans are relatively faster than other ethnic groups or citizens of other countries in various aspects. A proper recognition and evaluation of the leadership's role in harnessing this ability as a growth energy is also necessary.

Due to the excessively fast pace so far, it can be interpreted that various side effects have emerged in many sectors such as politics, economy, and society in the 21st century. For example, it took the UK 200 years, the US 120 years, and Japan over 80 years to achieve industrialization in its early stage, whereas Korea took only 30 years. Furthermore, since Korea has achieved democracy following industrialization, the accompanying side effects were inevitable. If this pace was due to the anthropological or cultural factors discussed earlier, it would be an unavoidable result even for Koreans themselves. Instead, it would be better to recognize and take appropriate measures to enhance or maintain competitiveness. All relative advantages come with explicit or hidden costs and side effects.

It's a universal phenomenon that as income increases and living standards improve, the intensity of one's work tends to decline. Korea is no exception in this regard. Even in such cases, the presence or absence of speed and willpower will lead to different results. Especially since speed and willpower are relative concepts, one cannot discuss the current state based on past instances. Countries that weren't so fast in the past may have changed now. However, changing fundamental bases is difficult.

For reference, it wasn't always like this in Korea. The fact is, in the past, Korea was very low in terms of task processing speed and customer response. The customer service in many sectors such as public offices, banks, and airlines in Korea was not very good, either in absolute or relative terms. It wasn't because they couldn't do it, but because they didn't or didn't need to do it. In contrast, these days, banks and public offices show a level of kindness that could be considered excessive. There are concerns that this now has a reverse effect on speed management.

Chapter 7

Conditions For the Realization of K-Speed and a Trial For Its Generalization

7-1 Conditions for the Realization of K-Speed

So far, we have explained that Koreans are a people who possess a relative advantage in speed and that this advantage has enabled the remarkable development and achievements we see today. A logical question that arises from this is, if that is the case, why did Korea historically live as one of the poorest countries in the world, inevitably falling behind as a colony and a divided nation? This is a logical question. Another related yet different question is whether the industrialization and democratization achieved by Korea in a short period of time is a general process that other developing countries can follow if they try, regardless of the presence or absence of the speed characteristic. And if simultaneous achievement is realistically difficult, what should be the order of progression?

The two questions mentioned above are fundamentally important and require separate academic verification and discussion. However, we will approach them here primarily on an intuition base.

First, let's consider the conditions for realizing K-speed. These can be explained within the framework of necessary and sufficient conditions. To achieve anything, necessary conditions are needed first. It is certain that our ancestors, the Koreans of the past, could think and act quickly due to their physique, constitution, ethnic traits, and culture. That's why they survived for a long time in difficult conditions and challenging circumstances. They had the necessary conditions, but the sufficient conditions did not follow.

Consider the 500 years of the Joseon Dynasty period. The ruling class that ran the country adamantly refused to break out of the framework to which they bound themselves, the ideology of the scholarly learning called Neo-Confucianism, and the worldview of the Sinocentric belief. Concepts or attempts of development, change, and productivity were seen as hazardous materials threatening the system and the status quo. The way to survive in this regime was to hide or suppress the speed instinct that calls for change.

In particular, the social system of Joseon played a decisive role in suppressing the speed instinct. Paradoxically speaking, Joseon could be described as a country of slaves. The slave class population accounted for more than 30% of the total population.[168] Some argue that the ratio was even higher. Slaves were a class in which human rights and property rights were not recognized, and their status was hereditary. If instinctual human desires for upward mobility, wealth accumulation, and improvements in living conditions are ignored, and if attempts to do so bring about punishment or even threats to one's own and their family's lives and survival, there's no need to even contemplate making an effort. Hiding oneself becomes a survival strategy. What is more surprising is the fact that there were quite a few commoners who sold themselves and their families into slavery status due to extreme poverty.[169] It was a closed and desperate situation where innovation or change could not be expected.

Development and growth are the products of innovation. Innovation is an attempt to change existing thoughts or methods, and although it may inevitably lead to conflict and clash at times, it ultimately becomes the driving force of change and development. Therefore, the history of Joseon can be seen as a result of generations of ruling class power preserving and protecting the inherited system, institutions, and ways of thinking. The fact that Hangul, one of the world's greatest innovative inventions in history, was not successfully distributed and used even after the King personally created it, serves as a critical example. If Hangul had been widely distributed and combined with the printing technology, which was at the world's leading level at the time, the status and fate of Joseon in the world thereafter would have been entirely different. Although there were occasional attempts at other innovations and changes, they were rejected and suppressed, and none could succeed. The term 'preservation of oneself' became a survival method for all classes, and this expression is still widely used today.

---

[168] Kwon Nae-Hyun, From Slavery to Nobility, The Long Journey, History Critics, 2021.

[169] Jong-In Park, History of the Land, Chosun Ilbo, July 28th, 2021, A34

The ownership structure also played a decisive role. If none of the results I achieved through my effort and swift action can become mine, why should I work harder and take a risk more than others? The ownership structure was directly linked to the social system. The strict class (caste) system branded any attempt for change as heresy and punished them. Efforts or attempts to innovate were reckless and risky.

The same logic applies in the realms of art and culture. It is worth noting that as Korea made economic advancement and growth, the wide-ranging and simultaneous manifestation of Koreans' cultural and artistic talents also took place. The low social status and perception of professionals in arts and physical abilities, coupled with the traditional suffering from generations of poverty and starvation, resulted in parents firmly opposing their children's decisions to major in or engage in arts, music, or sports. This opposition came through parental authority or refusal of financial support. This was because of an experiential and probabilistic judgment that their beloved children might find it difficult to maintain a livelihood and properly manage a household in the future as well as in the current social atmosphere. It was a rational decision in situations where a stable life, where one can properly feed oneself throughout their entire life, was not guaranteed for their children.

Exemplifying talent in these fields was quite the opposite of today's circumstances where wealth, honor, and social status are assured together. This rapid transition occurred within a generation. The turning point coincides with the period when Korea began to grow significantly.

Alongside economic conditions, social and cultural conditions, particularly those related to a free social system, are also needed. Without a system where freedom of the press and freedom of expression are guaranteed, the new cultural power, referred to as 'soft power' cannot emerge. As there have been no new sprouts or attempts in culture and art from socialist or communist countries until now, it is unlikely to be possible in the future either. This is because diversity is opposite to totalitarian thinking.

At the same time, market demand also needs to be considered. If the demand market for culture, arts, and physical abilities is not broadly developed or formed, it cannot function properly even if there is supply. The fact that the works of impoverished genius artists of the past are now valued astronomically and traded in the market is proof. There can be many reasons for this, but the first is affordability and purchasing power. Additionally, the speed of such change should also be examined.

Unlike natural science or engineering, in social science, areas such as comparing social and political systems or their constituents are practically impossible to experiment. An experiment requires a comparison based on conditions, but it is impossible to deliberately set different social, political, or socio-economic conditions within the same country, test them over a long period, and compare the results. Therefore, it is difficult to make an empirical claim that genetic or individual factors inducing the changes and differences in speed truly exist and operate, and when and how such effects occur as a result.

In this context, the Korean Peninsula over the past 80 years has become a living laboratory, which is the first and probably the last experiment in human history, to verify the correlation between the social systems and their constituent factors, and the individual and collective ability and performance of the factors. Regardless of their intentions, the country was divided by capitalist and socialist forces, followed by a long period of mutually destructive warfare, and after being thoroughly severed, the result of each side's best efforts are the current state of South and North Korea today.

This experiment is so valuable because we can compare the result of the same ethnic group, who have lived together in the same country for over two thousand years, starting anew under similar conditions and adapting over a long period of about 80 years, equivalent to a human lifetime. There's no need to separately explain or provide statistical data for the experiment result and report card here. We can report a valuable experimental result that the outcome varies completely depending on which system (condition) or environment, the same people (raw materials) operate under.

For the unfamiliar reader, the following only four statistical facts are provided by the Korea Statistics Office and others. 1) Per capita GNI: South KRW 40.4 million vs North KRW 1.4 million. 2) Export: South US$ 683.5 billion vs North US$ 0.16 billion. 3)Vehicle Registration: South 24.9 million vs North 0.25 million. 4) Mobile Communication Subscribers: South 70.5 million vs North 6.0 million in 2022. Up to the 1960s the economic condition of the North was better than the South.

Even with the same material, the result can greatly vary depending on how and when it's used and under what conditions. In other words, it leads to the irrefutable conclusion that even individuals and societies with the same potential and ability for speed can produce completely different results personally and collectively, depending on the given environment and conditions.

Through this experiment, it was first proven that Koreans innately or constitutionally possess the ability of speed, and even so, the experimental result shows that these characteristics can only fully manifest when the right conditions are provided. Even if we cannot definitively assert the competitiveness of speed, comparing the potential outcomes from this experiment makes the answer more apparent.[170]

In addition to genetic and cultural attributes, and the political and social conditions raised earlier, there are other conditions required. As previously explained, a certain level of economic and social foundation needs to be established for the advantage of speed to manifest as a sufficient condition. In other words, innovation and substantial change can only start to show proper effect when a certain level of economic, technological infrastructure, and social conditions are in place.

This does not happen suddenly. Rather, it's like the gradual rise of water temperature until reaching its boiling point as internal changes progress and the atmosphere and conditions mature. Various industrial achievements are obvious evidence. A few examples on K-wave (and Hallyu) introduced in Chapter 5 adds more evidence. These results do not suddenly appear or materialize from the parties involved alone. Rather, they are the result of sporadic efforts and attempts in various forms in various fields, until starting to bloom at the right time (boiling point).

As the natural scientific concept and measurement of speed introduced in

---

170 Countries with conditions similar to Korea in the past include East and West Germany and North and South Vietnam.

Chapter 1, Section 1-3-(4), the similar formula $C=\Sigma E \times T$ can be used for culture. The level and size of culture (C) are determined in proportion to the size of energy (E, economic capacity) and the efficiency of technical means (T, both soft and hard technological capabilities). This formula effectively explains the development of Korean culture up to date.

Utilizing this logical framework, more achievements of various forms will continue to appear in the same fields within Korea or many other fields in the future. The intensity and frequency of society's surprise or excitement about these achievements will gradually weaken and become normal, becoming a part of everyday life. This is possible due to the reciprocal upward effect influenced by income, economic power, social atmosphere, and other various conditions. Soon, not only in culture and art, but also in non-peace-related fields, Nobel laureates will start to emerge.

The ripple effects and related effects after the blooming are larger and more widespread than expected. As introduced in Section 5-8 of Chapter 5, the Hallyu (Korean Wave) craze globally sparked a boom in Korean language learning, and as of 2020, Korean is being taught in schools in 43 countries. In particular, during 2020, about 160,000 students learned Korean in 1,699 elementary, middle, and high schools in 36 countries. Vietnam adopted Korean as the first foreign language, and India chose it as the second foreign language instead of Chinese.[171] Sri Lanka adopted Korean as a foreign language course subject for senior high school students in 2021. Of the 115 enrolled students in the Graduate School of Korean Language and Literature at Seoul National University for the 2021 academic year, 41 were international students from 18 countries. In all Korean graduate schools, 39% of Korean language major students are international students[172]. This is a phenomenon that was hard to imagine in the past and is still hard to believe. Choosing to major in a discipline is a decision made based on a medium to long-term plan for one's personal life. It's even more surprising for non-nationals. It would be the result of their judgment that it has value for their future use.

In conclusion, once again, borrowing the lens of necessary and sufficient

---

[171] Sri Lanka adopted Korean as a subject for high school senior foreign language courses in the 2021 academic year. Chosun Ilbo, March 15th, 2021 A6

[172] Maeil Business, May 14th, 2021, A2

conditions, the genuine display of economies of speed or speed instinct requires the intrinsic characteristics of actors (the people and the state) and a certain level of the social and political system. These would be necessary conditions. A certain level of economic achievement, social and educational level, environment and experiential factors would be sufficient conditions.

Therefore, it is difficult to suggest a general path or method for other developing countries to follow Korea, but efficient leadership and a self-reliant spirit of 'it can be done,' along with consensus during the initial stage of industrialization in Korea's past, can be shared and referred to as valuable assets. Korea's precedent regarding the sequential relationship between industrialization and democratization discussed below can serve as a significant reference for any country or individual.

7-2 The Sequential Relationship between Industrialization and Democratization - A Hypothesis for Generalization

Furthermore, since the last century, Korea can be considered the only country in the world that has almost simultaneously achieved industrialization and democratization within the shortest time span, albeit with some time difference. Many countries that still haven't achieved either find it difficult to properly establish even one, which is a global reality. As Korea has set a precedent, it would be beneficial to consider whether other developing countries can follow suit. Naturally, the speed of achievement and the sequence of execution are of interest. However, this section will conclude by suggesting an experience-based hypothesis regarding the sequence of the two.

Firstly, it is essential to define the measures of industrialization and democratization. Industrialization may be viewed as maintaining an economic development level that meets the basic needs of all citizens, along with a suitable economic growth rate that sustains it. A feasible way to determine this could be by achieving a certain level of per capita income (for instance, $15,000 or more or less). Democratization, on the other hand, can be defined as reaching a stage where a regime selection and replacement are possible through free, fair elections.

While it would be most desirable for all developing countries to achieve these two things within a short period of time, if this proves practically impossible and we have to prioritize, what order or relationship could we suggest? It is impossible to prove this through experimentation, so one has to infer based on Korea's precedent and experiential results.

Firstly, we can consider what might have happened if Korea had started with democratization before entering the full-scale industrialization phase. Hypothetically, would Korea have experienced the same growth and prosperity today without the military coup in 1961, which started industrialization immediately after the coup? Those who directly experienced that era would resolutely say it would have been impossible. Only those who lived through the era of chaos following the democratization achieved by the student uprising (April 19) protesting against the presidential election process in 1960 truly understand. This rise gave the term 'Republic of Demonstration', and even saw a situation where demonstrators occupied the national assembly.

In a society where assured democracy precedes industrialization, it is virtually impossible to convince the various social strata of voters to endure and hold out until the completion of industrialization with respect to their desires. This is because a democratic electoral process is already in place. Radical measures that changed the constitution of the Korean economy, like the bond freeze on August 3, 1972, were possible because it was a military regime elected by the public. The groundbreaking and preemptive measure of unilaterally setting a 'green belt' before the onset of urban planning in Korea required foresight of the leader, but the conditions for its implementation were also necessary.

The Bond Freeze and Green Belt Implementation - Korean Experience

One of the problems with the Korean economy until the early 1970s was the inherent vulnerability of the financial structure due to a lack of savings and capital. Financial institutions were largely ineffective, and private financing (bonds) prevailed, creating a structure where business management and economic activities relied entirely on private bonds, making normal business operations almost impossible. At that time, the government suddenly declared a freeze on all private bonds for a certain period and undertook a groundbreaking measure to give businesses some breathing room, marking the beginning of a shift in the economic structure. One may only imagine what would have happened if the government had opted to follow normal and legal procedures.

The unilateral establishment of the Green Belt at that time was also a measure based on the foresight of the leader. Setting aside the rationality of the Belt's boundary decisions, if we imagine what our national landscape would look like today if we had continued national and urban development at the same speed without the Green Belt, if the economy had developed as it has today. The original plans and ideas inevitably become distorted from the moment we opt for a democratic consensus process. It's a similar dimension to currency reform(change) or other similar reform measures. At the time of the Green Belt announcement, there were some landowners who wished their land to be included in the Green Belt area. It was a time when economic and real estate development had not yet begun in earnest, and the concept of nature conservation was considered a desirable thing. Noteworthy is that it was a preemptive measure before the Urban Planning Act was first established.

As industrialization progressed, the plan to construct a highway was established. One of the opposition party leaders at the time, who became the president after the achievement of democratization, physically sprawled out , laying down at construction sites in vehement opposition. It's an experience in Korea that forces us to think about the order of industrialization and democratization.

Among academic research on this issue, Professor Benjamin Friedman of Harvard University (2006) explains the relationship between economic growth, democracy, openness, tolerance, and other moral values, historically demonstrating that economic growth and rise of income promote and support democracy, but the reverse relationship does not hold true.[173] In reality, there is no example in the world after the 20th century where democratization led to industrialization.

Professors Kim Tae-yoo and Kim Yeon-bae of Seoul National University

---

[173] Friedman, Benjamin, The Moral Consequences of Economic Growth, Harvard Business Review, 2006

also emphasize that without successful industrialization, democratic values such as freedom, equality, and fraternity could not have been realized.[174] Furthermore, as the world has experienced so far, successful industrialization from an economically lagging state does not necessarily guarantee a smooth transition to democratization in the next stage either.

The question of the order of industrialization and democratization is similar to that of growth and distribution. Both growth and distribution are important. It is a proposition that neither should be overlooked or neglected. The simultaneous achievement of both is most desirable, but if that is realistically impossible, the decision on the order of the two is not different from deciding the order of industrialization and democratization. Moreover, in most fields such as economy, culture, and academia, they generally develop together, not individually. Of course, there could be a certain time lag in each field. In this process, it is logical and empirical that the economy leads the sequence.

In Korea, the declaration of democratization in 1987 and the end of military dictatorship was the result of a burst of desire for democracy and freedom, as the problem of making a living was definitely solved by rapid industrialization in less than 30 years. Of course, the fierce democratization movement, accompanied by the sacrifice mainly of university students, accelerated the process and shortened the time required. However, it can be inferred that this process is difficult to apply equally to other developing countries today. So, if we were to speak of order, proper industrialization should be the first feasible stage. As an old Korean saying goes, 'one needs to be satiated to know courtesy'. If we accept this realistic order, it is contradictory for the so-called democratic forces to unilaterally denounce and disparage the industrialization generation or the leaders of that time, thereby denying their present.

In this respect, the global fusion of Korean culture, which is referred to as the Korean Wave and also called soft power, can be defined as the third phenomenon following industrialization and democratization. What the leadership of North Korea, the only closed country in the world, fears most is not the economic power, military power, or democratic system of South Korea, but the infiltration and popularity of the soft power.

---

174 Kim Tae-yoo, Kim Yeon-bae, The Time of Korea, Sam & Parkers, 2021

Figure 7-1 *Per Capita Income and Democracy Development in the World(2017)*

As another piece of evidence, if we look at the quartile graph made by the World Bank, which associates per capita national income and the degree of democratic development in the current world as a whole, there are quite a number of countries where the degree of democratization is relatively high, but industrialization lags behind, with India being representative. There are also cases where industrialization is taking place, but democratization is lagging behind, with China being an extreme example.[175] Most of the countries that satisfy both are the so-called advanced countries in Europe and the United States, including the three or four Asian Tigers including Korea, but the only country with a certain level of national scale is Korea (and Taiwan).

During the early stages of Korea's modernization and industrialization, accidents of varying magnitudes were frequent at construction sites, mainly public buildings. This was the result of various factors, but an undoubtedly significant one was the hasty sense of urgency to complete tasks quickly. In the same vein, the phenomenon of achieving democratization shortly

---

175 Dae-Hwan Jang, 'The Korea We Don't Know', Maeil Business Newspaper Publishing, 2019, p424

after industrialization, and the continuous realization of regime change through elections across the left-wing and right-wing paradigms defining the social system, all within an absolutely or relatively short period, is a dramatic scenario and pace that is rarely seen anywhere in the world other than Korea.

Therefore, what we now need is a safe speed, a reliable speed, and an honest speed. Nevertheless, the achievements and advantages brought about by the 'quick-quick' mentality following the early development of the Korean economy should never be denied. However, as we look at the stages of economic development, once a certain stage is passed, we need wisdom and change that continues to capitalize on the advantages of speed while also emphasizing safety, trust, and accuracy.

Chapter 8

Paradox of K-Speed and Declining Competitiveness

8-1 Personal Speed and Social Speed – A Demographic Aspect

Humans are economic and social beings. They make various decisions and actions for the present and the future, considering their own and their family's convenience, utility, happiness, and future. However, the form and conditions of societal advancement achieved by the swift actions of all these individuals can manifest in ways and outcomes different from their expectations and intentions. At such times, some individuals discern or anticipate the change and quickly adapt to the situation. However, overall, or for the majority, they may be bewildered by the unexpectedly different situation, unable to exercise their own adjustment abilities, and eventually have no choice but to passively accept the results that have deviated from their predictions. This is the conflict between the micro and macro aspects, or the contradiction of composition that is introduced in the later section 9-1.

The speed at which Korea has unprecedentedly grown can actually cause problems and unintended consequences due to excessive acceleration in specific areas. This can also lead to crises occurring more rapidly. Among these examples, the most prominent and serious issue is the population problem.

(1) Low Birth Rate and Population Decrease

The best efforts of all individuals, as constituents of a nation, to adapt to changing conditions can result in entirely undesirable outcomes or unexpected side effects for society as a whole. Consequently, in the long term and on the whole, this could manifest in a rather negative light. This outcome can be expressed as the 'paradox of speed' or, in extreme cases, the 'curse of speed'.

The aforementioned explanation and development can serve as a framework or tool to explain two significant structural changes that Korea has been experiencing over the past 30 years. The first is the phenomenon of rapid decline in fertility rate, resulting in a population stabilization or decrease, while the second is the rapid aging of population due to significant increase in life expectancy. Let us first explore the decline in birth rate in Korea, its manifestation, and examine the impact and implication it has on Korean society.

In its early stages of economic development, Korea implemented strict policies for population control, such as the 'two-child policy' to cope with excessive population size in comparison to its economic capacity. She achieved remarkable success within a short period of time and became a globally recognized role model. However, due to the unprecedented rapid economic growth over a short period, the country became entangled in voluntary birth control measures, resulting in a decline in population growth rate and recording the world's lowest birth rate. Eventually, from 2020 onwards, the absolute population began to decrease. The start of the absolute population decrease was brought forward by 8 years than initially predicted, and if the aging that increases average life expectancy had not been achieved rapidly, that time would have arrived even much sooner.

The total fertility rate[176] in Korea it is the lowest in the world, recorded 0.78 in 2022, making it inevitable for the total population to decline even faster as time passes. This is the stark reality today. In fact, the number of births in Korea plummeted to 357,000 for the first time in 2017, and by 2021, it dropped further to 260,000. This represents a reduction to one-third of the number of births recorded in 1992 (731,000 births) within a single generation. Professor Cho Young-tae of Seoul National University stated, "Korea is the only country in the world where such a significant population difference between generations exists, excluding wartime situations."[177] Furthermore, if we do not consider the increased proportion of non-native births resulting from international marriage, immigration, and naturalization, the decline rate will be even faster. It is evident that Korea is entering a phase of population contraction. According to a projection by Washington

[176] Total fertility rate is a statistically estimated average number of children a woman can give birth to during her lifetime.
[177] Chosun Ilbo, January 4th, 2021, A3

University in the United States, by 2100, the Korean population is predicted to decrease by 53% to 26.78 million, compared to 2017.[178]

When marriage and childbirth shift from being natural phenomena to options, the individuals involved have no choice but to plan and predict from a long-term perspective. Particularly, childbirth entails a sense of responsibility for one's future generation, which makes it even more challenging as individuals have to consider their prospects in both the micro and macro outlook.

(2) Decreasing Marriages and Increasing Divorces

Such a speed of decline can bring about fundamental changes in the social structure, causing individual issues to change, and these changing individual issues also cause changes in social structure and scale. This phenomenon is more astonishingly apparent in the related statistics. In 1983, there were 412,984 marriages and 28,549 divorces. In 2020, there were 213,502 marriages and 106,500 divorces. Simply comparing the numbers for the two years carries the risk of distorting the characteristics of the comparison population, but if we simply calculate for comparison, the number of divorces in 1983 was 7.0% of the number of marriages. This figure, having passed through 36.0% in 2000, reached 49.8% in 2020, meaning half of the marriages ended in divorce. Regardless of whether we approve or disapprove of the reasons and processes, this is an astonishing speed.

First of all, if the number of marriages decreases, it is natural for birth to decrease as well. The divorce also has a negative impact on the number of children. As the number of marriages rapidly declines and the number of divorces dramatically increases, coupled with the mutual influence on the average fertility rate, all these factors contribute to a cumulative effect of population decline. Once again, the focus is on the speed of Korea. Even without considering the decreasing trend in marriage rate due to economic growth and development, as well as the increasing divorce rates due to societal changes, the speed at which these changes occur in Korea is not only absolute but also relatively faster compared to other countries.

---

[178] Maeil Business, July 16th, 2020

Another characteristic of divorce is the rapid increase in twilight divorces. In 2020, in the case of Seoul, divorces after 30 years of marriage (20.6%) exceeded divorces within four years of marriage (17.6%). This is another example of the speed in Korea from a different perspective.

The decrease in marriage rate and the increase in divorce rate naturally lead to an increase in single-person households. The proportion of single-person households in Korea was 15.5% in 2000, at the beginning of the 21st century, but it rose to 30.2% in 2019 and further to 31.7% in 2020, more than doubling in just two decades. The sharp increase in single-person households is undoubtedly intertwined with the decline in marriage rate and the resulting decrease in birth rate. Another factor contributing to the increase in single-person households is the growing proportion of the elderly population. The proportion of single-person households aged 60 and above increased rapidly from 7.3% in 2000 to 33.1% in 2020.

The deceleration of population growth or absolute population decline directly and indirectly affects both macro and micro economy, leading to side effects that weaken or decrease economic growth. In a situation where other conditions do not change significantly, a decrease in population and labor force inevitably leads to a decrease in potential growth rate.[179]

(3) Analysis on Population Decrease Phenomenon and Its Impact

Let us discuss the process, background, and consequences of rapid population decline and the increasing speed of aging in Korean society and economy.

1) There is an old saying that 'If half of your children survive, that's a success.' This implies that due to poor nutritional conditions, hygiene, and medical services, infant mortality rates were extremely high and young children were susceptible to various diseases. Even if only half of the children survived, it was considered a great success in child rearing. Under these circumstances, it was instinctively advantageous to have as many

[179] The potential economic growth rate means a theoretical growth rate under given conditions such as population, and other factors.

children as possible. Nowadays, the level of medical care has risen even higher than the standard of living, so we live in a world where virtually no one anticipates infant mortality. In other words, people hardly consider the possibility of early death or mental and physical disabilities in their children. These circumstances become a very important factor in the choice and decision about the number of children.

Currently, among the elderly population aged 60 and above, there are a considerable number of individuals whose registered birth year differs from their actual birth year, with many cases where birth registrations were delayed by 1 to 2 years or even more. There were various reasons for this, such as the sudden liberation, the Korean War, and deficiencies in the administrative system. However, a significant number of cases included delayed registrations due to high infant mortality rates. The registration was postponed until the chances of survival increased because birth registration was cumbersome and difficult at the time. In most cases, the birth year at the time of late registration was applied. As the country rapidly grew and developed afterwards, many people benefited from the rules applying the registered age for retirement, due to the discrepancies in their registered age.

2) As the gross domestic product (GDP) rapidly increased and individual income rose, living conditions improved, leading to rapid changes in lifestyle patterns and the way of thinking. In Korea, one of the most elastic components of household expenditure is child education expenses. In the minds of Korean parents, it is natural to invest more in their children's education and upbringing as soon as their financial situation improves, with the belief that 'even if we starve, we must provide education for our children' and 'we should do as much for our children as others do for theirs.' According to the market principle, education expenses increase not only in absolute amounts but also as a larger proportion of household expenditures. Additionally, as women's participation in economic activities increases and a higher income is needed to match the improved living standard, the dual-income earning in a household gradually becomes a necessary condition in decision-making.

In reality, in Korea, the birth rate and the cost of child education are moving in opposite directions. This phenomenon signifies that conditions for having more children are blocked. In 2020, an inverse phenomenon occurred where the number of births was less than the number of deaths. As a result, from now on, the absolute population will decrease.

3) If the number of children remains the same as in the past, most families cannot afford the drastically increased cost of children's education, and the situation becomes difficult to properly raise even a single child in a competitive society. If dual-income is chosen for the purpose of supplementing income, childcare becomes the biggest obstacle for young couples, forcing them to give up further childbirth or reconsider having children from the start. Statistically, among couples who married between 1980 and 1984, 2% did not have any children. However, among couples who married between 2005 and 2009, one out of ten couples (9%) were childless. This is a more severe phenomenon than the decrease in the number of children in households. In more recent years, among couples who married between 2010 and 2015, one out of three couples (37.2%) were childless.[180]

As a result, the proportion of newborns born to mothers in their 20s decreased from 80.7% of the total in 1990 to 22.1% (60,200 births) in 2020. The proportion of newborns born to mothers in their 40s also increased from 0.4% in 1993 to 5.1% in 2020. The proportion of fathers aged 50 and above also doubled in the past five years. These are the outcomes of the K-speed, resulting from unmarried, childless, or delayed marriages.

4) From 1982 to 2020, 3,843 elementary, middle, and high schools closed. There are schools that continue to operate despite having an absolute or relative shortage of students. Currently, there are 1,488 elementary schools with fewer than 60 students in the entire country.[181] Private academies also face unsustainable levels of operation, but schools, due to the need for compulsory education, have to be maintained. Half a century ago, the country faced challenges with overcrowded classrooms and insufficient facilities, leading to a necessary two-shift class system. Now, we are experiencing the paradoxical phenomenon of worrying about the idle facilities due to the continuously decreasing number of school-aged students. All regions in Korea are experiencing similar situations, albeit at different speeds.

---

[180] 'Korean Birth Report', Chosun Ilbo, February 13th, 2018, A9

[181] Maeil Business, January 16th, 2021, A5

The impact extends to higher education as well. In 2020, the number of applicants for the college entrance test (490,522) was around 60,000 fewer than the total admission capacity of universities and colleges (555,577). This highlights the rapid pace at which the future of Korean higher education and higher education policy face a difficult challenge. Many local universities struggle with an undersubscribed enrollment quota. This issue is not new, but a well-known fact based on statistics. It is also a consequence of the wait till the last minute hold out attitude.

5) The speed of educational attainment among the population is also remarkable. As of 2019, over half of the Korean population aged 25 to 64 had attained at least a bachelor's degree. This represents an increase of more than double compared to 23.8% in 2000, after a span of 19 years.[182] Among OECD countries in 2020, only four countries had a higher tertiary education attainment rate for the entire population, with Canada being the highest at 59.4%. Particularly, the tertiary education attainment rate for Koreans aged 25 to 34 is already at 69.8%, which is globally one of the highest. However, due to the limited availability of quality jobs, issues such as job mismatches and high-skilled unemployment persist.

6) In the past, society expected people to marry as they aged, whether they liked it or not. However, today, as women's social status increases and societal and domestic conditions do not support this trend, marriage becomes a difficult choice when women gain economic capability. Furthermore, in a society where poverty isn't normalized as it once was, men who can't fully provide economically and meet certain conditions fall behind in the competition for marriage, regardless of their personal intentions. These results are another cause for the drastic decrease in marriages.

The proportion of unmarried individuals in their 30s, who should be the prime age for marriage and childbirth, is also sharply increasing. For men, it increased from 9.5% in 1990 to 50.8% in 2020, while for women, it increased from 4.1% to 33.6% during the same period. This trend is undesirable not only for individuals but also for the entire society.

As mentioned earlier, the trend of a significant increase in single-person households among Korean men in their 20s and women in their 30s

[182] Maeil Business, February 27th, 2021, A16

continues. While it can be seen as a result of improved economic power leading to independent living away from parents, it is also evidence of a shift towards living alone without marriage. Moreover, the crucial aspect lies in the speed at which this trend is increasing.

7) As income increases and living standard improves, values regarding marriage, life, and children also change. Furthermore, with the sharp increase in the average age at marriage for both men and women, the probability and possibility of pregnancy decrease biologically. Consequently, the number of obstetric hospitals and specialists rapidly decreases, while fertility clinics, on the contrary, see an increase. The decrease in the number of infants and adolescents also affects the pediatric healthcare system. When demand decreases, the supply is bound to react sensitively. The decreasing number of children, their health status, and disease occurrence are not correlated.

8) Similarly, humans have lived with the expectation that families and descendants will increase through generations. The common expressions we use, such as 'a prosperous household' or 'a declining household,' presupposes an increase in the number of family members or children. Now, even if individuals achieve significant success economically or socially, it is no longer assumed to ensure the enlargement of future generations. Instead, it becomes a personal desire or posthumous hope for the individual or their respective family. The revolutionary change in the concept and expectations of home or family relationship in the context of nuclear families seems inevitable.

9) Of course, the first seven phenomena mentioned above are logical processes that can exist in any country depending on the degree of development, and they provide a clear reason why Korea's birth rate can only decrease further. However, even here, the speed is the issue. Korea is a prime example of a country where the fertility rate, which was once at a very high global level, has dramatically reduced to one of the world's lowest levels in a short period due to rapid economic growth and quickly increasing income.

As mentioned before, Korea implemented policies to actively suppress birth rates while establishing an economic development plan in the early

1960s. However, not even a decade later, due to the suddenly reduced fertility rate, massive budget allocations and various birth-encouragement measures were implemented. There is a need to verify whether the fertility rate would have fallen further if the government hadn't invested over KRW 120 trillion for birth encouragement. There may be problematic issues with the direction and effectiveness of the policy. Fundamentally, it reflects the representative contradiction between the personal speed and social speed in Korea, which may be an unavoidable paradoxical situation.

Governments sensitive to elections tend to focus on short-term measures, leading to policies that provide various incentives for childbirth. However, for individuals in this era, decisions about childbirth and childcare are rational choices based on long-term perspectives. It depends on macro factors such as whether the economy and society will grow stably in the long run and the confidence in parenting, children, and their own lives. Therefore, this issue truly requires a proper combination of long-term perspectives and mid-term strategies to yield effective results.

Since ancient times, in the history of East and West, a developing nation has generated a large population and economic power, and economic power has been linked to military power.[183] In countries where the population remains stagnant or relatively and consistently decreasing, there is no history of continuing strength. One direct factor that led to changes in the power and landscape of European countries in the 19th century was population change.

The same applies to issues within a single country. Outside of the Seoul metropolitan area in Korea, there are serious concerns about the consolidation and potential extinction of local self-governing bodies. As of 2020, 89 cities, counties, and districts faced the 'extinction crisis due to the population decline and were designated as recipients of special support from the central government. In addition, all 250 cities, counties, and districts have entered an aging society with a population aged 65 or older accounting for more than 7%. This also exacerbates the difficulty of finding solutions due to the issue of speed. It is possible that, by political reasons, the population threshold for local self-governing bodies would

[183] Paul Morland (Translated by Seo Jeong-ah), The Power of Population, Window into the Future, 2020

be lowered, potentially acting as a shield to delay extinction or consolidation as a self- governing unit.

While the power of the population may not be a sufficient condition to create a major or strong country, it is undoubtedly a necessary condition. One can imagine whether a country like the United States can maintain its current influence while its population is declining. In the digital age, both in the present and in the future, the level of population will become a key indicator of a country's strength. It is an important condition both absolutely and relatively.

According to mathematical reasoning, once the population starts to decrease, the rate of decline will naturally increase. When coupled with aging due to extended lifespan, the rate of increase in average age grows. The decline in population is a matter directly related to a country's future and fortune, distinct from the reduction in income or other variables. Given the various conditions explained before or after, it is practically difficult for the population to increase again in a short period, making Korea's national power and competitiveness unlikely to be bright or optimistic in the long run unless immigration or other measures are seriously implemented.

A prime example right in front of us, experiencing a decline in birth rates and a declining trend in economic growth, is Japan. In the 1980s, there was a global movement led by the United States, to learn from Japan's emergence as a manufacturing powerhouse. At one point, there was even a strong prediction that Japan would follow the United States as the next global economic leader.[184] However, for over four decades, Japan has been gradually experiencing a decline and deceleration in both population growth and economic growth. In the current situation where China is emerging as a new powerhouse, the once highly anticipated resurgence of Japan in the world economy is now deemed impossible.

However, China is already entering an aging society, and it is predicted

[184] In the 1980s, while the competitiveness of the US manufacturing sector was declining, Japan continued to rise. China was still in a state of closed-off stagnation, and Europe had not yet established the EU. During a tumultuous era marked by the disintegration of the Soviet Union and the reunification of Germany, many experts predicted the rise of Japan with its industrial competitiveness.

that by 2033, it will become a super-aged society.[185] China is undergoing a rapid population decline and rapid aging at a pace similar to that of Korea. The difference between Korea and China is that China is experiencing simultaneous phenomena of population decline and aging, despite its per capita income still being around $10,000. This reality shows that the 'China Dream' may not be more than a dream, in its literal sense.

On the other hand, Israel, which shares similarities with Korea in many aspects, has the world's highest fertility rate, with 3.01 births per woman in 2020. This is due to the societal perception of childbirth, the national support system for childcare, and a nation that holds a strong hope for the future.[186]

This is a topic that cannot be thoroughly discussed here, but from a biological perspective, humans naturally possess the instinct of reproduction. However, in recent times, average lifespan and living standard have rapidly increased, and previously unpredictable mortality rates have significantly decreased. At the same time, artificial and man-made methods such as contraception and birth control have been widely accepted without much resistance. As developing countries achieve economic growth in the future, it can be predicted that countries in Asia and Africa, which are currently struggling with high population growth rates, will also experience a decline in birth rate. Of course, the key factor here also is the speed of change, and statistically speaking, Korea has had the fastest decline in birth rates so far. It is unlikely that there will be any other country surpassing Korea's speed and experiencing a more rapid decline in birth rates.

(4) Counterattack of Population Aging

While fertility can be influenced to some extent through planning, control, or active encouragement policies, etc., aging is an entirely different issue. The increase in human average lifespan is undoubtedly a significant blessing. One of the common changes that humanity has experienced over the past century is the increase in longevity. Although there are still many countries and individuals suffering from hunger or malnutrition, the 20th

185 Son Il-seon, "The Most Dangerous Enemy of Sinicization: Aging," Maeil Business, March 16th, 2021, A33.
186 Kim Se-hyeong, Column, Maeil Business, March 3rd, 2021

century, on a global scale, can be seen as the century when the issue of food production, supply, and overall capacity to sustain human lives was resolved at a macro level as explained before. In other words, when considering the world as a whole, we have reached a stage where actual food production or production capacity can meet the demand for food.

Furthermore, thanks to advancement in medical technology, improvement in nutrition and hygiene, the average life expectancy has increased by 20 to 30 years not only in advanced countries but also in most nations. Korea, which achieved rapid economic growth and recently caught up with advanced countries, has also seen an increase in average life expectancy of more than 30 years over the past three decades. The projected life expectancy for a child born in 2020 was announced as 83.6 years. International comparisons of life expectancy are explained in Figure 3-6. At the time of liberation of Korea in 1945, the average life expectancy for Koreans was 45 years.

This increase places an immense burden not only on a national and societal level but also on individuals and families. Despite an increase in life expectancy, if a country's absolute population starts to decrease, it can lead to undesirable results, potentially sowing the seeds of self-inflicted disaster.

To summarize the changing situation:

1) Due to increased income, improved nutrition, advancement in medical services, the average life expectancy of Koreans has significantly increased in the past 30 years. This has led to paradigm shifts in national politics, society, and family dynamics. According to the Population Census, the proportion of people aged 65 and older accounted for 14% of the Korean population in 2017, and it is projected to reach 25% by 2030.[187] Approximately 1 out of 4 individuals will be elderly. Statistics Korea predicts that by 2060, 44% of the population will be aged 65 and older, nearing half of the population. The rapid pace of population aging, combined with the ultra-low birth rate phenomenon, is reshaping social structure. Some even predict that people will live up to 120 years. If the pace is not rapid, adaptation and adjustment are possible, but sudden changes become impossible to cope with.

---

[187] The aging index also varies significantly by region, with rural areas having higher indices and significant disparities between urban areas.

2) In terms of the speed of aging, Korea is the top country in the world. It took only 17 years for Korea to transition from a society where the elderly population aged 65 and older accounted for 7% of the total population in 2000 to a society with an aging population exceeding 14%, which is an aging society. In comparison, France took 118 years, the United States took 73 years, Germany took 40 years, and even Japan, a representative longevity country, took 24 years. It is an extraordinary record. According to the Population Census, it is predicted that by 2025, Korea will become a super-aging society where the elderly population exceeds 20% of the total population. Japan, which is ahead of us, took 11 years. This is an astonishing outcome. Based on the Population Census, it was projected that by 2040, one out of three individuals in Korea will be aged 65 or older. This will transform our country into an entirely new society. It is an undeniable statistical prediction. 2040 is not a distant future but a reality that a significant portion of the current surviving population will face.[188]

3) In the past, there were grand celebrations and feasts for the sixtieth birthday, as not many people lived beyond the age of 60. The sixtieth birthday, called 'Hoe-gap' in Korean, symbolized a new beginning. The early celebration of the Hoe-gap, even before reaching the actual age of 60, might have been motivated by the possibility that the person might not survive until their next birthday. Nowadays, we no longer hear of Hoe-gap celebrations. As people often live more than 20 years beyond their 60th birthday, it can feel odd to separately celebrate that specific day. The same applies to retirement ceremonies in workplaces, where the concept of a mandatory retirement age is becoming less relevant.[189]

4) In the past, the old saying 'living 70 years is rare and extraordinary' was often used. Even in the Bible, there is a verse that says, "The length of our days is seventy years or eighty, if we have the strength" (Psalm 90:10).

---

188 Lee Byung-moon, Maeil Business, February 3rd, 2021, A14

189 The author joined Pusan National University in 1984 and retired at the statutory retirement age in 2010. In the early days of his tenure, retiring professors would hold grand retirement ceremonies at the main hall, attended by families, relatives, former students, and many others. Back then, it was relatively rare for people to survive until the retirement age of 65, which might have been why such ceremonies were held. Since then, retirement ceremonies are conducted in accordance with increased life expectancy trends. Today, while there may be various forms of retirement commemoration, the grand feast-like celebrations of the past have disappeared completely.

the traditional housing forms such as Han-ok or thatched-roof houses are rapidly disappearing all across the country. It's an inevitable and rational choice to that individual, and it appears as the result of Korea's rapid speed of change.

In 2020, due to the COVID-19 crisis, an income policy based on fiscal deficit was implemented under the guise of disaster support fund for the entire population, followed by a second policy using a selective support method. The third round of support fund has been distributed, and continuous distribution like the fourth round would have been carried out, probably with elections in mind. While one cannot oppose the necessity stemming from an unexpected disaster situation, such an income policy and economic stimulus policy based on fiscal deficit inevitably come at a cost. When the regime's term expires or is not re-elected, the regime can simply step down, but the deficit remains as the nation's debt, passed onto the next generation.

Therefore, it's crucial to consider individual speed and social speed separately. In other words, what may be inevitable or good on a personal level may not always be beneficial for society as a whole, and vice versa. But the whole, society and the individual, its constituent part, are like the two sides of a coin. Although they face opposite directions on the surface, we should not forget that they are of the same entity. If one emphasizes and exerts force on one side, the opposite side diminishes more or less, and if the whole is over emphasized, some parts may struggle or become suppressed, as seen throughout human history.

Chapter 9

Factors Hindering K-Speed - Dragging Down Competitiveness

9-1 Metaphorical Relationship between Development and Speed

Economic development or national power growth refers to an increase or expansion in the capacity of an economy or nation compared to the past. It is measured by the rate at which its output and scale expands. Development or growth is usually a relative concept, so there's always a comparison point. If you are faster than others and that speed is sustained for a considerable period of time, you will feel it yourself, and others will also acknowledge it.

The economic development of all nations in the same era can be likened to a marathon race. A marathon race proceeds with a lead runner or group, followed by the formation of the next runner or group, and this similar phenomenon continues sequentially. After World War II, a country like the United States could maintain the lead for a long period, and in some cases, a late runner could catch up, joining in the lead group in terms of total volume (Gross National Product) being formed by multiple countries like G2 or G7, etc. This group may be classified by different criteria such as per capita income, and growth rate, etc. Within a group, there might be mutual check and balance, but at least within the same group, there is a competitive urge not to fall behind or drop out and join the subsequent group, so naturally, a broad range of groups are formed over a quite long period. Occasionally, a competitor emerges who breaks away from the current group or makes an effort to enter the group ahead. However, as this race is like a long-distance race without a finish line, if you push too hard, like a sprint at the end of a short distance race, or if you speed up excessively, it often results in a breakdown, leading to the risk of dropout or falling further behind.

Attempts are also made to artificially form a group, as in the case of the EU, where they join hands and run together, or try to maintain the group artificially like Euro by encouraging or helping each other through agreements or alliances. This is because they believe that it will ultimately be more beneficial for everyone. However, there's no way to carry and go with a tired or injured colleague, so the reorganization of the group is inevitable in the long run.

In this process, the most important factor is speed. If you can't maintain a constant or similar speed to others, you will gradually fall behind, or eventually leave the group and run alone or change to a lower group. Conversely, due to the inertia of the race, the runner's own physical strength, driving skills and equipment, mental strength, and so on, it is extremely difficult to increase the current pace and enter an unexpected group ahead. All competitors running together within a group share the same goal and are making efforts, so it's not a temporary spur but a very difficult or rare event to constantly increase the speed, first get out of the current group, and continue to enter the upper group. Not falling behind even after dropping out could be a praiseworthy situation.

Speed and stamina are determined by various conditions. For example, there are currently economically advanced countries that have inherited relatively advantageous physiques and constitutions and run in the lead or front groups under favorable conditions. They have relatively abundant supplies and equipment that they have saved, or they can easily borrow, and they also have fat stored in their bodies for emergencies, and they have received systematic running training too.

Unlike actual marathon races, the race between nations has historically been a long one, where it has been difficult and rare for one runner to overtake another and join a more advanced group. Looking at the 20th century alone, several South American nations that were trying to leap into the advanced group ended up self-imploding, not only failing to join, but unable to maintain their position within the group they initially belonged to, in effect, continuing to fall back.

In other words, it is not easy for a runner who was running in the rear group to decide to increase the speed and enter the front group when they judge that the right conditions are prepared. This becomes a necessary condition for development. For instance, conditions such as a thin but strong physique, the endurance and stamina to endure at least for the time being, and promptness to quickly judge and deal with the situation at hand are required. If you decide to leap forward, saving current expenses, purchasing and preparing good equipment, even though borrowed, and learning to run quickly become sufficient conditions for overcoming current weaknesses. This is the case with Korea, which is very rare in the history of the world economy.

Also, if you look a little longer, in a race with no finish line, the nature of this game tends to slow down the average speed. This phenomenon is common to all runners. This tendency becomes more distinct as you belong to the front group. While running ahead for a long time, the body weight increases significantly, and as a result, the body structure and shape change. If there is no other front group or competitor, the urgency to increase the speed and the patience and determination also weaken, so there occurs a sense of relief that you just need to maintain the current group or position. Of course, thanks to good equipment and operation know-how, basic physical strength, excellent food and supplements, and the inertia of speed, maintaining the current position is possible for a certain period.

Historically, no country or region has continuously maintained the leader position or group. There were only differences in the length of time that position was maintained, and this applies to the future as well. The point to note is whether the position of a runner or group is accelerating or at a generally constant speed but still in an upward phase, or whether it is gradually decelerating or in a downward phase. It should naturally be judged comprehensively considering the average speed or trend of the group to which the relevant runner belongs.

Since the 1960s, Korea started to speed up from the bottom group and escaped from that group in a record short period of time, and then continuously increased its speed and maintained above the average speed of the newly caught up group, repeatedly overtaking and now, in terms of per capita gross national income (GNI), it has achieved a miracle-like result of belonging to almost the leading group, and even in the broad sense of gross domestic product (GDP). The problem is that the race does not end here awaiting an award ceremony, but it continues endlessly, so it is always possible for the position to be changed to the front or rear group according to the current speed. Obviously, it is hard to catch up, but not difficult to slow down and fall behind.

In the 1960s, the Philippines was a leading country in Asia. At that time, per capita income exceeded twice that of Korea, and the establishment of the Asian Development Bank in Manila reflected the country's status as second in Asia after Japan. Since then, the Philippines has not been able to maintain its group and has been pushed down to a lower group. If the status of Korea and the Philippines at that time remained the same, Korean workers might now be working as housemaids or wage workers in the Philippines. It's about acknowledging the harsh reality that money explains everything (money talks).

As previously explained, it is not easy for a runner in the leading group to maintain their fast speed from the past or align their speed with the average of the runners in the group. In the case of Korea, who entered the leading group without a significant adaptation period, fundamental factors such as an increased body size, physique, weight gain, diet, and the required change in equipment and technical conditions may play the role of reducing speed. Various regulations and other internal and external disturbances that prevent focus on speed maintenance continue to arise. Justifications and reasons are behind these regulations related to speed and are equivalent to an order to artificially reduce speed.

In many races, including the marathon of today and tomorrow, victory or defeat is determined by speed, that is, being fast. Maintaining a group and position not to fall behind is difficult enough but acceleration cannot be applied. The body size and weight have already grown large, and the palate has become high end and demanding. Furthermore, with so much to consider and prepare for, including newer equipment, maintaining the already decreased speed or preventing further deceleration even within the moved group becomes relatively difficult.

9-2 Principle of Relativity of Speed

In the previous sections, we have demonstrated and inferred that Koreans have a fast attribute and ability compared to other ethnic groups. Based on this speed, over the past half century, Korea has achieved unprecedented growth and development in the history of the global economy in a very short time. It is almost a miracle that, even before half a century has passed, Korea has reached the level of developed countries from the status of the least developed. And we are currently enjoying the benefits of this achievement.

Leadership at that time had a vision for the future generation and interacted with various factors and circumstances, enabling growth in a short period of time. More than anything else, in a nutshell, it was due to the competitiveness of Koreans and Korean industries. Several pieces of evidence are provided to show that the essential foundation of such competitiveness lies in the speed of Korea and Koreans.

However, this speed is relative. In various aspects, if you are faster than others, it translates into competitiveness. But if you become slower than others, it can become a hindrance. The speed of an individual or group is basically determined by genetic factors, education, training and the current situation and environment, but it also has a direct or indirect relationship with the economic level at that point of time, social laws and systems, and various conditions, which can make the speed faster or slower.

The issue at hand is that in the case of Korea, as a result of rapid growth, the economy and standard of living have improved in an unprecedentedly short period of time. Consequently, there is now less urgency or desire to maintain the speed of the past. Conversely, there are now more things to protect, enjoy, and share, making it harder to maintain the original speed. We continue to find ourselves in a situation where it is becoming increasingly difficult to maintain our original pace.

We are not living in a world where we have achieved all our initial goals and can simply enjoy our achievements without burden. Instead, we are living in a world that is even more fiercely competitive and harsher than before. Furthermore, because our standards in all aspects have improved significantly compared to before, we are not at a stage where we need to discover and develop other forms of competitiveness apart from speed and find ways to utilize them.

Whether you are an adult or a child, a business or an organization, in the past or present, the most assured way to succeed is to discover what you can do best and to do it properly and diligently. There are no exceptions.

At the same time, no matter what work or sector in this world, it is not only just the positive aspects that exist, but also the negative, dangerous and opposing aspects. The world is fair. However, a sentiment of giving up the competitive edge we have maintained so far, declaring it too difficult, troublesome, and now risky, and opting for an easier path, is continuously appearing in aspects of Korean society. Speed is clearly a competitive factor, and losing it implies giving up the competitiveness derived from speed. Let me explain the reasons and causes for such phenomena in several ways. First, using the general characteristics and attitudes that humans possess, and second, using concepts and terms from Economics.

9-3 Hungry Pigs and Satiated Pigs

People, by nature, certainly feel differently when they need to use the restroom for physiological necessities versus after the urgency is resolved. The feeling and attitude when it's urgent and difficult to bear cannot be the same when considering things from another perspective once that urgent physiological need is resolved. This is not something to condemn or blame, but rather should be accepted as natural. However, the degree to which this happens could be problematic.

Our ancestors have lived in agony since the dawn of time, unable to resolve the issue of securing food. The fact that this problem was solved for the first time after the 1970s is nothing short of a miracle. The issue of nourishment is a more fundamental problem, different from the physiological discomfort. While physiological issues can be resolved even on the road if it's truly urgent, the issue of hunger cannot be resolved by any other means—it is a tough problem on which life and death hang. And finally, we have been liberated from starvation.

Has this historic milestone led all Koreans to perceive their country as more satisfactory and happier than before? There would not be many people who say 'yes' now. Despite the fastest achievements, the level of happiness among Koreans is at the lower end among OECD countries. There is a far greater dissatisfaction and complaint compared to when living conditions were difficult. New conflicts and resentment of a different dimension have arisen. That's because the way of thinking and attitude before and after difficult times naturally change.

The Bible teaches us that 'man does not live on bread alone,' and there is an old Korean saying, 'One can endure hunger, but not a stomach ache.' After resolving such desperate and urgent problems, more difficult challenges of a different dimension are presented to us all.

This is not an event unique to Korea, but can happen anywhere, anytime in this world. However, the reason why it is particularly severe and rapid in the case of Korea is that all these processes and events happened within a generation, in an extremely short period of time. It's due to the speed of everything happening all at once in a very short time, rather than gradually over generations for a longer period. All of us have suffered from similar hunger and hardship, and while the problem of securing food has been quickly solved, if each person's situation and status become too different within a short period, a new dimension of conflict, dissatisfaction, and anger arises.

That's why there's the expression 'Koreans like to compare themselves with others.' If they feel unfairness, they start to express anger towards others, leading to a routinization of anger. Deep down, they develop an attitude of never wanting to be at a disadvantaged position. Although inequality exists in every country and society, in our society, the sentiment of comparing oneself with others is greater, hence the perception of inequality is amplified. This is because, as explained above, rapid changes occur in a very short period, making it difficult to adapt.

Humans, surprisingly, are forgetful creatures, so we easily forget the past and judge past matters with the lens of present circumstances. It is not easy to compare and make decisions on pressing current issues with reference to the past. Therefore, it's hard, or practically impossible, to ask someone to endure the current situation by thinking what predecessors endured in a much more difficult circumstance.

9-4 Collision of Micro and Macro - Fallacy of Composition and Market Failure

Micro and Macro perspectives involve looking at the same entity or issue from different standpoint. Macro is the whole, and micro is the divided whole, so mathematically, when you combine the micro elements, they should form the macro characteristic. However, if you cut up an apple, you get apple pieces, but the taste and usage of apple pieces may quite differ from that of a whole apple. That is to say, depending on where you stand or look, two perspectives can be in conflict.

A classic example of the contradictory situation referred to as the 'fallacy of composition' in microeconomics is a baseball stadium on a rainy day. When it suddenly starts to rain, all the spectators need to open their umbrellas to avoid the rain. But if everyone opens their umbrellas at the same time, everyone, except for those sitting in the front row, can't properly watch the game. Everyone came to watch the game in the same way, but a contradiction arises when it becomes impossible for everyone to do so. This is a classic example of a collision between micro and macro. While it is correct to open an umbrella when it starts to rain, if everyone does so, it becomes impossible to achieve the original purpose, and instead, everyone ends up with a loss.

In this case, if everyone brings a raincoat in advance and does not open their umbrellas, everyone might be uncomfortable and slightly inconvenienced, but it could also be an optimal solution. However, if even a few do not cooperate or insist on their right not to get wet, it's hard to enforce. Also, it's difficult to ask someone not to use an umbrella while most other people are using one, or to endure wearing a relatively uncomfortable and imperfect raincoat compared to an umbrella. Furthermore, if all the spectators possess rights equivalent to a single vote in an election, there's no need to say more. Even if a raincoat is provided for free to those who have no umbrella, it's hard to get them to wear it without complaint.

Another classic example is a movie theater with a single emergency exit. If a fire suddenly breaks out, it would be best for each individual to quickly escape through the emergency exit, but if all spectators rush at once, no one can escape, resulting in injuries or deaths from stumbling or suffocation. This is a case where the micro-optimal leads to the macro-worst or a disaster.

In the current situation of Korea, although livelihood issues are being resolved, there is a constant clash between the micro and macro. Individually or partially, there are clearly necessary and justified reasons for protection, but these issues often become obstacles on a national or societal scale.

Consequently, they either slow down the speed or completely hold it back, leading to a loss of competitiveness.

The economic system that has been proven to work properly and most efficiently in the entirety of human life, historically verified and proven through various forms of experiments, is the market economy system. China - a socialist country that couldn't escape economic hardship after communization - is prospering today due to the adoption of the market economy system, championed by leaders like Deng Xiaoping. Under Mao Zedong's socialist economic system from the beginning, there were tragic events where tens of millions of people starved to death. Of course, how long and how harmoniously the socialist system and the market economy can coexist in the future remains an experimental situation that requires further observation. The clear conclusion is that the economy moves most efficiently through the market economy[193]

The market economy is fundamentally speed-centric. In every aspect, those who are faster have a competitive edge over those who are slower. However, within the same country or society, those who are slower end up falling behind, resulting in societal problems as they incur losses or damages. Also, unchecked competitiveness can destroy the market ecosystem in the form of monopolies and bring about harmful consequences in the mid to long term. This is referred to as 'market failure', and the role of the state or society is to intervene, primarily through institutional means, to remedy these flaws. This is how market capitalism continues to survive.

However, expecting a government akin to a surgeon, skilled in appropriately operating and suturing the necessary part at the right time, ultimately enhancing the overall health of a patient, is incredibly challenging. In most cases, surgeries, treatments, and interventions are necessary and inevitable on a micro-level, but the effects of these procedures are often inefficient on a macro-level, causing side effects or unintended problems. Also, in many instances, even though the prescribed medicine is unavoidable, it often carries addictive properties. Once the administration of such drugs begins,

[193] Of course, the market economy is not a panacea that solves all problems. The Gini coefficient of the Chinese economy, which has achieved high growth through a market economy, was 0.467 in 2017, already the highest level in the world, and is facing severe income and wealth inequality (Chosun Economy, July 27th, 2021, B1)

it becomes almost impossible to stop, which is a prevalent reality.

In the real world, the market economy is not a panacea that solves all problems. In reality, micro-level measures may treat a specific disease (or problem), yet they do not improve, or rather, might worsen the overall health (or situation). An example of this is the three Fair Economy Laws revised in the first half of 2021 in Korea. They essentially divide companies into conglomerates and big ones, and businesses of other sizes, viewing them in a competitive relationship. Capitalists and workers are perceived in a confrontational relationship. Small businesses and workers are seen as the weak or victims, and large corporations, capitalists, or individuals with high incomes are considered the powerful without goodwill, thus warranting stronger regulation. However, these enhanced protective measures for the vulnerable can only result in slowing down the pace, reducing efficiency. Korea, which ranks within the top ten in global economic power, is ranked 102nd out of 141 countries in terms of employment and dismissal flexibility based on OECD standards, and 84th in wage flexibility. Its economic freedom is rated at 25th.[194]

Conversely, measures intended to treat the macro (overall) situation can cause contradictions and conflicts on a micro (partial) level. For example, the 52-hour workweek law, created to enhance the welfare of workers, has positive aspects in achieving its aim of improving the quality of workers' lives. However, it also negatively impacts competitiveness by ignoring the seasonal influences and the need for concentrated production in certain industries, as well as technical requirements. It also has the adverse effect of stifling the individual hope of small businesses or workers who voluntarily wish to work more and earn more. This is an example of a policy that disregards partial or micro-level circumstances in order to achieve macro-level objectives.

9-5 Institutions and Environments that Hinder Speed

On the other side of the coin, there are customs, laws, or institutional mechanisms that stop or slow down the pace of development. These mechanisms have been working tirelessly to restrict competition from the past

[194] Chosun Ilbo, October 6th, 2020, A3

to the present day. The Luddite movement, which resisted and sought to destroy the mechanization brought about by the Industrial Revolution, is a prime example. From a political or institutional perspective, institutions are a vital factor in determining the speed of progress, as exemplified by the Far Eastern Russian checkpoint operation introduced in Story Box of Section 1-9.

Inherently, institutions tend to suppress, interfere with, and prohibit rather than promote and assist. New things generally clash with the status quo, and the institutions created to accommodate them often have the structure and characteristics protecting what already exists. When running faster than others or during a period of expansion, minor issues or side effects are easily overshadowed. However, when the pace slows down, they manifest in various forms.

Let's revisit the marathon analogy. As a runner's diet improves and nutrition becomes relatively better than before, body weight naturally increases. There are more things to consider and take care of, which makes it harder to maintain the previous speed. Changing to heavier and sturdier shoes, wearing more clothes, and attaching decorative items or markers that weigh down different parts of the body, especially the arms and legs, undoubtedly affect speed. If a complaint arises asking why an item was attached to the right foot but not the left, then it would also have to be attached to the left, further reducing the speed. The bag which the runner carries starts to fill with items to be taken care of, adding more weight. This is where the various regulations born out of growth come into play.

As pointed out earlier, in these cases, there are reasons and justifications for wearing such shoes and clothes, and attaching all decorations or add-ons, most of which have been added through struggles or legislative processes. However, these seemingly inevitable individual add-ons or burdens inevitably slow down the pace. This is precisely the case of the clash between the micro and the macro. In a marathon race, if all other runners are wearing the same or similar decorations or add-ons, the problem might be different. However, if one particular runner keeps increasing the weight of one's decorations or backpack, the speed will inevitably fall, absolutely and relatively. As in the previous example, when it rains, I (we) need to open or prepare an umbrella, and if the person next to me is using an umbrella when I don't even have a raincoat, I certainly need to get an umbrella in addition to a raincoat too.

The most representative example is the labor union. In a market economy, labor unions are essential and can be likened to a shirt that a runner is wearing. The ideal shirt is lightweight, absorbs sweat well, and sometimes provides good insulation. Therefore, if the shirt helps the runner run faster and plays a role in adjusting body temperature or physical condition, it benefits both. Also, due to competition rules, the shirt must be worn, so the runner can't take it off, even temporarily, even though it's hot or uncomfortable.

However, if one chooses to wear thick, heavy clothing that is unfit for one's weight or function, or continues to wear outdated, expensive clothing adorned with various decorations or outer layers like a vest instead of breathable clothes that absorb sweat, it inevitably interferes with their speed. That outfit has a hard-earned history and tradition, making it very difficult to take off or change, and practically impossible to replace with new materials and better designs. Other competitors increase their competitiveness by changing to new shirts or adjusting their add-ons through long historical experiences or compromise, but this is not yet the case for Korea, who entered the front group so quickly.

There can be new ideas to improve the runner's running method, physical ability, nutrients to enhance physical strength or constitution, food for condition control, and methods to assist the body's metabolism and running efficiency. In most cases, they need to obtain permission for adoption or use in accordance with laws, systems, or rules. This is where the clash between the micro and the macro occurs. Due to a variety of reasons, this, that, and these(system, method and rules) were established, and the persons directly involved have been adhering and taking advantage of it. Even if a more effective method can be applied, a strong opposition arises saying that you cannot randomly remove it, change it, or consume it differently. Also, such opposition is mostly initiated by those with vested interests against new innovation attempts. Among the numerous examples that Korea is currently facing, let's briefly discuss three of them.

(1) Telemedicine Case

With the advancement of digital communication technology and AI, there are emerging areas where all diagnoses and prescriptions do not necessarily require face-to-face interaction with doctors. Particularly, in regions where patients and hospitals are far apart unlike in cities, the need for and inevitability of telemedicine increases. As a country with global medical technology and ICT infrastructure, Korea is able to technically support video examination, diagnosis, prescription, and monitoring. However, even patients who need only a prescription during a regular visit, not their first visit, must go to the hospital and meet their primary care physician.

Technically, it is possible to monitor atrial fibrillation or measure electrocardiograms via smartphones or wearable devices, and to provide medical consultation and advice over the wire, but it's prohibited domestically. Domestic hospitals can provide telemedicine abroad, but must turn off the regulatory devices domestically.

The medical community has clear reasons for their staunch opposition. Medical practice is directly connected to human life and health, so mistakes and side effects should be minimized as much as possible. Also, there may be empathy for the opposition since in cases of medical accidents, the system often places more responsibility on medical personnel. However, the fact that medical practices have not been able to take a single step forward even after the long-term experiment of the non-face-to-face method, which was unimaginable in many sectors due to the COVID-19 situation, implies a lack of consideration for competitiveness. One of the opposition's arguments and logic is the fear of patient concentration in large hospitals, which is similar to other industries. In addition, the medical community's devoted service and contribution throughout the recent pandemic crisis have been significant, so this will likely be an additional factor strengthening their position and voice for a while. To quote an old saying in Korea, 'there are no graves in this world without a reason' translates in a sarcastic nuance, any single thing and event has a reason attached to it.

Telemedicine systems have been officially introduced and are growing rapidly in the United States and France, with doctors and medical associations even demanding a relaxation of regulations.[195] In China, remote surgeries targeting patients over 3000 km away are being performed using 5G technology and robots.[196] Collaborations with delivery companies and online vendors have also made consultations and medication delivery possible. We have previously looked at the status of telemedicine in Korea compared to OECD countries.

The global telemedicine market size is expected to increase from $61.4 billion in 2019 to $559.5 billion in 2027.[197] It is a reality that Korea, boasting world-class medical technology and leading information and communication technology, is tying its own hands, unable to lead or follow the global trend due to group interests and social regulations.

In the past, there was a case of deep conflict due to the separation of dispensing and prescribing drugs, and the pharmaceutical industry lost the case at that time. But the pharmaceutical industry is also adamant about protecting its interests. Following the flow of the times, a large supermarket applied to register the trademark 'No Pharmacy' for products such as probiotics, dietary supplements, nutrient-enhanced drinks, and over-the-counter drugs, but withdrew following the threat of a boycott by the Pharmacist Association. Large supermarkets had already launched many products at low prices under the 'No Brand' trademark, so the 'No' trademark was already in use, but the particular supermarket surrendered to the organizational resistance of the Pharmacist Association stating that it was impossible in 'our' territory. Naturally, competition is abandoned or restricted.

(2) Tada Taxi Service Case

The revocation of the Tada taxi service license in 2019 is a similar case. A venture's attempt to improve the efficiency and convenience of the transport industry through a business model of new rental-car-based vehicle call service was halted by vehement opposition from the taxi industry, including suicide of taxi drivers. It was an attempt at innovation within the scope of

---

[195] Chosun Ilbo. June 3rd, 2021. A1, A6
[196] Chosun Ilbo. June 2nd, 2021. A1, A3
[197] Chosun Ilbo. June 2nd, 2021. A1, A6.

the existing passenger automobile transportation business act, but even this was unacceptable to opposition, resulting in political submission to the fierce backlash. Of course, the interest and livelihood of taxi industry workers are important and should be considered but this case is a typical collision of micro and macro issues that contrasts with the United States during the Uber incident explained below. Innovative mobility attempts such as Tada and others are currently dormant, but in reality where mobile platforms continue to develop, franchise taxis that manage the quality of taxi call services through the platform and receive compensation are filling the void.

The American Uber, the original vehicle sharing service, also experienced conflict early on. In New York, USA, eight taxi drivers committed suicide and over 950 filed for personal bankruptcy. Of course, when the New York taxi market collapsed, the city authorities stepped in with regulation, but they adhered to the principle of respecting consumer choice, and Uber even went public on the New York Stock Exchange in May 2019. In Korea, it becomes an example of 'lack of ability to adjust social conflicts'.[198] As another foreign example, Estonia's ride-sharing company Bolt has already entered 35 countries, and the words of the President are impressive: "The role of the government is not to intervene in the market, but to create legal space for new services and create services."

In the case of Korea, the government predicted that more innovative services would emerge by creating a law prohibiting Tada, but of course, this did not happen. Instead, the assessment was that the number of franchise taxis centered on large corporations has increased. For example, after Tada, Kakao has taken over a significant portion of the taxi market, but the cost of passengers' calls and the commission of taxi drivers are causing a loss.[199] The Korean Supreme Court decided that the Tada Taxi service is not illegal after a long period of trials and disputes. But the original innovator has lost the energy and momentum.

There was a case where the taxi industry was put in a contradictory position in the opposite case. They tried to use taxis for delivery service as a means to overcome the recession in the taxi business, but when the courier and quick motorcycle business sectors opposed, regulatory authorities did not

---

[198] Chosun Ilbo, October 30th, 2019, A3
[199] Chosun Ilbo. June 14th, 2019, A1

allow it.[200] It's difficult to see the taxi delivery idea as a result of innovation, but it is an example of a vicious cycle showing that incumbents cannot step back from the current vested interests in the face of attempts at innovation.

(3) Law-Talk Case

The third example of a conflict between traditional industries and new industries is the relationship between the Korean Bar Association (KBA) and the nascent legal intermediary platform, Law-Talk. The KBA has called for a ban on Law-Talk's online advertising and has demanded that its members not join Law-Talk, citing reasons such as the Prohibition of Broker Interference Law, and the need to prevent the disruption of sound legal service order and market order. In response, Law-Talk, a startup, has put forward the necessity of providing information and portal services to increase public convenience and service accessibility, and has even lodged a constitutional appeal against the KBA's actions.[201] The Ministry of Justice has ruled that Law-Talk is legal. The services provided by Law-Talk include attorney search and appointment platforms by field and case, online legal consultation, and sentencing prediction services. From an industrial perspective, this is an innovative attempt to utilize the gaps in the existing market. The essence of conflict is similar to the two previous cases, which ultimately boils down to the matters of choice and judgment.

Rather than debating the morality of the three examples above, the point here is to highlight that such conflicts and contradictions have inevitably become a universal phenomenon in Korean society. Consequently, these factors are slowing us down and weighing us down in the marathon race. Furthermore, the trend of such conflicts and power struggles is expected to increase in the future.

Innovation is an attempt to experiment and explore different methods, different ideas, and more efficient practice. Anything that deviates from the status quo often changes the existing framework and vested interest. As a result, even if the pie (or share) enlarges and the overall gains increase, it is inevitable that some existing parties suffer loss or damage like the above

---

[200] Maeil Business, April 9th, 2021, A20

[201] Maeil Business, June 1rst, 2021, A2, A29

three examples. The change is a desperate issue for them, as their very livelihood is at stake.

Unlike in the past, we now have too many things to protect and care for. Our jobs, income, assets, and interests are no longer what they used to be. Therefore, new changes can be perceived as threatening and may result in unwelcome outcomes. Thus, there are reasons and justifications for defending and protecting certain sectors where power and influence reside. The stage for ignoring, yielding or requesting compromises has passed. Additionally, it's practically difficult to impose exceptions or sacrifices on a certain group or minority, so the majority of conclusions are reached on the level where society as a whole bears the burden. This could be seen as the price of rapid growth and development, where there is a lack of adaptation and adjustment process.

Competitiveness is not just a domestic issue; it's a shared concern for all countries. As an example the semiconductor industry, which Korean companies independently initiated and now possess the top class production technology and have an absolute advantage in domestic production, employment and exports, needs to construct a new factory or expand existing factories to meet the new demand. However, because of regulations and permit procedures, this reportedly takes six months longer than it does for competitors in other countries.[202] Given equal conditions, this inevitably leads to a loss of competitiveness. We are creating a rigid phenomenon that restricts development and denies ourselves the opportunity for faster and more efficient methods outside the designated path.

Of course, these phenomena are not unique to Korea. They are part of the growth process and seen as a price we have to bear for development. However, the speed of these changes should be monitored. Even from the perspective of adjusting and inevitable slowdown, Korea's pace is certainly among the fastest. Furthermore, as a front-runner in the global marathon race, we have no choice but to pay more attention to competitiveness. If we run in our own way, without considering competitors, the outcome of the race is bound to change.

As emphasized repeatedly, everything is evaluated relatively. If others also

---

[202] Maeil Business, March 26th, 2021, A6.

slow down or falter, no major problem arises. Therefore, comparison and impartial assessment are needed. According to the 2020 Global Innovation Index announced annually by a joint research team from France's INSEAD, Cornell University in the US, and the World Intellectual Property Organization, Korea ranked 10th out of 131 countries surveyed, in line with its macroeconomic status. While it continually improved its record, ranking first in human capital and research in the category-wise innovation index assessment, it displayed an imbalance, ranking 29th in the institutional sector. This is actual proof of the existing problems.

9-6 Conflict Between Innovation and Regulation

Innovation, by nature, is the process or outcome of creating something new, better, and cheaper that didn't exist or wasn't done before. The process and result of innovation are directly or indirectly related to speed, and can even be speed itself. As repeatedly explained, speed is inversely correlated with cost under the given conditions. Therefore, speed implies market competitiveness.

On the other hand, regulation, by its nature, serves to slow down things - it doesn't have the opposite function like facilitation. In other words, regulation is a legal and institutional mechanism that prevents doing things differently from now or that stops such attempts. Of course, there are reasons and circumstances for this, and in most cases, there is a micro-level validity. Furthermore, since political power and processes are inevitably involved, a logical conclusion is not easy to reach.

Moreover, most regulations are created and implemented by laws and systems. It takes time to create and amend these laws, and naturally, the process takes up time. Therefore, the more frequent and faster beneficial innovations occur, the more it establishes a relationship of conflict with regulations, which exist in the opposite dimension. Regulation essentially aims to prevent doing things differently, while innovation is an attempt to do things in a new or different way.

A famous economist of the 20th century, Joseph Schumpeter, defined innovation as 'creative destruction'. He stated that economic development is driven by innovation. Most new things do not fit into the existing framework. Innovation is an attempt to do things differently somehow, and regulation is a mandate not to do things differently from existence. Some argue that laws or regulations are not useful for creative stimuli that improve economic productivity (Friedman, previous book, p22). It has also been argued that if Korea escapes being a heavily regulated country, her GDP could increase by 1.2 percentage points.[203] This is a remarkable figure, considering it's challenging to predict an annual growth rate of around 2% in Korea these days.

Innovation, in definition, implies an improvement over what was before, and benefits not only the innovator but also the broader society. Regulation is a mechanism that aims to prohibit change or difference from the current state, whether it concerns a specific part or sometimes the whole. There are reasons and causes, as well as historical backgrounds and scars from struggles and efforts. Therefore, creating new regulations might be easier than changing existing ones.

So, should we encourage innovation and allow competition? Or should we prohibit and prevent the disruption or destruction of the current state or order that we have maintained so far? Among numerous cases, which should be considered, and which should be excluded? Isn't there a harmony and point of contact between the two? How should we adjust and resolve the conflict of interests between parts and the whole? Furthermore, as in the marathon example mentioned earlier, we should also watch our competitors if we don't want to fall behind.

There are quite a few cases where 'what is good in the short run is not good in the long run', and history has shown that societies that progress often involve an individual that takes on the difficult villainous role and pays the price. There are many medicines that are good for the body but bitter or unpleasant to take. Conversely, there are things that are harmful to the body but immediately appealing to the palate.

The remarkable global convergence of Korean culture, arts, performances, sports, and other achievements can be described in economic terms as the result of relentless innovation and competition. It has been possible because consumers at home and abroad appreciate these innovative attempts and

---

[203] Jun-Kyung Kim Chosun Ilbo, WB, March 4th, 2017

recognize their competitiveness. If we consider the interests of individuals or groups already established attempting to standardize and institutionalize the innovative effort, it's clear what the outcome would be. It's inconsistent to encourage innovation in areas like culture and sports but not in the industry sector.

When a Korean entertainment agency planned to establish a global K-pop educational institution in Seoul, it garnered enthusiastic responses and expectations from young people worldwide. However, due to regulations on establishing school and course curriculum, they reportedly gave up and instead decided to establish a digital school, an online high school, in California, USA.[204] In this case, it was not a conflict with traditional industries, but rather Korea's rigid education system that fundamentally prevented it. Of course, there are clear issues and potential abuses that may arise if such regulations are hastily relaxed. However, as emphasized several times before, innovation mostly involves trying something new and different that was not done before, so if we stubbornly stick to the old framework and judge accordingly, most cases will not be acknowledged, and competitiveness will inevitably decrease or disappear.

This issue is merely a small example, and it is a well-known fact that Korea's education system itself has been shifting in a direction that excludes competition and difference. Yet the irony is that while indirectly preventing competition, educational authorities and politicians are touting the achievement of leading industrial nations and welfare states.

The function of politics and administration is expected to solve such difficult problems wisely and strive for harmony. Yet, in reality, the opposite happens. Politicians often stand at the forefront of conflicts, amplifying them, and ultimately exacerbating situations. If political forces pursue political gains based on division and opposition, problem-solving becomes even more difficult and challenging.

In a fiercely competitive global world, it is crucial to consider the future of the nation while simultaneously considering the lives of all its members striving in the present. Not only the conflicts between micro and macro levels, but also the conflicts and contradictions between short-term and

---

[204] Chosun Ilbo, January 16th, 2021, A6

long-term perspectives require the desperate need for leadership that cannot be ignored. It is almost universal in human life to be willing to sacrifice oneself or suffer loss for one's own children. However, attempts or decisions to sacrifice or concede for the future of the community or future generations on a macro scale are hard to find. This is yet another case of the clash between micro and macro.

As introduced in Chapter 4, Korea is at the forefront of digitalization and administrative computerization, befitting K-Speed. Now, due to reduction in transaction cost and administrative expense, policies that were unthinkable in the past can be implemented. For instance, in income policy, welfare policy, real estate policy, and tax policy, it's now possible to selectively or partially implement or apply measures based on data and evidence. This shift allows for major changes in policy direction, efficiency, and implementation speed. Despite the improved environment that overcomes the past necessity for uniform application, regulations and controls that ignore market principles are continuously increasing.

Another point to be cautious of and be aware of at this juncture, discussing once again, is the blatant realization of the Big Brother from George Orwell's novel "1984". Some of this experiment was conducted during the recent COVID-19 crisis, with compulsory alerts being sent to the screens of all citizens' cell phones, delivering government notices and enabling tracking and control of individual citizens' lives for infection tracing. It's like a test run for a totalitarian or controlled socialist state. The fact that China is already identifying criminal suspects and anti-government figures through facial recognition technology is worth noting.

The relationship between the market and regulation can be likened to the relationship between players and referee (government) in a sport game (for example, a soccer match). The referee's role is to ensure that the game proceeds properly and according to the rules, but the referee is not the main character in the game. If there were no referees, foul plays and excesses could proliferate, preventing a proper game from taking place. However, if the referee continuously interrupts the game by blowing the whistle or by consecutively expelling players for fouls, the game itself cannot take place, the flow is interrupted, or it ultimately falls apart. Furthermore, if there are as many referees as players strictly judging, the purpose of the game would be lost.

An even more serious case is when the referee shows bias in a decision due to having preconceived intentions or emotions towards a team or individual players. An unfair football match can end in one round, but the game in the market economy is related to the fate of the participants and can disrupt the balance of the entire market, hence the role of the referee (policy and regulation) is extremely important.

Regulation must be objective and fair, and there should be consistency in judgment and application for it to be sustainable. In the spring of 2021, ahead of the by-elections for the mayors of Seoul and Busan, the ruling party and the government, with the cooperation of the opposition party, hastily changed the predetermined location of the new airport in Busan to Gadeok Island, bypassing the review of 37 related laws and regulations and ignoring cost-benefit analysis. This set a precedent suggesting that if you push forward around election time, you can achieve what you want regardless of regulations or costs. It's a precedent that is difficult to block if someone asks, 'Why are we the only ones not receiving benefits?'

Currently, almost all of the legislation or amendments proposed by the National Assembly or the government are related to regulation either directly or indirectly. There are inevitable aspects due to the election system, but only the emergence of a leader or group with a future-oriented perspective can attempt a balance that revives competitiveness and benefits the whole. As was the case of the neo-Confucian scholars in the Joseon era, metaphorically it is not desirable to force people to fit their bodies into intended pre-made clothes, as our bodies or physical conditions continually change. Another important point to recognize is an old Korean saying that 'one cannot please both of a sister and her husband at the same time.' You can't please everyone.

The Case of Makgeolli (Traditional Rice Wine) Market

The Wingless Fall of Makgeolli, in spite of Being Loved by the People.

Makgeolli is a traditional Korean alcohol made from rice and yeast, and its name is derived from the phrase 'roughly strained'. During the Joseon Dynasty, alcohol was brewed at home, known as the traditional home brewing practice. However, this tradition was disrupted when the Japanese colonial authorities only allowed licensed brewers to exclusively produce and sell alcohol, and cracked down on home brewing. After liberation, the government, facing severe food shortages such as the spring famine period, also prohibited individual households from brewing alcohol and prohibited brewers from making makgeolli using rice. Since then, makgeolli made with flour as the main ingredient was sold in the market.

The 1970s is referred to as the golden age of makgeolli. In 1974, it accounted for 77% of the Korean alcohol market. Makgeolli was truly a national drink. Accordingly, makgeolli was subject to intense regulation. The regional monopoly sale system was implemented because of the difficulties in distribution management and also to avoid the production of low-quality alcohol due to excessive competition and the risk of tax evasion. As a result, the makgeolli industry was mainly composed of small-scale businesses in each region. Amid this, makgeolli adulterated with water to increase production volume, or with impurities such as industrial saccharin and carbide, was also sold. From this point, makgeolli established a negative perception as an alcohol that causes a painfully splitting headache the next day. The market was flooded with low quality makgeolli, and by the 1980s, it ceded the throne to beer, which experienced hyper growth, and by the 1990s, its production volume even fell below that of soju (Korean traditional liquor).

The Brilliant Revival of Makgeolli and Its Designation as a Suitable Industry for Small and Medium Enterprises

Amid the decline of the makgeolli industry, the government began to reconsider various regulations imposed under the pretext of protecting the makgeolli industry. In 1991, it became possible to produce makgeolli using rice, and the regional monopoly sales system was eventually abolished, as the problem of chronic food shortages disappeared due to increased rice production.

In the 2000s, the so-called new makgeolli began to be actively distributed in the market. This new makgeolli was a different product from the murky makgeolli with many impurities that had been ingrained in consumers' perception. This was thanks to technological developments such as production automation, low temperature fermentation, and packaging innovation. With the advent of new fermentation technology, the shelf life of fresh makgeolli in a shop, preferred by consumers, increased from 10 to 30 days, moving from the alcohol display corner to the refrigerated section.

By the late 2000s, the popularity of makgeolli among college students began to rise rapidly, riding the wave of well-being. Its popularity did not just increase domestically. Makgeolli, canned through sterilization technology, began to be exported and gained explosive popularity among Japanese women, riding the Korean Wave, and referred to as 'Makori' (the Japanese pronunciation of makgeolli). Korean canned makgeolli made a large-scale entry into Japanese supermarkets and convenience stores, and makgeolli exports exceeded $50 million in 2011. The release of makgeolli soared from 260,000 kl in 2009 to 450,000 kl in 2011.

The chairman of the Fair Trade Commission at the time evaluated at a 2009 press conference that this makgeolli boom was due to the relaxation of regulation. He stated that the easing of entry regulation and others had enabled quality improvement, diversification, and globalization. Large corporations, recognizing the potential of the market at the time, also eagerly entered the market. Companies such as CJ CheilJedang, Orion, and others jumped into the makgeolli business. Hite-Jinro and Lotte also participated in export or export agencies. Other big food companies considered entering the makgeolli market.

As expected, when the large corporations jumped in, small scale makgeolli manufacturers began to protest. In response, the government designated makgeolli as a 'suitable' industry for small and medium sized enterprises in October 2011. This decision falls under a size dependent policy where support of business activity or regulation is decided based on the size of the company. A few years after makgeolli was designated a suitable industry, the large corporations wound up either folding their business or barely sustaining themselves through overseas export.

A Return to Recession

Just as it seemed the makgeolli industry was rebounding, it entered a path of decline after 2012. The size of the makgeolli market, which was 507.5 billion KRW in 2011, shrank to 421.1 billion KRW in 2013. Especially in the case of export, 36.89 million US$ in 2012 plummeted to 18.86 million US$ in 2013, decreasing by 48.9%.

As the initial designation period of three years as a suitable industry for small and medium sized enterprise nearly ended, controversy arose over whether makgeolli should be re-designated as a suitable industry. Those opposing the re-designation criticized that the designation did not significantly enhance the competitiveness of small breweries but only reduced the market size. Although small and medium sized businesses had expected to improve profitability when makgeolli was designated a suitable industry, they showed weakness in securing capital, distribution network, and marketing, resulting in cases where they had to reduce sales or cease operations. One manufacturing executive said, "If large corporations had actively marketed and pushed R&D, the market would have continued to grow, and the situation for small and medium sized businesses would have improved."

On the other hand, those supporting the redesignation, including the Korea Makgeolli Association, argued that the decrease in makgeolli consumption was due to changes in consumer trend (market change) and had nothing to do with the restraint of large corporations from entering the market due to the designation as a suitable industry.

Some pointed out that consumers quickly lost interest as the industry failed to keep up with market preference, such as delays in launching new products with unique taste or premium products. Many products primarily used imported rice to cut cost, which was also mentioned. Despite the variety of products, the issue was that they all tasted similar due to the industry's lack of effort towards differentiation. One expert said that to expect a revival, most makgeolli should use less sweeteners and utilize local microbes to preserve the authentic taste of makgeolli from that region.

One of the venture operators running a brewery in the region posted an article titled "Makgeolli Industry That Needs to Grow Together" on the homepage of the Mutual Growth Committee, which is involved in the designation of the suitable industry. This operator stated the following:

"When this policy was first established, I considered whether it was right to prohibit large corporations from accessing makgeolli. However, I think the reality has turned out to be the opposite, and the existence of makgeolli from both an economic and cultural standpoint as a traditional industry is seriously threatened. I assert that traditional alcohol has almost no place in

the market as large corporations dominate the liquor market with beer and soju, as well as importing whiskey, wine, and sake, based on their capital. If the government is not willing to support the industry, I think we should strive to continue to expose the existence of the product in order to attract consumer interest, developing as a corporate form based on market logic and capital investment.

Most of the fresh makgeolli products are distributed by so-called agents, who operate under a specific liquor sales license. As the makgeolli market shrinks, the tyranny of these specific liquor sales license holders, with no exaggeration, are destroying the manufacturers. In order to provide a fair profit, a systematic manufacturing and distribution system is necessary, but this will only be possible when approached with the logic of a company with capital.

Alcohol advertising is regulated by several laws such as the Youth Protection Act, but marketing is necessary to inform consumers of the product's existence and to inspire more trust. Small-scale breweries need a nurturing policy that maintains the diversity and cultural aspects of makgeolli, finding their existence by being renowned as a tourist spot through the selection of regionally distinctive ingredients and fermentation methods. If we keep shrinking the pie while expanding small businesses, there will be no laughter for anyone."

In the case of makgeolli, the implementation of the system (designation of suitability) was found to have minimal impact on sales, profitability, and technological innovation efforts of small and medium sized manufacturers.

Another criticism of the medium size suitable industry system was that it inadvertently gave foreign companies reflexive benefits. In the case of the 'kimchi' industry, Chinese kimchi dominated the dining table after being designated as a suitable industry in 2011. Criticism was also raised that the system harmed the relevant industry. 'Tofu', whose market size shrank immediately after the suitable industry designation, is similar to the case of makgeolli. Before the designation, medium and small sized companies also grew in sales together with big companies like Pulmuone, CJ, and Daesang, launching packaged tofu made from Korean soybeans. After the designation, large corporations, which primarily used domestic soybeans, had to force sales to decrease by using cheaper imported soybeans, causing losses to domestic soybean farmers.

After all the controversy, makgeolli was not re-designated as a suitable industry. This is because the industry voluntarily concluded a mutual growth agreement before being re-designated by the government. The agreement included large corporations restraining from direct manufacturing in the domestic market and supporting investment, marketing, and technological development with small and medium sized makgeolli manufacturing companies, while pioneering domestic and foreign markets using their distribution networks. Despite the mutual growth agreement, the market's slump did not improve. Large corporations, afraid of criticism that they were infringing on the traditional market, hesitated to return. The makgeolli market returned to its former regional market situation.

The Spring Breeze Blows Again (Korean saying on hope)... This time...

In 2019, another makgeolli regulation was abolished. The total acidity limit for makgeolli was removed. The higher the acidity, the sourer it tastes, but traditionally, makgeolli was regulated not to manufacture and sell above a certain acidity level. The following year, the consignment production (OEM) of alcoholic beverages, including makgeolli, was also allowed. For small scale makgeolli manufacturers producing small quantities of various types, the display items of their tax proof labels were changed so that they could be replaced with the name of the alcohol manufacturer instead of the trademark name and specifications.

In 2020, as the RETRO (Newtro) culture craze emerged, interest in makgeolli began to rise again amongst the younger generation. Following the COVID-19 situation, unlike other alcohols, makgeolli which can be purchased online, also gained popularity as a house drink. According to an online shopping mall, 11th Street, makgeolli sales increased by 324% from January 1, 2020, to April 28, 2020. BGF retailing, which operates CU convenience stores, launched 'Tes-style Makgeolli'(trade mark after an old singer's song). In the case of the age group sales proportion for Tes-style Makgeolli, the 20s and 30s age group accounted for 61.4%, and the average age of all Tes-style Makgeolli buyers was 32.5, which is about 20 years younger than the average makgeolli consumer. Sparkling makgeolli and various collaboration makgeolli are emerging, becoming the main players of the new alcohol trend, attracting the interest of the MZ generation.

Recently, with the growing global interest in fermented low-alcohol content beverages, makgeolli exports are also on the rise. In addition, due to the effects of COVID-19 and the focus on strengthening immunity, makgeolli companies are developing products with added nutritional ingredients including probiotics, and exporting them. Technology to control fermentation has been developed, which allows the use of completely sealed caps, making it possible to export fresh makgeolli. Kooksoondang (makgeolli manufacturer) announced that its export sales in the first two months of 2021 increased by 201.6% in Southeast Asia (excluding Vietnam) compared to the same period of the previous year.

In May 2021, the National Tax Service announced to lift another regulation. Through a revision of the notification, the sales container volume limit for makgeolli will be relaxed from 'up to 2 liters' to 'up to 5 liters'. This is a first in 20 years since the introduction of packaging volume regulations in 2001. An industry insider stated, "With the relaxation of volume limit regulations, large scale supplies of traditional alcohol like makgeolli become possible, reducing production costs and social costs like disposal of waste containers," and added, "With the supply of large volumes for businesses, sales of traditional tavern makgeolli could spread in large pitcher sizes or in the form of leftover alcohol sales, similar to draft beer in beer houses."

According to the Commission for Shared Growth, a request has recently been received to designate the makgeolli industry as a livelihood appropriate business, and it is currently under review. A livelihood-appropriate business is a system that designates and nurtures specific industries to protect the livelihood of small business owners with less than five employees. If designated, the acquisition, commencement, or expansion of the designated business by a large corporation is principally prohibited for five years. The Commission for Shared Growth stated that the review is being conducted considering the small-scale nature and protection needs of the industry, the impact on stakeholders in the upstream and downstream sectors, and consumer welfare.

The Korean Makgeolli Association, which requested the designation as a livelihood appropriate business, stated, "The kimchi market was also started by small business owners and small and medium enterprises, but now it is dominated by large corporations." They added that the makgeolli market in the liquor industry is "the only area not yet invaded by large corporations," and thus the request is made in order "to prevent domination by large corporations in advance." The association continued, "for the makgeolli industry to grow, it should reflect the characteristics of each region, rather than being dominated by a single company."

Those opposing the designation are worried about the reenactment of the nightmare of 2011. An industry insider said, "We must not forget the experience of an industry, which recorded exports of 50 million dollars, becoming irrecoverable due to a moment of regulation."

Source: Summarized sentences from the final exam of a law course, 2021, Seoul National University Law School.

9-7 Cases of Inversion and Change in Relation Between Part and Whole

There are numerous instances where the opposite of such conflicts between the micro and macro occurs. A macro level decision stimulates the micro elements, leading to the development and leap of both the micro and macro elements. In the early stages of Korea's economic development, due to the frailty of Korea's industrial competitiveness and the lack of foreign currency, all imports from foreign countries were subject to a positive system that required government approval, with the exception of certain permitted items.

As a result, the import permit itself was a tremendous privilege, and those who obtained it reaped huge benefits. Considering the situation at the time, this might have been a reasonable policy. However, as the economy began to grow, the government reversed this policy in one stroke, shifting to a negative system. With the exception of certain designated items, import was fully liberalized. This initially came as a huge shock. However, the drastic decision stimulated domestic competitiveness, leading to an increase in exports and enabled the Korean economy to enter the global economic system more quickly.

Another example is the Screen Quota System in place to protect the Korean film industry as mentioned before. This mechanism obligated movie theaters to screen a certain percentage of domestic films to protect the domestically frail film industry. In 1967, to prevent the erosion of domestic films by Hollywood movies, movie theaters were required to screen domestic films for more than 146 days a year. Incentives were even implemented, such as granting the right to import foreign films for those making successful domestic art films. About 40 years later, in 2006, this number was reduced to half, 73 days, which was strongly opposed by the domestic film industry. There were sufficient reasons and grounds, and it was an unavoidable measure. The result of reducing this system, despite the expected risk and severe opposition, is the present-day performance of the Korean film and video industry that now holds sway over the world. As a result, the existence and necessity of the screen quota is no longer recognized due to the qualitative and quantitative growth of Korean films. The most certain way to quickly unleash hidden talents is to expose them to competition, making them faster and stronger.

A recent example appeared when Netflix entered the domestic market in 2016. There were concerns that 'Korean dramas would all die.' However, the result was quite the opposite. Many Korean works are spreading worldwide through the Netflix platform and gaining great popularity. The recent example is the drama "Squid Game," which received production investment from Netflix and achieved global success.

There are two major ways to reduce the gap or distance between opposite spectrums within a society. One method is slowing the fast spectrum, and the other method would be speeding up the slow spectrum to narrow the gap. There is a significant difference in the feasibility and result of these two methods. It is easier and politically more secure to slow down the fast by inhibiting (tripping) them, than it is to speed up the slow. However, as history and experience have shown, the outcome of these two methods appear in opposite directions, becoming another case of contradiction of the micro and macro perspective. The policy direction pursued by socialist-leaning regime in many fields, including industrial, educational, and distribution policies, tend to inhibit (trip) the fast, to a somewhat standardized speed.

In the early 1960s, when Korea began industrialization based on exports, the policies adopted by several South American countries, including

Argentina, (who had a much higher income and better living conditions than Korea at the time) were to abandon openness and suppress imports, thereby protecting vulnerable domestic industries. That policy gained popularity and support from citizens by advocating protection and regulation policies instead of openness and competition. The result is what we see and experience today. In the early stage of industrialization, the Korean government encouraged export, even using extreme measures such as allocating import permit licenses proportional to companies with an export letter of credit.

The economic experiment of South and North Korea, both Koreas with the same ethnicity, serves as another example. Theoretically, the seemingly noble ideology and system that North Korea promotes, should give a stable economy to the residents of North Korea, instead of the poverty it's in. The reason is simple. North Korea refused to implement the market principle that humans inherently move according to. Sustainable speed and spontaneous acceleration are only possible by the market principle. The side effects that inevitably follow market failure must be corrected without damaging the principle itself.

Chapter 10

Creating a Sustainable K-Speed

10-1 Looking into the Future of Korean Competitiveness

As discussed in several parts of this book, competitiveness is often expressed by speed. The factors of competitiveness are determined by an individual's or society's given abilities and training, historical tradition and culture, accumulated human and physical capital, technology and the social system. Most of these factors are directly or indirectly linked to speed. The source of competitiveness lies mainly with people. Manufacturing, service systems, machines, devices, or systems including artificial intelligence can increase competitiveness through speed, but ultimately, it is the human touch that recognizes and creates a method or system of speed.

Of course, there are other opinions as well. Speed remains important, but the progression of time and technology also demands a new change. "About a decade after digital technology permeated the world of atoms, an awareness began to arise that the entities using the technology are humans, and they are highly diverse. Therefore, the smart era is not an era of speed but an era of creativity... Until now, Korea has risen to its current position through diligence and speed. It said to invest diligently because it will evolve quickly in one direction. However, such an era is slowly coming to an end."[205] This quote means that competitiveness derived simply from physical speed can quickly and widely become commonplace, and its effectiveness may be weaker than in the past.

The era of artificial intelligence (AI) is arriving faster than expected, and there is a possibility that an AI surpassing humans could appear soon. If that happens, the definition given earlier would need to be revised, and it should be said that the source of competitiveness is artificial intelligence. However, the entity developing AI is still human. The discussion about development after that stage is beyond the scope of this book.

---

[205] Requoted from LG Economic Research Institute, "A New Future is Coming, 2020," Hans Media, Chosun Ilbo, December 25th, 2010

We have looked at how people (nation) or society hold competitiveness in natural, social environments and conditions, systems and cultures. We have also discussed that competitiveness derived from speed can vary depending on the individual or country. Even now, as the world rapidly globalizes and geographical and temporal distances are shortened, competitiveness remains the most crucial factor in economic development, regardless of the cause or process. This principle applies equally to individuals and organizations.

Competitiveness is a relative concept, so the past becomes history, and by comparing and reviewing the current state, it is possible to predict sustainability for the future. According to the results of a survey conducted by the World Economic Forum in 2021 with experts and entrepreneurs from 42 countries, the potential for Korean speed to leverage its advantages and outpace other countries in competition does not appear in these survey results. Rather, it concludes that Korea is lagging in preparation for economic transition in the future.[206] This is due to the current attitude of avoiding competition while bulking in size, as discussed earlier.

10-2 Reconstruction of the Foundation of Korean Competitiveness

What this book has repeatedly demonstrated through various discussions, is that speed is the greatest and most certain aspect of the competitiveness possessed by Koreans. This speed has been a driving force that led to rapid growth from one of the world's poorest countries to an advanced country level since the mid-20th century. However, if this speed is underestimated or disregarded, it results in lowering one's own competitiveness. The most reliable competitiveness is born by focusing on what one can do best.

However, if this speed does not improve qualitatively and is simply fast but inaccurate, improvised without consistency, and unreliable, it is inevitable that although temporarily effective in the short run it will lead to worse results in the medium and long run, resulting in decline. Competitiveness, in the future cannot be measured by mere physical speed alone, and must be considered and emphasized along with qualities such as reli-

[206] World Economic Forum, Global Competitiveness Report, Special Edition 2020

ability, safety, and honesty of that speed. This is what leads to genuine and sustainable competitiveness.

Adding social capital to competitive speed accomplishes qualitative depth. In other words, social capital can be thought of as polishing the physical and human capital already accumulated. With this refinement we can truly become a society and an individual using competitiveness with a solid foundation.

Consideration of the following three aspects is mandatory for a healthy society.

(1) Safety

In the beginning of Korea's economic development, a number of accidents occurred, starting with the collapse of the Wow Apartment built in Sinchon, Seoul in the 1960s, the collapse of the Sampoong Department Store in Seoul, and the collapse of the Seongsu Bridge over the Han River in the 1970s. One of the common causes was due to haste that led to shortening the construction period. There were several reasons for the shoddy construction that led to the accidents, such as low construction budget, insufficient construction technology, irresponsible construction and supervision, so it would be difficult to blame hastiness alone. However, it is clear that ability enabled the haste. One of the slogans that were popular at the time and resonated with many people in thought and action was 'Just do it, it will be done', and it goes without saying that speed was a major factor in this mentality.

In fact, speed is essentially related to risk. Increasing the speed of a human, car, or machine inevitably increases the risk of an accident. However, if caution is added the risk automatically decreases. While speed belongs to an instinctual attribute, attention is the realm of training and education. Rather than being afraid and giving up one's advantages by reducing speed altogether, the idea is to train oneself early on to have the habit of safety consideration. This is not impossible.

Therefore, if the emphasis on speed inevitably caused accidents that were not intended, we now have no choice but to demand 'safe speed.' However, this does not mean abandoning speed itself but to exert the abilities we've originally had while keeping safety in mind. A true upgrading of speed.

This is not limited to physical speed. The suicide rate in Korea ranks highest in the world, although the country has become more affluent and better to live in than before. Whatever the reason, it is not desirable to have a quick pace in frustration and despair and to be speedy in ending one's life. Life is the only thing human beings possess and the most precious thing that cannot be retrieved once lost. The concept of safe speed now needs to be applied, and we need to start from the fundamental question about speed, that is, thinking about the ultimate purpose of speediness.

It's unfortunate that Korea's politics and government have shown little interest or concern about these issues so far. Since there is a high likelihood of repeating past behaviors of temporarily making headlines and then being forgotten, the society as a whole, should consider it everyone's business and revive the value of the community.

(2) Reliability

The speed of production, delivery, and pricing is the important source of competitiveness of goods and services. While speed is an important factor determining price, if a product or service loses the user's trust, they will not be able to maintain competitiveness. If there is no other choice, the consumers may reluctantly use them. However, in a broad globalized market economy like today, trust is the 'it' factor. Therefore, speed should be reliable.

Reflecting on our rapid development process, it is true that there have been many cases where consistency and sustainability were deliberately or inevitably ignored for the sake of a fast finish. If one were to make excuses, there was a time when the general social atmosphere prioritized the result rather than the process and quantity over quality in order to 'catch up'. By stressing the result or so called 'performance', neglect of quality was inevitable.

In the past, taking up again, most domestic products were untrustworthy. Not to mention various machines and devices, even items like pencils or matches were only deemed reliable to use if they were made in the USA,

Germany, or Japan. The case was the same for food, where foreign-made was considered safe to eat, but domestic grown was hard to trust. This speed of change is hard to believe considering the stark contrast to today's phenomenon where, in most cases of food or electronic products, the domestic is preferred and even priced higher.

Korea is not the nation of the past. In about a quarter of a century, a very short time, it has achieved growth by world standards. The thoughts and actions we had as a child must change as we grow older. If an adult does not change the habits and routines from childhood, they won't be received properly. In other words, they won't be trusted. Such trust manifests itself in our attitude towards others.

A reliable speed is needed for the same reasons as safe speed. When discussing reliable speed, the first thing that comes to mind is the delivery service industry. This is a smoothly developing example of reliable speed in Korea. The internet provides many options and what you see is what you get reliability, ensures a thriving business model in the non-face-to-face era.

(3) Honesty

Safe speed and reliable speed ultimately stem from honesty. Honesty comes from responsibility, compliance with laws (or rules), transparency, and so on. If honesty is recognized, whether it's an individual's work, an organization's work, or a product or service created, it is acknowledged as trustworthy. As previously mentioned, the symbol of that trust can be a country, a company, a religion, a group, or a specific individual.

If a company providing a product or service gives consumers the impression of honesty, then all the products or services it produces or provides will be acknowledged for their value, even if the cost is relatively expensive. The scope can extend to the country or region that the company belongs to. There can be various explanations for the phenomenon of high-end or luxury goods preferred by certain classes being sold at high prices, but it goes without saying that belief in the respective product is presupposed.

We still say things like 'X is a trustworthy person', 'products by company Y are reliable,' or 'people from country Z are generally honest, and there are many cases where such consciousness is actual or potential, so we can see that the concept of honesty becomes a large asset for individuals, corporations, groups, and even societies or nations.

We can find evidence of such possibilities in the history of the world and in Korea today. Prominent conglomerates in Korea are implementing a policy that products or services bearing their brand are trustworthy, emphasizing their brands, and achieving considerable success both domestically and internationally. For example, they emphasize brands like Samsung and LG, rather than individual products.

Through such a success, the national brand and image must also improve. As 'Korea' and 'Made in Korea' become widely recognized, the country truly becomes successful. From now on, the impression that 'products and services made or provided by Koreans or Korean companies are as reliable as those from other first-rate countries' needs to be highlighted globally in order for us to truly become an advanced country and progress to the next stage. It's self-evident that the image of Korea, represented by the Korean Wave, can have an uplifting effect.

Thus, our crucial task is to upgrade speed competitiveness into honest speed. As we've continually emphasized, speed is an asset we can never give up; it only becomes truly competitive when it turns into honest speed. This honest speed must permeate all areas: politics, society, culture, industry and business, and everyday life. In simpler terms, not only should one avoid deceiving others or oneself, but being stricter with oneself is the real integrity and the source of sustainable competitiveness.

An Experience on Implementing Proactive Integrity

For Korea to expect sustainable growth and advantage of speed, she needs to become a more honest and upright society than it is now. In reality, making every sector of society more honest and upright is a tremendously difficult task. While there may be multiple avenues to approach this, a realistic solution might be for changes to begin in the public sector, then spread to other sectors. Rather than grandiose campaigns, expanding influence gradually from a smaller part to a wider range is a method that could increase the probability of success.

In 2014, I was appointed as the auditor of Korea Southern Power Co., Ltd. While it wasn't something I expected or hoped for, it provided me with an opportunity to put my everyday thoughts into practice. In other words, I began to have hopes and plans for a ripple effect that could spread from one public corporation to another in the same sector, then to public corporations of a different kind, and further to the whole public sector.

Upon my appointment as auditor, I was greeted with the good news that the company had been selected as the top company for three consecutive years in a public enterprise integrity survey conducted by the Anti-Corruption and Civil Rights Commission. My response was to define 'no giving, no receiving, no taking' as 'passive integrity,' and to assert that we should now move forward to the stage of 'proactive integrity'. It was a concept to go beyond the stage of not being caught, in other words, beyond the stage of passively possessing integrity, to actively realizing and practicing it in life and work.

The proactive integrity entails upholding fairness in one's own or the organization's tasks and decisions, furthermore practicing honesty and integrity in one's life and execution of daily tasks. Thus, the concept aims to yield greater efficiency and performance results that ultimately benefit the whole. Efficiency is no different from innovation as understood in a corporate context. Innovation is not just the result of laboratory experiments; it is directly linked to efficiency in the work and accurate judgment in business. Therefore, proactive integrity ultimately leads to innovation. If fairness is added to the task performed by public enterprise employees, and if honesty and integrity are practiced as a change of habit and way of thinking, the Korean public sector will definitely change, and this will also be reflected in visible and quantitative performance.

During my tenure as auditor, I conducted lectures numerous times at the headquarter and branch, department or function, and at each business location, in collaboration with the auditing team, I published and distributed a book titled 'Proactive Integrity - A Prerequisite for Public Enterprise Innovation' by the cooperation of staffs of auditor's office. Subsequently, we widely collected and rewarded book reviews and essays on personal implementation experience from all employees. Since the auditor's term is only two years, there was not enough time to properly check the changes, so I published a book titled 'Interim Report on the Practice of Proactive Integrity' to record book reports, individual achievements and changes during the campaign by that time. Among various practical cases, an especially memorable one includes a person who decided to quit smoking to maintain time integrity (the company headquarter is located on a floor higher than the 36th story), and another one who bought a new color printer for home for personal use instead of free loading the company facilities. I saw these as an astonishing change.

The follow-up is expected to be in progress, so there's not much more to report by this time from my side. However, what can certainly be said is that although it was a short and limited experiment, the result is that awareness and practice are possible if there's a firm will and commitment. I truly believe that proactive integrity can be a new source of competitiveness for Korea in the future.

Of course, safety, trust, and honesty are not concepts that must be strictly separated. Trust comes from honesty, and one can trust only when one feels safe. Being honest can easily build trust, and an honest speed cannot but be mindful of safety. Thus, these three elements must support each other like the three legs of a tripod and should form an interconnected pathway.

The fact is, there is a dilemma. Sometimes, accurate and trustworthy methods of handling work may require sacrificing speed, or there might be situations where tasks need to be done regardless of speed. Also, there may be side effects of losing the unconscious or instinctive sense of speed that we originally possessed when we consciously maintain a safe or trustworthy speed. Furthermore, although not measured empirically or statistically, there can be a hypothesis or logic that the speed of handling work slows down as income increases. Comparing Korea's past and present, this hypothesis may prove to be valid.

Our task is to achieve safety, reliability, and honesty while not damaging our inherent trait of speed or quickness. This is indeed the key to Korea's successful and sustainable presence on the international stage.

10-3 A Correction of Misunderstanding on Speed

Speed is not efficiency in itself. There may be a higher cost for speed. For instance, sports cars focus on increasing speed regardless of cost, which can result in more fuel consumption and doesn't necessarily represent efficiency in an economic sense. Therefore, being faster is not always better. It should bring competitiveness by being relatively faster under the same conditions.

Another factor to consider is the cost manifesting in the present and the cost that is yet to reveal itself in the future. Speeding up the present without considering the future could ultimately lead to higher cost and more sacrifice. There's a story in ancient Chinese literature about this. A farmer, impatient for his crops to grow faster, pulled on the stalks a little bit in the evening. However, when he went out the next day, they had all wilted.[207] In Korean old sayings, there's a phrase that says, 'If it's on credit a cow can be consumed.' This is a warning against the foolishness of not considering future costs and burdens. From another perspective, it also means not to fall into the trap of prioritizing visible quantity or superficial speed without considering quality or content. These are words of wisdom we need to remember as 'K-speed' is once again coming to the forefront in various sectors.

A correct understanding of the difference between haste and diligence is also necessary. Speed is often associated with diligence, but the two do not necessarily go hand in hand. At the same time, speed and haste are not in the same category.

Nonetheless, speed has been, is, and will continue to be a necessary competitive advantage for Koreans. As explained in various ways and provided examples and assertions, there are countless reasons, pretexts, and political demands pushing aside and disregarding speed, yet we cannot deny that speed is the source of our competitiveness. For instance, BTS, which has emerged as a symbolic existence of the current Hallyu wave, continues to demonstrate enormous growth in corporate value and revenue, comparable

---

[207] From this perspective, it may not necessarily be a desirable phenomenon that the number of doctoral recipients in domestic universities has tripled compared to 20 years ago, standing at 16,000 as of 2020.

to leading groups in other growing industries. However, if people start to argue that this group, which has become as large and significant as Korea's conglomerates, should now be subjected to various regulations and sanctions, or conversely, if they lobby or protest that BTS should be protected and thus no other competitors should be allowed to enter the race because of gained vested interests, one should consider what the outcome might be. To put it in extreme terms, the BTS phenomenon could be a product of a situation where sanctions and vested interests have not been properly formed.

10-4 Rise and Fall of a Nation

Every nation, ethnicity, enterprise, and individual inevitably experiences a process of rise and fall. The duration and speed of this process can vary greatly, and it's challenging for anyone to escape this cycle. In some cases, there could be an eternal downfall or a prolonged period of weakness, eventually leading to disappearance. An essential lesson we all need to keep in mind is: 'the flower that blooms quickly, withers quickly.'

The past half-century of Korea, viewed on a global scale, could be seen as a period of rising from prolonged frustration and stagnation. For a nation, as opposed to an individual, a downfall or period of weakness could require a considerable amount of time to recover, even if it manages to rise again. Korea is an exceptional case where it managed to recover miraculously in a very short period. Such speed is hard to find in world or economic history.

However, as previously pointed out, we are not in a position to slow down while enjoying achievements. On the contrary, there are many areas that require speed more than before. For example, the era of Software 1.0 has ended, and we are already in the era of Software 2.0 where artificial intelligence develops and creates software. It's uncertain how far ahead Korea can get in such a fast-paced era.

This book has endeavored to prove that Koreans inherently possess competitiveness due to their physical, genetic, or cultural characteristics, or other aspects. It also emphasized that such speed needs to be utilized to solve current and future problems. However, it has illustrated with examples that fast speed is not always beneficial, and could be dangerous with side effects associated with excessive speed.

The world and history teach us that if we fail to adequately control the side effects or risks of speed, or if we become complacent, the rate of decline can only accelerate. The historical lesson that those who rise or prosper quickly decline or fail quickly carries profound meaning. It is the duty and responsibility of all of us to maintain and further develop our status, having risen among the ranks of the world's leading nations for the first time in our long national history. Now that we have officially joined the ranks of advanced countries, we must guard against complacency.

Simultaneously, we must consider our ability to adapt to a slow-paced environment. Everything changes depending on whether we are moving fast or slow. Yet, what is even more challenging is the difficulty of moving slowly. Issues or side effects that were unseen or un-manifested when moving fast can emerge as difficulties when we slow down, and they are not easily resolved. This is akin to the idea that retreating or falling back in war is more challenging than attacking or advancing. As Korea now inevitably has to accept a low-growth economy characteristic of advanced countries, we need wisdom to revive Korea's speed and adapt to these changes.

10-5. Final Remark – Speed is an Essential Element of Innovation

So far, through logic, evidence, examples, and comparisons, I have emphasized that Korea's competitiveness lies in its speed. However, speed is not a panacea. No matter how good a medicine is, long-term use can lead to resistance and side effects. We now want to find and embrace other medicines, tools, or methods without forgetting the need for the original medicine. Once basic physiological or survival issues are resolved by the medicine, our thoughts naturally change. A medicine taken for a long time can become tiresome.

Speed is fundamentally an essential element of innovation. In terms of politics or social systems, market capitalism maintains and develops on the basis of recognizing the competitiveness of speed. In contrast, social communism strives to grow and develop by prioritizing equality and leveling over speed. Both methods continuously exhibit their own contradictions and side effects, leading to attempts at revisions and improvements.

However, the basis cannot be changed, because changing it would mean altering the system itself. I have reported the process and results of scientifically testing these two systems for the first time in world history. An important point to note from current events in Korea is whether we fundamentally acknowledge and emphasize 'speed' or whether we respect 'equity' and 'privilege' more than speed. Equity and privilege are contradictory concepts, yet some of us often use them interchangeably.

In all of history, the decisive factor for a country, group, or individual to survive, prosper, develop, or decline is competitiveness. This competitiveness can be influenced by various conditions and the capacity and efforts of the group or individual. From the perspective of speed, history can be seen as a process and result where the fast surpasses and conquers the slow. Humans often wish to ignore or forget this principle, which applies without exception to all animals, plants, and ecosystems, not just societies and humans.

This book asks from the outset what Korea's competitiveness is and emphasizes that the only way to save Korea's sustainability is to recognize that speed and speediness are the source of competitiveness and to utilize them. Since nothing is perfectly good in this world, speed is bound to have side effects, withdrawal, and fatigue. It is our responsibility to accept these and utilize the advantages. As explained in the text, the competition between countries is like a marathon race with no set finish line.

Contrary to the initial stages of industrialization, now, with economic capacity (capital), genetic factors (intelligence and speed), and environmental factors (digital and cultural ecosystems), we have reached a state where we can grow naturally even when left alone. Nevertheless, if we block innovation and change for all sorts of reasons, we can no longer expect rapid development. The role and function of politics, which directly or indirectly controls and intervenes in the economy and industry, is not discussed separately because it is not included in the scope of this book, but is perhaps a more important factor. Therefore, the disparity between the pace of technological and social change and the pace of political change should be pointed out as the most important issue.

In this world, and especially in a country, there are reasons and causes for everything that is not going well. And the blame is likely to be placed more on others than on oneself. However, in a democratic system where voting rights are in the hands of the people, there is no room for excuses. It is therefore important to make correct and honest choices while acknowledging that we are a community for which we ultimately have to take responsibility.

www.ingramcontent.com/pod-product-compliance
Ingram Content Group UK Ltd.
Pitfield, Milton Keynes, MK11 3LW, UK
UKHW041643031026
15587UKWH00001B/467

9 781804 411797